DETAILED CONTENTS

PREFACE

In 2012, about 1.8 zettabytes (or 1.8 trillion gigabytes) of data were created, the equivalent to having every U.S. citizen write three tweets per minute for 26,976 years. And over the next decade, the number of servers managing the world's data stores will grow by ten times. It should come as no surprise then, that the results of tens of thousands of studies appear online and in print.

How can an individual identify and make sense of the voluminous amount of currently available information on every topic in education, health, social welfare, psychology, and business? What standards can be used to distinguish good and poor studies?

This book, like the previous three editions, is for anyone who wants answers to these questions. Its primary purposes are to teach readers to identify, interpret, and analyze the published and unpublished research literature. Specifically, readers are instructed in how to do the following:

- Identify valid online bibliographic/articles databases
- Determine how to search for literature using key words, descriptors, identifiers, and thesauruses
- Use Boolean operators to refine a search
- Identify and deal with unpublished studies
- Organize the research literature by using bibliographic software
- Set inclusion and exclusion criteria to produce useful and valid information
- Justify a method for identifying and reviewing only the "highest quality" literature
- Prepare a structured abstraction form
- Create evidence tables
- Ensure and measure the reliability and validity of the review
- Synthesize and report results as part of proposals and papers or as a stand-alone report

- Evaluate qualitative research studies
- Conduct and evaluate descriptive literature reviews
- Understand and evaluate meta-analytic research

The book provides flow diagrams to assist the reader in linking each step of the review to the contents of each chapter and offers exercises linked to the goals.

NEW TO THE FOURTH EDITION

- Nearly a hundred online examples and references from the social, behavioral, and health sciences
- A revised and updated list of online articles databases
- Case studies in the use of major online databases
- Expansion of the exercises at the end of the chapter to include more online searching
- Clarification of some of the basic concepts of research that are essential in making judgments about the quality of research methods
- Explanation of the major available formal systems (such as CONSORT, TREND, PRISMA) for evaluating the literature's transparency and quality
- More qualitative research examples and guidelines and checklists for evaluating their quality
- Discussion and examples of mixed-methods research
- Additional examples of how to write up reviews and how others have done it

This book is written for all who want to uncover the current status of knowledge about social, educational, business, and health problems. This includes students, researchers, marketers, planners, and policy makers who design and manage public and private agencies, conduct studies, and prepare strategic plans and grant proposals. Every grant proposal, for instance, requires applicants to provide evidence that they know the literature and can justify the need for the grant on the basis of what is and is not known about a topic. Also, strategic and program planners are interested in finding out what is known about "best practices" in order to define programmatic missions and plan activities as diverse as marketing goods and services, preventing child abuse, and setting up school voucher systems. Any individual with admittance to a virtual or real library can use this book.

ACKNOWLEDGMENTS

I appreciate the constructive comments and suggestions provided by all of the reviewers: JaMuir M. Robinson, Suzanne Sinclair, Julia L. Sloan, Dr. Gail Thompson, and Walter J. Ullrich. Their suggestions were invaluable to me in creating the fourth edition.

ABOUT THE AUTHOR

Arlene Fink (PhD) is Professor of Medicine and Public Health at the University of California, Los Angeles, and president of the Langley Research Institute. Her main interests include evaluation and survey research and the conduct of research literature reviews as well as the evaluation of their quality. Dr. Fink has conducted scores of literature reviews and evaluation studies in public health, medicine, and education. She is on the faculty of UCLA's Robert Wood Johnson Clinical Scholars Program and is a scientific and evaluation advisor to UCLA's Gambling Studies and IMPACT (Improving Access, Counseling & Treatment for Californians with Prostate Cancer) programs. She consults nationally and internationally for agencies such as L'institut de Promotion del la Prévention Secondaire en Addictologie (IPPSA) in Paris, France, and Peninsula Health in Victoria, Australia. Professor Fink has taught and lectured extensively all over the world and is the author of over 135 peer-reviewed articles and 15 textbooks.

✵ ONE ✵

REVIEWING THE LITERATURE

Why? For Whom? How?

A Reader's Guide

ॐ

Purpose of This Chapter

This chapter gives an overview of the process of doing research reviews and illustrates how they are used. A main objective is to demonstrate how to do online searches of the research literature using major bibliographic or article databases. The chapter provides guidelines on how to ask specific questions of these databases and how to search for information using key words, thesauruses, and Boolean logic. The chapter also discusses methods for supplementing online searches with manual or hand searches of references lists and guidance from experts. Finally, the chapter concludes with a discussion of how to organize and store literature using bibliographic or reference software.

Research literature reviews have many uses. You find them in proposals for funding and for academic degrees, in research articles, in guidelines for professional and evidence-based practice, and in reports to satisfy personal curiosity. Research reviews, unlike subjective reviews, are comprehensive and easily reproducible.

Research reviewers are explicit about their research questions, search strategy, inclusion and exclusion criteria, data extraction methods, standards for evaluating study quality, and techniques for synthesizing and analyzing their findings. Subjective reviewers choose articles without justifying their search strategy, and they may give equal credence to good and poor studies. The results of subjective reviews are often based on a partial examination of the available literature, and the findings may be inaccurate or even false.

Figure 1.1 shows the steps involved in conducting a research literature review. This chapter covers the shaded portions of the figure: selecting research questions and bibliographic databases and Web sites, choosing search terms, and asking experts to review your methods.

WHAT IS A RESEARCH LITERATURE REVIEW? WHY DO ONE?

A research literature review is a systematic, explicit, and reproducible method for identifying, evaluating, and synthesizing the existing body of completed and recorded work produced by researchers, scholars, and practitioners.

The scholarship and research on which you base the review comes from individuals in diverse professions, including health, education, psychology, business, finance, law, and social services. A research review bases its conclusions on the original work of scholars and researchers. Focusing on high-quality original research rather than on interpretations of the findings is the only guarantee you have that the results of the review will be under your supervision and accurate.

A research literature review can be divided into seven tasks:

1. Selecting research questions. A research question is a precisely stated question that guides the review.

2. Selecting bibliographic or article databases, Web sites, and other sources. A bibliographic database is a collection of articles, books, and reports that can provide data to answer research questions. The database is usually accessed online. The bibliographic databases of interest in research reviews often contain full reports of original studies. Other sources for literature reviews include experts in the field of interest, the Web, and the reference lists contained in articles.

3. Choosing search terms. Search terms are the words and phrases that you use to get appropriate articles, books, and reports. You base them on the words and concepts that frame the research questions and you use a particular grammar and logic to conduct the search.

Figure 1.1   Steps Involved in Conducting a Research Literature Review

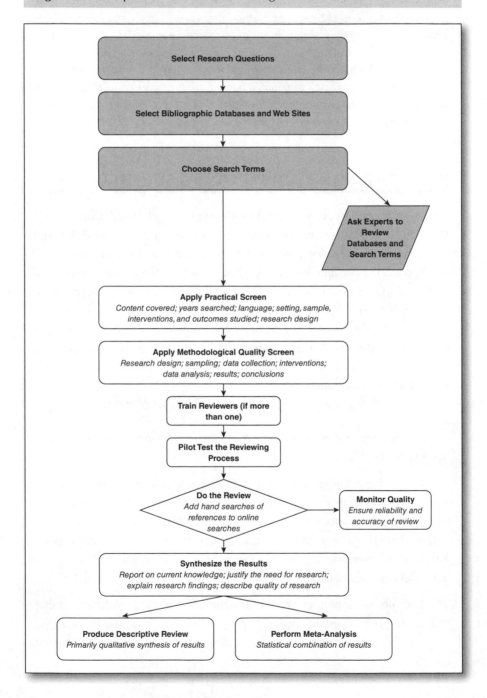

4. Applying practical screening criteria. Preliminary literature searches always yield many articles, but only a few are relevant. You screen the literature to get at the relevant articles by setting criteria for inclusion into and exclusion from the review. Practical screening criteria include factors such as the language in which the article is printed, type of article (journal article, clinical trial), date of publication, and funding source.

5. Applying methodological screening criteria. Methodological criteria include criteria for evaluating scientific quality.

6. Doing the review. Reliable and valid reviews involve using a standardized form for abstracting data from articles, training reviewers (if more than one) to do the abstraction, monitoring the quality of the review, and pilot testing the process.

7. Synthesizing the results. Literature review results may be synthesized descriptively. Descriptive syntheses are interpretations of the review's findings based on the reviewers' experience and the quality and content of the available literature. A special type of synthesis—a meta-analysis—involves the use of statistical methods to combine the results of two or more studies.

Why should you do a literature review? You may do one for personal or intellectual reasons or because you need to understand what is currently known about a topic and cannot or do not want to do a study of your own. Practical reasons also exist for doing reviews. You will be asked to include one in an honor's or a master's thesis, a dissertation proposal or dissertation, and to get funding for program planning, development, and evaluation. Consider this example.

Write Proposals for Funding

Example. The Fund for Consumer Education is interested in health promotion and disease prevention. One of its current funding priorities is preventing drug and alcohol abuse in older adults. The Community Health Plan decides to apply for a grant from the fund to develop educational materials for the elderly. The fund has specified that all grant proposals include a literature review that proves that the proposed research or education is innovative and evidence based.

The Community Health Plan grant writers do a comprehensive literature review. They first search for evidence to support their hypothesis that the risks of alcohol use are different in older and younger people. Numerous research studies provide them with the compelling confirmatory evidence they need. The grant writers also find that currently available educational programs do not make this distinction adequately. Using this information, the Community Health Plan establishes a basis for its proposal to develop, implement, and evaluate an alcohol use consumer education program specifically for people who are 65 years of age and older. The program will use educational methods that the literature suggests are particularly effective in this population. That is, the program will rely on evidence-based educational methods.

The fund reviewers agree that the grant writers have done a good job of reviewing the literature but ask for more information about the specific educational methods that are being proposed. The grant writers expand their literature review to identify methods of learning and instruction that are particularly appropriate for older persons.

When writing proposals for funding, you are almost always asked to use the literature to justify the need for your study. You must either prove that nothing or very little can be found in the literature that effectively addresses your study's topic or that the studies that can be identified do not address the topic as well as you will in your proposed research. In intervention studies, you will need to provide evidence that the methods you propose to use are likely to be effective.

In the preceding example, the proposal writers use the literature to justify their consumer education program by demonstrating that existing materials do not adequately distinguish between the risks of alcohol use in older and younger people. They also use the literature to support their hypothesis that the risks are different and to identify methods of learning and instruction that are specifically pertinent to older people.

Literature reviews are also used in proposals for academic degrees.

Write Proposals for Academic Degrees

Example. A student in a doctoral program in education plans to write a proposal to prepare a high school curriculum aiming to modify AIDS-related knowledge, beliefs, and self-efficacy related to AIDS preventive actions and involvement in AIDS risk behaviors. The student is told that the proposal will be accepted only if a literature review is conducted that answers these questions:

1. What curricula are currently available? Are they meeting the current needs of high school students for AIDS education? Have they been formally evaluated, and if so, are they effective?

2. What measures of knowledge, beliefs, self-efficacy, and behaviors related to AIDS are available? Are they reliable? Are they valid?

The student performs the review and concludes that currently available curricula do not focus on prevention, although some have brief prevention units. The student also finds that valid measures of knowledge, beliefs, and behaviors related to AIDS are available in the literature. Good measures of self-efficacy, however, are not. The student concludes that developing a detailed AIDS prevention curriculum is worthwhile. He plans to use available measures of knowledge, beliefs, and behaviors and will validate a measure of self-efficacy in relation to AIDS preventive actions.

The student's adviser remains unconvinced by the review. How effective are current curricula in meeting the needs of today's students? Are behaviors more or less risky than a previous generation's? What does the literature say about the prevalence of AIDS among adolescents? The student expands his review of the literature to answer these questions.

Literature reviews are also used to guide current professional practices, as is illustrated in the next example.

Describe and Explain Current Knowledge to Guide Professional Practice

Example. A group of physicians reviews the literature to provide a basis for a set of guidelines or recommended practices for treating depressed patients. First, they use the literature to help define depression and the different forms it takes (e.g., major depressive disorder and dysthymic disorder). Next, the physicians rely on the literature for data on effective treatments. They find that the literature supports distinguishing among treatments for different populations of depressed patients (such as children and the elderly), types of depression, gender, and methods of treatment (including medication and psychotherapy).

Using the literature review's results, the physicians divide the guidelines into separate categories for each different population of concern and base their recommendations for treatment on gender and type of depression. For example, the recommendations suggest that the treatment for elderly patients with major depressive disorder may be different from the treatment for major depressive disorder in younger patients; treatment for each type of depression, regardless of age, may differ for males and females.

Increasingly, practitioners in occupations such as health and medicine, education, psychology, and social welfare are required to base their activities and programs on demonstrably effective practices. For example, suppose a school district wanted to implement a new reading program. Before it could do so, the district would have to provide proof that the new program "worked." If resources are available, the district can conduct a research study to demonstrate the reading program's effectiveness among its students. Another option is for the district to find evidence of effectiveness in the literature. Practices, interventions, programs, and policies that have proof of effectiveness are said to be *evidence based.* In the preceding example, the literature review is used in selecting definitions, organizing the guidelines for depression, and linking treatment to type of depression, gender, and age.

The literature also can be used to identify methods of doing research or developing and implementing programs, as shown in this example.

Identify Effective Research and Development Methods

Example. A review of the literature reveals a validated Web-based assessment of alcohol use. The assessment has been used with people 65 years of age and older and measures alcohol consumption alone and also in combination with diminished health, medical conditions, and functional status. The writers of a proposal to develop and evaluate an alcohol use curriculum plan to purchase the computer assessment instrument for their study because the cost of purchasing the instrument is less than the costs of developing and validating a new one. Identifying and using an existing instrument will make the proposal more competitive.

Why reinvent the wheel? A great deal of work has gone into producing methods and instruments that can be adapted to meet your specific needs. For instance, if you are interested in assessing customer or patient satisfaction, health status, or educational knowledge, attitudes, or behavior, the literature is filled with examples for you to copy.

A literature review may produce conflicting or ambiguous results or may not adequately cover a topic. Experts—persons who are knowledgeable and prominent—are often called in to help resolve the uncertainty that arises when data are inconclusive or missing, as illustrated next.

Identify Experts to Help Interpret Existing Literature and Identify Unpublished Sources of Information

Example. After reviewing the literature, three people were found who had published five or more studies on the topic and who also worked in our city. Two agreed to consult with our project and helped us identify other publications of interest.

Example. A review of the literature on depression left many questions unanswered. For example, the long-term effects of certain medications were not investigated adequately in the literature, nor was the effectiveness of certain types of "talking therapy." A panel of physicians, nurses, and psychiatric social workers was convened. The panel was asked to supplement the review of the literature with their clinical and other expertise. A major criterion in selecting members of the panel was their publication record as revealed in the literature review.

The literature can also be used to help you find out where to get support for your research. You can also learn about the type of studies being done at the present time. Following is an example of these uses.

Identify Funding Sources and Works in Progress

Example. We found 100 relevant studies through our literature search. The Office of Education funded about half of them. We contacted the office to ask if we could place our name on their list for future studies. We contacted the project managers of current projects for as-yet unpublished information to supplement our literature review.

As consumers of health care, education, and social services, we want to make certain that we receive the best services and treatment. The literature can help in this regard by providing access to evaluated programs and helping us to select criteria to do our own assessments. Also, sometimes we are simply curious about an issue, and knowing how to do a literature review can help satisfy our curiosity.

Satisfy Personal Curiosity

Example. Voters are being asked to make decisions on the merits of school vouchers. These vouchers are given to parents who can use them to enroll their children in any school of their choosing. The idea is that schools whose performance is currently relatively low will have to do better to "sell" themselves to students. Do school vouchers encourage competition? How do increased choices affect children's intellectual and social well-being? A literature review can be useful in answering questions like these.

Example. Some parents have observed that their children appear restless or even agitated after eating very sugary foods. Does eating "too much" sugar induce aggressive behavior in children? A literature review will help you answer this question.

Look at these three case studies. Select the literature review(s).

Three Case Studies: Literature Review or Not?

Case 1: Policy Making and Program Planning—State-of-the-Art Knowledge. The Department of Human Services is considering the adoption of a program of family preservation services. These programs aim to prevent children who are at risk for abuse and neglect from being taken from their families. Program participants—families and children—receive emotional, educational, and financial support. Family preservation programs are considered by many practitioners to be worthwhile. Others are not so sure and ask, "Are all equally effective, or are some programs more effective than others?" "If some are more effective, which of their activities makes them more effective?" "Would such activities be appropriate for implementation by the department?" "If the department decides to adopt or adapt an existing family preservation program, what methods and criteria should be used subsequently to evaluate its outcomes and effectiveness?" "Who are the experts in the family preservation field who might be consulted to help with the evaluation?" The department asks for a literature review to get the answers to these questions.

The Research Division goes online using three bibliographic databases dealing with social and psychological studies. Researchers identify 200 studies regarding family preservation programs. After evaluating the relevance of the investigators' findings to the needs of the community, they answer the department's questions.

Case 2: Preparing Guidelines for Treating Infections and Fever in Nursing Homes. Infections are a major cause of morbidity and mortality and a leading cause of hospitalization for nursing home residents. Each year, more than 1.5 million infections occur in the institutional long-term care setting. Among elderly nursing home residents, the overwhelming majority of fever episodes are caused by serious infection, which, if inappropriately treated, may result in unnecessary morbidity, mortality, and expenditures.

Despite the magnitude of this problem, guidelines for detecting and treating fever in nursing homes are not readily available. To remedy this deficiency, Atlantic Health Care convened a panel of experts, each of whom had published extensively on the subjects of fever, infectious disease, the elderly, and nursing home care. The panelists were asked to distribute their published and unpublished research studies before the meeting to facilitate discussion and consensus. Nurses and physicians used a validated "expert panel group process method" to develop practice guidelines for the detection and treatment of fever. The panel also helped to set standards for evaluating quality of care. Both the guidelines and the quality-of-care methods were based on the findings of the panelists' research and their own experience in detecting and treating elderly people with fever.

Case 3: What Is Known and Not Known—Justifying the Need for New Studies to Fill in the Gaps. Alcohol use in people 65 years of age and older is a growing public health problem. Even if the rate stays the same, doctors and other health professionals can count on seeing an increase in the number of alcoholics, simply because the number of older people in the population will increase. Traditional surveys of alcohol use focus on issues pertaining to young people, such as work and family matters. Very few surveys are available that take into account the concerns of older adults.

Alcohol use in older people can impair function, cause or exacerbate illness, or increase the difficulty of treatment. Alcohol also interacts with more than 100 of the medications most commonly used by older persons. Finally, older people metabolize alcohol differently from younger people and may suffer adverse effects with relatively few drinks.

To address the special needs of older adults, public health workers conducted a literature review to find methods for physicians and other health workers to use in identifying older persons who are at risk for alcohol-related problems or who already have them. The reviewers first went to experts in the field of geriatric medicine and alcohol abuse research and asked for a list of studies they considered to be important. The reviewers examined those studies the experts recommended as well as the references contained within them. Finally, they did an online search of two major medical bibliographic databases to make certain they included all relevant data in their review.

The review revealed that comparatively little research has focused specifically on older people and that no validated method of measuring alcohol consumption is available for their use in health settings. A main finding of the review was that more research is needed to identify methods for detecting risks for alcohol misuse in this growing segment of society.

Cases 1 and 3 use formal literature reviews. In Case 1, the Department of Health and Human Services is planning to depend on the literature to answer all its questions. Consultants will be called in later to help with the evaluation, but they will be identified by studying the literature to determine who they are. In Case 3, the literature review is done to justify research into methods for detecting risks for alcohol misuse in the elderly; no experts are consulted. In Case 2, experts select any studies they consider pertinent. Although literature is certainly used in this scenario, how it is used and its characteristics are not discussed. Are the study results synthesized? Are opinions (e.g., editorials and tutorials) included? Do the studies represent all or a meaningful sample of the available literature? Without answers to questions such as these, we cannot really call Case 2 a true literature review.

GAINING CONTROL: EXPERIMENTS AND OBSERVATIONS

Reviewing the research literature means identifying and interpreting what is known about a topic. High-quality literature reviews base their findings on the evidence from controlled experimentation and observation. They rely on the researcher's original studies for information rather than on other people's interpretations of the results. Editorials and testimonials are usually excluded from the review itself because they are subjective and prone to bias. They are not ignored, however. Expert views—when they come from credible sources—may be used to help interpret findings and answer questions such as these: What references should I include in the review? Have I included all the important references? Why do the findings of some studies contradict the findings of others?

To evaluate the research literature, you must learn some basic criteria for evaluating the quality of research. Not all research is equally good, and the reviewer must be able to distinguish high- from low-quality research. The objective of high-quality research is to produce accurate information. If your review is based on research that is less than high quality, the results will be less than accurate.

High-quality experimental and observational studies, the "gold standards" for systematic reviews, are characterized by study designs that have clearly formulated research objectives and questions, rigorous research plans, valid data collection, and exacting data analysis and interpretation. In an experimental study, the investigator actively intervenes and examines effects. In an observational study, the investigator takes a relatively passive role in observing events. Following are examples of experiments and observations.

An Experimental Study

Research Question. How effective is a school-based intervention for reducing children's symptoms of depression and posttraumatic stress disorder resulting from witnessing or being personally exposed to violence?

Some children who witness violence develop symptoms of depression or posttraumatic stress disorder (PTSD). Trained school-based mental health researchers used validated measures of depression and PTSD to assess sixth-grade students at two large schools. Sixty-one of 126 students with these symptoms who reported witnessing violence were randomly assigned to a standardized therapy program, and 65 were assigned to a waiting list. Students in the therapy program were tested before their participation and 3 months after it. The researchers found that when compared with the waiting list students, after 3 months of intervention, students who were in the program had significantly lower depression and PTSD scores. But at 6 months, after both groups had received the program, the differences disappeared. The researchers concluded that the program was effective and could be delivered on school campuses by trained school-based mental health personnel.

An Observational Study

Research Question. Who is at greatest risk for melanoma, the deadliest form of skin cancer?

To answer this question, researchers conducted a study in which 452 women who had melanoma were compared with 900 women from the general population who did not. The women lived in five counties that make up a major American city. All women were interviewed using a standardized interview schedule and highly trained interviewers. The interviewers asked about the women's history of exposure to the sun, medical history, and demographics (such as age). A statistical expert from the local university analyzed the data from the interviews. The researchers found that risk of melanoma increased with increasing tendency to get sunburned, with increased severity and/or frequency of sunburns up to age 12, and with lack of use of sunscreen.

The first study is an experimental study because the researchers are relatively in charge of the main events. In their study, they administer therapy to reduce symptoms of depression and PTSD in children. The researchers also evaluate the effects of the therapy by creating an experimental group and a waiting list from the same sample, selecting the methods for assigning students to groups, and choosing measures to record changes over time. In contrast, the researchers in the second study do not provide treatment, have no role in assigning people to the group being observed (people with melanoma), and are dependent on people's recall of their past sun exposure and use of sunscreen.

Because of the greater methodological control over events that experimenters have compared with observers, experimental studies are generally preferred to observational research. Only well-done studies belong in a literature review. Evaluating the rigor of a study's design is an essential feature of any valid literature review. Only good study designs produce good data.

SYSTEMATIC, EXPLICIT, COMPREHENSIVE, AND REPRODUCIBLE: FOUR KEY WORDS

Research literature reviews can be contrasted with more subjective examinations of recorded information. When doing a research review, you systematically examine all sources and describe and justify what you have done. This enables someone else to reproduce your methods and to determine objectively whether to accept the results of the review.

In contrast, subjective reviews tend to be idiosyncratic. Subjective reviewers choose articles without justifying why they are selected, and they may give equal credence to good and poor studies. The results of subjective reviews are often based on a partial examination of the available literature, and their findings may be inaccurate or even false. Subjective reviews should be distinguished from narrative reviews. Narratives may be appropriate for describing the history or development of a problem and its solution.

How can you produce a systematic, explicit, comprehensive, and reproducible review? You need to identify precisely what you need to know and decide on the best sources of information. You must also evaluate the quality of the information you find and synthesize the results. This chapter discusses where to go for information and how to ask for it. The next chapters tell you how to justify your choice of studies to review, abstract information from the studies, and analyze and synthesize the results.

CHOOSING AN ONLINE BIBLIOGRAPHIC DATABASE

Reviews of the literature depend on data from online bibliographic or article databases such as PubMed or specialized databases such as the Cochrane database of systematic reviews, government reports, and collections maintained by professionals in law, business, and the environment.

Online Bibliographic Databases

One of the most important (some would emphasize *most* important) assembly of articles can be found in online databases. Everyone with an Internet connection has free access to the world's scientific, social scientific, technological, artistic, and medical literature, thanks to the U.S. government that supports it, the scientific community that produces it, and the schools and public and private libraries that purchase access to bibliographic databases and other sources of information. The U.S. National Library of Medicine at the National Institutes of Health, for example, maintains the best site for published medical and health research. This site is called PubMed, and access is free from any computer with an Internet connection (http://www.ncbi.nlm.nih.gov/pubmed/). Although PubMed's focus is on the life and health sciences, you can find many articles in the database that deal with topics related to education, psychology, and other types of social and political science.

University and other libraries, including public libraries, usually provide free access to hundreds of government and nongovernment, private bibliographic databases.

A short list of available databases is given below to give you an idea of the range available.

Online Bibliographic Databases: A Sample

African Studies. Provides combined access to 17 bibliographic databases from Africa, Europe, and the United States providing access to multidisciplinary information on Africa, including African Studies Abstracts (1988–Present) and its predecessor—the library catalog of the Africa Institute (1981–Present).

Anthropology Plus. Brings together into one resource Anthropological Literature from Harvard University and the Anthropological Index from the Royal Anthropological Institute in the United Kingdom.

Arts & Humanities Citation Index. A multidisciplinary database covering the journal literature of the arts and humanities. It covers 1,144 of the world's leading arts and humanities journals.

BIOSIS Previews (Online). Contains citations to items in more than 6,000 journals, books, conference proceedings, and technical reports, in all areas of the life sciences and biology. Many citations include abstracts.

Child Abuse and Neglect Documents Database. Indexes journal articles, books, book chapters, proceedings, reports, and other materials on child abuse.

ERIC. Index to journal articles from 1969 to the present and ERIC documents since 1966 on educational research and practice. Searches combining different fields (e.g., descriptor with title, author).

Expanded Academic ASAP. Provides selected full-text articles and images from 2,600 scholarly journals, magazines, and newspapers, with the earliest citations dating back to 1980. Spans all academic disciplines.

LexisNexis Academic. Full-text news, business, legal, medical, and reference information. Also useful for finding full text of current performing arts and media industry news in major newspapers.

LexisNexis Academic Universe—Business. Includes detailed financial data about companies, annual and quarterly reports, news, and directories.

Linguistics and Language Behavior Abstracts: LLBA. Abstracts of articles from approximately 2,000 serials in the fields of linguistics, language behavior, and related disciplines, as well as books, book chapters, occasional papers, and technical reports.

POPLINE (via Johns Hopkins). Worldwide coverage of population, family planning, and related health issues, including family planning technology and programs, fertility, and population law and policy. Coverage: 1970–Present.

PsycINFO. Citations and abstracts for articles in 1,300 professional journals, conference proceedings, books, reports, and dissertations in psychology and related disciplines.

PubMed. This search system provides access to the PubMed database of bibliographic information, which is drawn primarily from MEDLINE, which indexes articles from about 3,900 journals in the life sciences (e.g., health, medicine, biology).

Science Direct. A database containing the full text of more than 1,700 journals in the life, physical, medical, technical, and social sciences available throughout the Internet. Contains abstracts and articles from the core journals in major scientific disciplines. Journals are arranged under subject areas for topical navigation. Keyword searching is also available.

Social Sciences Citation Index. A multidisciplinary database covering the journal literature of the social sciences, indexing more than 1,725 journals across 50 social sciences disciplines.

Sociological Abstracts. Database containing citations for articles from more than 2,600 journals, books, conference papers, and dissertations in sociology and related disciplines in the social sciences.

Web of Science. A multidisciplinary database, with searchable author abstracts, covering the journal literature of the sciences, social sciences, and arts and humanities. Indexes major journals across disciplines.

How does the reviewer determine which online databases may be relevant in reviewing a particular research topic? Some, such as PsycINFO or PubMed, have names that describe their content's orientation (psychology and medicine, respectively). Each library usually has a list of databases by subject areas, such as psychology or medicine. If you are unsure about the contents of a specific database, ask a librarian for information or go directly to the site to find out what topics and resources it includes.

How do you select among bibliographic databases? It all depends on the topic and research questions. For example, if you are interested in finding out what the literature has to say about the best way to teach reading to young children, then the literature in education is clearly an appropriate place to start. However, if you are interested in finding out about interactive reading programs, then a computer and information technology database may also be relevant. It helps to be precise about what you want and need to know so you can choose all relevant databases.

What Exactly Do You Need to Find?

We have almost instantaneous and worldwide access to research on practically any topic one can think of. Most literature reviews are limited in purpose and time, however. To ensure that you get the literature that you need and not just an unlimited number of somewhat related (and sometimes unrelated) articles, you must be precise about your research needs.

Systematic literature reviews start with very specific needs for knowledge or research questions. Examine these examples of three relatively nonspecific and specific questions:

Examples of Nonspecific and Specific Research Questions

Topic 1: Family Preservation

Less Specific

Research Question A. Which programs successfully keep families together?

More Specific

Research Question B. Which family preservation programs effectively prevent children from being placed out of home?

Comment

Question B is more specific because it describes what it means by the term *programs*—family preservation programs. Question B also defines what the questioner means by "successfully keeping families together"— keeping children from being placed out of home.

Topic 2: Curing the Common Cold

Less Specific

Research Question A. What can people do to cure a cold?

More Specific

Research Question B. Can antibiotics cure the common cold?

Comment

Question B is more specific than A because the vague word *do* is defined in B as meaning a definite action—taking antibiotics. This clarification may spare you from getting articles about antibiotics and temperature changes, if you use *antibiotics* AND *cold* as key words in your search. (See below for an explanation of the concept of key words.)

Topic 3: Alcohol, Women, and Breast Cancer

Less Specific

Research Question A. How does alcohol use affect breast cancer?

More Specific

Research Question B. What is the relationship between drinking two or more alcoholic beverages daily in women 65 years of age and older and breast cancer?

Comment

Question B is more specific because "alcohol use" is clarified to mean "two or more alcoholic beverages daily," and the targeted population of interest is specified to be women who are 65 years of age and older.

How Do You Search for What You Want to Find? Key Words, Descriptors, Identifiers, and the Thesaurus

Research Questions and Key Words

A precisely stated research question has the benefit of containing the words the reviewer needs to search online for applicable studies. These words or search terms are often referred to as **key words, descriptors,** or **identifiers.**

Consider this question (Research Question 1B above): Which family preservation programs effectively prevent children from being placed out of home? From the question, you can see that the important words—key words— include *family preservation programs, children,* and *out-of-home placement.*

What are the key words for Question 2B (above): Can antibiotics cure the common cold?

Answer: antibiotics, common cold, cure

What are the key words for Question 3B (above): What is the relationship between drinking two or more alcoholic beverages daily in women 65 years of age and older and breast cancer?

Answer: women 65 years of age and older, breast cancer, alcoholic beverages

Just knowing the key words is not always enough, unfortunately. For instance, suppose you are reviewing family preservation studies to find out which programs work best to prevent out-of-home placement.

You decide to use PsycINFO for your review because it is an online bibliographic database dealing with subjects in psychology. You also search the database using the exact phrase *out-of-home placement* and are given a list of 195 articles. You find that the articles contain data on out-of-home placement, but not all pertain to family preservation programs. To narrow your search and reduce the number of irrelevant studies, you decide to combine *out-of-home placement* with *family preservation,* and find that your reviewing task is reduced to 31 articles. However, on further investigation, you find that not all the 31 articles include data on effectiveness. You get data on effectiveness from evaluation studies. So you decide to further narrow the search by adding the term *evaluation* and find that the reviewing task is reduced to a mere 7 articles. This seems like a manageable number of articles to review.

Are fewer articles always better? Not necessarily. If your search is very narrow, you may miss out on some important ideas. However, if your search is very wide, then you can be faced with thousands of potentially irrelevant citations. Suppose you are interested in reviewing medical knowledge of the common cold. If on July 19, 2012, you entered the words *common cold* into the PubMed search field, you would be given a list of 284,840 citations! If, however, you asked for *antibiotics* AND *common cold,* you would get 49,106 citations. If you refine this search further by asking for *cure* AND *common cold,* you would be referred to 1,547 citations. (It may be interesting for you to try this now to see how many citations you get. Articles are published increasingly rapidly, especially because they are often first published online and later on in print. In 2008, a search for *antibiotics* AND *common cold*, resulted in 6,436 citations as compared to 284,840 citations found in 2012). The moral of the story is that to get the information you need from the literature, you must balance very specific research questions with justifiable limits or restrictions, or you will be flooded with thousands of irrelevant citations.

Suppose a researcher wants to find out what is known about the use of antibiotics in treating the common cold. The researcher speaks English and is interested in articles published in the last five years. Figure 1.2 illustrates the results of the researcher's effort. As you can see, the researcher uncovers 94 articles.

Figure 1.2   Results of a PubMed Search for Meta-Analytic Studies on the Common Cold and Antibiotics

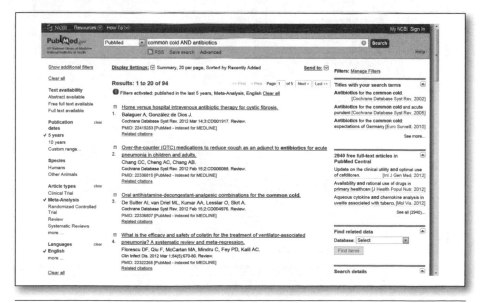

Source: US National Library of Medicine, Pubmed.gov

One way to achieve a balance between specificity and restriction is to check your planned search terms with those used by authors of articles you trust. Did you include all the terms in your search that they included? All online citations include additional search terms. Figure 1.3 gives an example of a citation for an article on family preservation from a search of PsycINFO. The citation includes descriptors, which are terms used by PsycINFO as part of its bibliographic indexing system or thesaurus.

Just going to the citation for one reference can help you greatly in your search because it provides additional descriptors to help you expand or narrow your search.

The Thesaurus as a Source: When Is Enough Really Enough?

One major source of search terms is a database's thesaurus or dictionary for indexing articles. In the case of PsycINFO, the indexing system is through *descriptors.* In PubMed, it is defined by the Medical Subjects Headings, or *MeSH,* database.

Figure 1.3   A Record From PsycINFO for One Article on Family Preservation

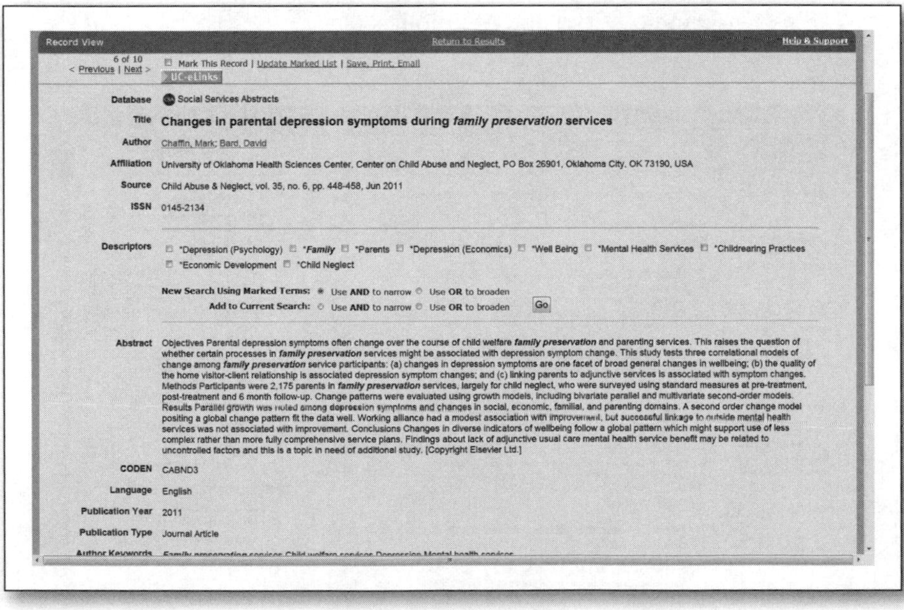

Source: American Psychological Association

The thesaurus is a controlled vocabulary that provides a consistent way to retrieve information across fields that may use different terms for the same concept. For instance, in studies of alcohol, investigators may refer to alcohol abuse as alcoholism, problem drinking, alcohol misuse, substance abuse, and so on. Each database's librarian assigns articles to categories that meet the system's requirements regardless of the investigator's preferences.

Suppose you are interested in finding out about workplace literacy but you want to be certain that you get all articles about workplace literacy, no matter what the investigators call it. Suppose also that you decide to start your search with the database ERIC (Education Resources Information Center) (Figure 1.4). As with most databases, ERIC gives you the opportunity to search other descriptors (as well as other options like author or date of publication to help you focus your search).

Remember! Thesauruses vary from database to database so check out each one.

Figure 1.4   Workplace Literacy Search Results Using ERIC

Source: U.S. Department of Education, Eric.ed.gov

Key Words or Thesaurus: Chicken or Egg?

A comprehensive search strategy probably requires combining key words and thesaurus terms. If you are certain of your research questions and the variables of interest, a key word search usually produces a relatively narrow range of articles.

A search that begins with official thesaurus terms will produce a wide range of articles, but breadth is important if you want your review to be comprehensive. In some fields, such as medicine, evidence exists that using thesaurus terms produces more of the available citations than does reliance on key words. For example, if a reviewer performs a PubMed search using the word *hyperlipidemia* but an author has used the narrower term *hypercholesterolemia,* then many relevant citations may be missed because only those articles with the word *hyperlipidemia* in their title or abstract will be retrieved. Using the appropriate subject heading will enable the reviewer to find all citations regardless of how the author uses the term.

Even More Search Terms: Authors, Titles, Title
Words, and Journals and Then Some—Limiting the Search

You can search for studies by asking for specific authors, titles of articles, words that you expect to be in the title (perhaps you forgot the exact title), and journals. Sometimes this is a useful way to identify key words and thesaurus terms. For instance, suppose you want to find out about programs to prevent child abuse. Asking for the thesaurus headings or key words from an article by any leading researcher in the field will enable you to conduct your search knowing that you are using commonly accepted terms.

Searching by specifics—authors, titles—also limits or narrows your search. This can be especially useful if you are not doing an inclusive review. Other methods of narrowing the search include type of publication (e.g., clinical trials, randomized trials), age groups (e.g., infants, adolescents, adults), language, date of publication, and whether the subjects of the study are male or female.

HOW DO YOU ASK FOR INFORMATION?
SEARCHING WITH BOOLEAN OPERATORS

Literature review searches often mean combining key words and other terms with words such as *and*, *or*, and *not*. These three words are called *Boolean* operators.

Look at these three examples of the use of Boolean logic.

Three Examples of Boolean Logic

Example 1: AND

common cold AND *antibiotics:* Use AND to retrieve a set of citations in which each citation contains all search terms. The terms can appear in any order—*antibiotics* may appear before *common cold.*

Example 2: OR

zinc OR *vitamin C:* Use OR to retrieve citations that contain one of the specified terms.

Example 3: NOT

antibiotics NOT *children:* Use NOT to exclude terms from your search.

Be careful when using NOT because you may inadvertently eliminate important articles. In Example 3, articles about children and antibiotics are eliminated, but so are studies that include children as part of a discussion of antibiotics and all age groups.

In addition to AND, OR, and NOT, an individual concept can be enclosed in parentheses, and the terms inside the parentheses will be processed as a unit. Figure 1.5 presents an efficient method of searching called *nesting.* The program will search for any articles on common cold AND zinc *or* common cold AND vitamin C. If both vitamin C and zinc are studied in a single article, the program will be able identify it, but the computer will not limit its search to just common cold and vitamin C and also zinc.

PAUSING DURING THE SEARCH

When your search is no longer fruitful, and you are not getting any new or relevant studies, review your collection of literature. Check the entire list for quality and comprehensiveness. Get assistance from someone who is interested in the topic or has worked in the field. Ask: Are all important investigators or writers included on the list? Have any major studies been excluded?

Figure 1.5   Nesting in PubMed

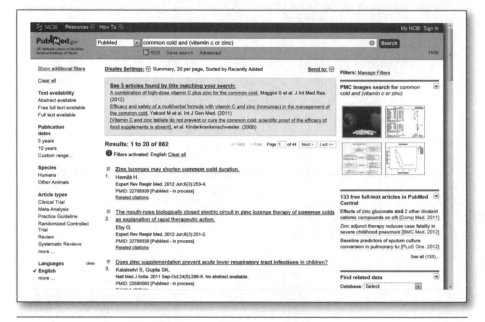

Source: US National Library of Medicine, Pubmed.gov

CHANGING THE COURSE OF THE SEARCH

You change course by considering new key words, subject headings, authors, and so on. A change in course may expand the scope of your review. Consider this example.

Changing the Course of a Literature Review Search: Expanding the Scope

Example. A psychologist reviewed the literature to find out how possible exposure to radiation affects people's psychological well-being. The review focused on catastrophes such as the Russian nuclear power plant disaster at Chernobyl in 1990. As part of the review, the psychologist discovered that the Chernobyl disaster subsequently affected more than 1 million immigrants to the United States and Israel. The psychologist expanded the review to consider the implications for policy makers of having to consider the needs of substantial numbers of immigrants who may have special life-long mental health problems resulting from participation in the disaster. This topic appeared especially pertinent given the number of immigrants throughout the world who have participated or witnessed wars and other disasters.

SUPPLEMENTING THE ONLINE SEARCH

Is the following statement true or false?

An experienced literature reviewer needs only access to the Internet to do a comprehensive literature review.

The answer is false. Experienced literature reviewers must know how to locate databases and use the correct language and syntax to identify key words, subjects, titles, and so on to identify pertinent studies. However, search processes are far from uniform or perfect, the databases and study authors may not use search terms uniformly (especially true with new topics), and even the most proficient reviewers may neglect to find one or more studies regardless of how careful they are. In addition, a reviewer may in actuality have access to just a few databases. Also, some studies may be in progress and not yet ready for publication. Finally, some potentially important studies may never get published.

The following summarizes the main reasons for supplementing computer searches of the literature with other data sources.

Reasons to Supplement Electronic Searches

The topic is new and its associated concepts have not yet been incorporated into official subject headings.

- Search terms are used inconsistently because definitions in the field are not uniform.
- There is reason to believe that many important studies are in progress or complete but not published.

Where do you go when being online is insufficient? Consider the following supplemental sources.

- Review the reference lists in high-quality studies.
- Talk to colleagues and other experts.
- Review major government, university, and foundation Web sites.

Reviewing References in High-Quality Studies

Believe it or not, after many, many hours of searching, you may fail to uncover all there is to know about a topic. This can easily happen if you rely on just one or two databases. For instance, if you are interested in the relationship between alcohol use and breast cancer in older women and rely on PubMed alone for information, you will get a great deal of clinical information, but you may not retrieve some of the available research on the psychosocial factors associated with alcohol drinking and breast cancer. If, however, you rely on a database that deals with research on psychosocial variables such as PsycINFO, you may not obtain some medical or health information. Even if you use both databases, you may fail to uncover some clinical and psychosocial articles. It is unclear why this happens, but it may happen.

One way to avoid missing out on important studies is to review the references in high-quality articles. You do not necessarily need to retrieve the article to do this because some databases (such as PsycINFO and Sociological Abstracts) provide a list of searchable references as part of the citation (if you ask for it).

Listen in on this conversation between a frustrated reviewer and a more experienced colleague to get a feeling for how references in articles can help provide coverage for a literature review.

*Searching the References: A Conversation Between
an Experienced and a Frustrated Reviewer*

Experienced Reviewer (ER):	I have been reviewing your list of references and notice that you do not include Monashe's experiment to find out how to teach young adults how to be better consumers.
Frustrated Reviewer (FR):	I did a search of 10 databases and asked specifically for Monashe. How did I miss that study?

ER:	Very simple. Monashe hasn't published it yet.
FR:	If Monashe hasn't published it, how could I find it?
ER:	If you had reviewed the references in my study of education and young adults, you would have found it. I knew that Monashe was working on the study and I asked her to tell me about it. She is currently working on the paper but was able to give me a monograph. She wrote the monograph to fulfill the obligations of the government contract that sponsored the study. The government insists that the monograph be made available at a nominal cost to other researchers. You can download the monograph from (hypothetical site) http://www.nixx.cdd.gov.
FR:	I wonder how many other studies I may have missed because I didn't study the references.
ER:	I wonder, too.

Is Everything Worthwhile Published?

Unpublished literature has two basic formats. The first consists of documents (final reports required by funding agencies, for example) that are written and available in print or online—with some detective work—from governments and foundations. Monashe's monograph, discussed in the preceding conversation between the experienced and frustrated reviewers, is an example. But some studies do not get published at all.

Although some unpublished studies are most certainly terrible or are the products of lazy researchers, some important ones are neither. These studies are not published because their conclusions are unremarkable or even negative, and journals tend to publish research with positive and interesting findings.

Much has been written about the effects of failing to publish studies with negative findings. The fear is that because only exciting studies (i.e., those that find that a treatment works, for example) are published, invalid conclusions inevitably result because less provocative studies with negative or contrary findings are not published. That is, if Reading Program A has one positive study and two negative ones, but we only get to know about the positive one, then Program A will look more effective than it may be in actuality.

This phenomenon—publication of positive findings only—is called *publication bias.*

The general rule in estimating the extent of publication bias is to consider that if the available data uncovered by the review are from high-quality studies and reasonably consistent in direction, then the number of opposite findings will have to be extremely large to overturn the results.

Bring in the Experts

Experts are individuals who are knowledgeable about the main topic addressed in the literature search. You can find experts by examining the literature to determine who has published extensively on the topic and who is cited often. You can also ask one set of experts to nominate another. Experts can help guide you to unpublished studies and work in progress.

They may also help interpret and expand on your review's findings. They help answer questions such as these: Do my literature review findings apply to everyone or to only a particular group of people? How confident can I be in the strength of the evidence? What are the practical or clinical implications of the findings?

Following are abstracts of two literature reviews that illustrate the use of experts. The first review is concerned with the risks associated with the treatment of depression in pregnant women. In that review, experts are called in to discuss references identified by reviewers. In the second review, experts are asked for references and books regarding the optimal treatment of urinary tract infections in older women. Their recommendations are supplemented by online searches.

Expert Guidance: How to Use It

Literature Review 1: Pharmacologic Treatment of Depression During Pregnancy[1]

Background

Depression is common among women of childbearing age. Even so, not much information is available that can help patients and physicians decide on treatment during pregnancy.

Objective

This study aimed to identify risks associated with treating major depression during pregnancy. Having this information can help physicians come up with plans for treatment.

Data Sources

The researchers searched MEDLINE and HealthSTAR for 1989 through 1999 using the search terms *antidepressant during pregnancy* and *depression during pregnancy*. They also manually searched the references in review articles and had discussions with investigators. To be included, a study had to be reported in English and a prospective controlled trial.

Literature Review 2: Antibiotics for Urinary Tract Infections[2]

Background

Urinary tract infections are common in elderly patients. Authors of nonsystematic literature reviews often recommend longer treatment durations (7–14 days) for older patients than for younger women, but the researchers in this review start with the premise that the scientific evidence for such recommendations is not clear.

Objectives

The researchers aimed to determine the optimal duration of antibiotic treatment for uncomplicated symptomatic lower urinary tract infections in elderly women.

Data Sources

The researchers relied on PubMed, EMBASE, CINAHL, HealthSTAR, POPLINE, Gerolit, BioethicsLine, the Cochrane Library, Dissertation Abstracts International, and Index to Scientific & Technical Proceedings. They also contacted known investigators and pharmaceutical companies that sell antibiotics used to treat urinary tract infections. The researchers screened the reference list of identified articles, reviews, and books.

Cautiously Approach the Web

The Internet contains a vast amount of information on just about any topic under the sun. As a source of credible, experimentally derived information, however, it is a mixed blessing. Its greatest advantage is that the world's literature is available to anyone who knows how to get to it. But even experienced reviewers can find themselves confronted with a mass of information of dubious quality, and quality controls for Internet sites are practically impossible to oversee.

The Geneva-based Health on the Net Foundation's voluntary set of ethical standards for health Web sites can help consumers discern the veracity of online information, but some say the standards are not always the best way to find reliable health information online.

The HON code, created in 1995 (http://www.hon.ch), is the oldest and most widely used Internet information code, covering more than 3,500 Web sites based in 67 countries. The HON (Health on the Net Foundation) site also features a search engine for medical information, and results come only from HON-accredited sites. The group accredits sites that abide by a set of eight principles; these sites are then allowed to display the HON code logo. The standards require that information providers reveal potential conflicts of interest, list credentials for authors relaying medical information, and reference their information sources.

Administrators of HON say they have trouble keeping up with information on complementary and alternative medicine (CAM) on Web sites, some of which display the HON code seal but are not accredited.

Healthfinder.gov, for example, a health information clearinghouse funded by the U.S. government, includes the HON code and links to more than 1,700 sites, most of which are HON compliant. The site links to government Web sites, federally funded research centers, and national professional associations of licensed health care practitioners.

Remember that in using the Internet, unless you have a specific address that you know will get you the data you need (e.g., http://findlit.com.nih.xxx .edu), you must be prepared to spend time performing detective work. If you just rely on the first page of results from a search engine, you may miss out on the information you really need. Even if your search is precise, you may find hundreds of pages to sort through before you get where you want to go. To add insult to injury, even if you do locate a great site, saving it for future review may be useless because unless the site is stable, it may disappear without warning. Many sites simply vanish.

Thus, the Internet is not an efficient source for a comprehensive review of the literature. It is extremely time consuming to use because all sites and publications must be evaluated carefully.

If you do decide to search the Web for literature, make sure you get a satisfactory answer to EACH of the following questions.

Standards for Believing Web Sites

- Who supports or funds the site? Does the funder have any financial interest in the outcomes of the study?
- When was the site last updated? Are the findings still relevant?
- What authority do the authors/investigators have to do the study? Interpret the findings?
- Do the investigators give sufficient information so that you can evaluate their qualifications?
- Are the investigators likely to profit from the outcomes of the study?
- Do the investigators have peer-reviewed publications in good journals?
- Is the study an experimental or a high-quality observational study?
- Do the investigators describe what they did, how they did it, and the weaknesses or biases that might be present in their findings?

You should be able to get answers to each of these questions without having to leave the site. If you have any trouble using the site or finding the information you need to answer each question, raise your index of suspicion to its highest level, and leave the site for a better one.

ORGANIZING THE RESEARCH LITERATURE: BUILDING A VIRTUAL FILING CABINET

Articles and abstracts can be stored in several places. You can print out hard copies and file them in a cabinet. The fact is that after most reviews are completed, large numbers of stored paper articles are usually left to disintegrate.

An additional storage method focuses on creating reference lists by hand entering titles, authors, and so on in word-processing programs, spreadsheets, database manager programs (such as Access), and statistical programs. Hand entry is tedious, however, and prone to error due to typing. Moreover, unless the reference list is short, it is costly to spend time manually entering supplementary information for each article such as the key words or descriptors, abstract, and authors' affiliations.

Fortunately, you do not have to hand enter references or store them in steel or wooden file cabinets. Software exists that enables you to store the results of your search in a virtual file cabinet. These programs enable you to download references (including the abstract and URL) from hundreds of online databases. For instance, suppose you ask the software for PubMed. You will be automatically connected to that database and asked for titles, or authors, or key words, and so on. Once you supply this information, the computer will generate a list of references. You click on each reference that you want, and the full citation is inserted into a library that you create on your computer. The citation includes the abstract and the URL or other links so that you can access the full article (if it is available to you and you are online).

You can also hand enter references into the library and download references directly from journals. Suppose you are searching PubMed and find an interesting article. You can download the reference into the virtual file cabinet in your computer by clicking on an instruction such as "download to reference manager" as can be seen in this example (Figure 1.6) from PubMed in the second column.

Some databases (Figure 1.7) place the "download to citation manager" function next to the article itself. Look at the right-hand column.

Bibliographic software is essential. Programs, such as EndNote, ProCite, BibTex, Bookkeeper, Zotero, and Mendeley, have many features beyond serving as a virtual file cabinet. They provide the means for you to save your search strategy (so that you can continue your search over time and others can use it), insert references from your library directly into reports and scholarly articles, and analyze the references by thematic content.

Figure 1.6   Download to Citation Manager in PubMed

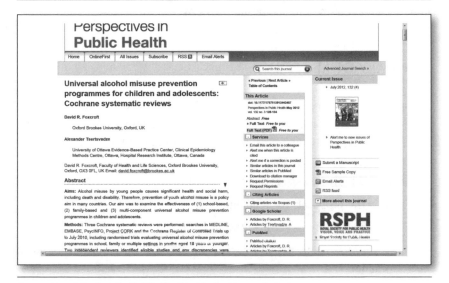

Source: Royal Society for Public Health. Used with permission.

Figure 1.7   Download to Citation Manager in the Sage Database of Journals

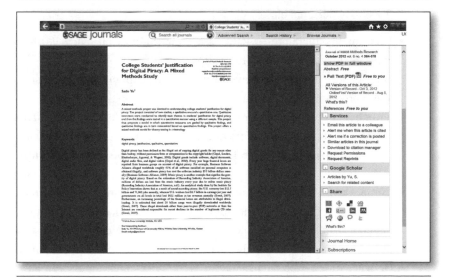

Source: Sagepub.com

An important reason to use bibliographic software management programs is because they help ensure accuracy and reproducibility. You can easily update a library, e-mail it, and post it on the Web.

SUMMARY OF KEY POINTS

- A literature review is a systematic, explicit, comprehensive, and reproducible method for identifying, evaluating, and interpreting the existing body of original work produced by researchers and scholars.
- Literature reviews are used for the following reasons:

  To write proposals for funding

  To write proposals for degrees

  To describe and explain current knowledge to guide professional practice

  To identify effective research and development methods

  To identify experts to help interpret existing literature and identify unpublished sources of information

  To identify funding sources and works in progress

  To satisfy personal curiosity

- High-quality literature reviews base their findings on evidence from experiments or controlled observations.
- High-quality literature reviews are systematic, explicit, comprehensive, and reproducible.
- Online searches usually are the most efficient. To use them effectively, you must have specific questions, key words, identifiers, and/or descriptors; learn to use Boolean logic; and be prepared to take tutorials.
- Comprehensive literature reviews mean supplementing the electronic search with reviews of the references in the identified literature, manual searches of references and journals, and consultation with experts to learn about unpublished and published studies and reports.
- Be wary of the Web as a source of credible research unless you have evidence that a site of interest is stable and unbiased.

- Reference management programs provide you with the means to set up virtual file cabinets, and they help ensure accuracy and reproducibility. You can easily update a library and e-mail it to other people who are interested in the same topic.

EXERCISES

1. You have been asked to design an educational and counseling program for people who are fearful of heights. Your research question is this: What are the determinants of and treatments for adults and older people who have a fear of heights? Before you begin to develop the program, you decide to do a literature review to ensure that the content of the proposed program will be up to date. You decide to use PubMed and PsycINFO (or similar databases) for your search. List at least 10 other key words or subject or thesaurus terms that you can use to find out what is currently known about the determinants and treatments for adults who are afraid of heights.

2. You are writing a proposal to do research into the prevention of common colds or rhinoviruses. Use a medical or health database to do your search. You propose to review only clinical studies in English, and you want abstracts of the articles. Which search terms do you use? How many citations result?

3. The following are sample abstracts retrieved from the PubMed and PsycINFO databases for your study of the prevention and spread of common colds. You decide to review the abstract first and then, based on the abstract, you will review only those studies that sound promising. Select the abstracts that are potentially appropriate for your review and justify your selection.

Prevention and Control of the Common Cold: Selected Abstracts

Abstract 1

Author: Smith AP

Title: Respiratory virus infections and performance

Source: In: Broadbent DE, Reason JT, Baddeley AD, eds. *Human Factors in Hazardous Situations.* Oxford, UK: Clarendon/ Oxford University Press; 1990. 71–80 of vii, 147 pp.

In this chapter, the author maintains that minor illnesses, such as colds and influenza, are frequent, widespread, and a major cause of absenteeism from work and education. Because of this, it is important to determine whether these viral infections alter the efficiency with which people perform certain tasks. To find out, the author reviewed studies from the Medical Research Centre Common Cold Unit and found that colds and influenza have selective effects on performance. In fact, the studies that the author reviewed showed that even sub-clinical infections can produce performance impairments, performance may be impaired during the incubation period of the illness, and performance impairments may still be observed after the clinical symptoms have gone. The author concludes that the findings from these studies have strong implications for occupational safety and efficiency.

Abstract 2

Author: Hemila H

Address: Department of Public Health, University of Helsinki, Finland

Title: Does vitamin C alleviate the symptoms of the common cold? A review of current evidence

Journal: Scandinavian Journal of Infectious Diseases. 1994;26(1): 1–6

In this article, the author reviews 21 placebo-controlled studies that have been done to find out if vitamin C at a dosage of 1 g/day affects the common cold. According to the author, the 21 studies did not provide consistent evidence that vitamin C supplementation reduces the incidence of the common cold in the general population. However, the author also points out that in each of the 21 studies, vitamin C reduced the duration of episodes and the severity of the symptoms of the common cold by an average of 23%. Because there have been large variations in the benefits observed, the author notes that clinical significance cannot be clearly inferred from the results.

Abstract 3

Author: Sattar SA, Jacobsen H, Springthorpe VS, Cusack TM, Rubino JR

Title: Chemical disinfection to interrupt transfer of rhinovirus type from environmental surfaces to hands

Journal: Applied and Environmental Microbiology. 1993;59(5): 1579–1585

The researchers in this study point out that rhinoviruses [which cause colds] can survive on environmental surfaces for several hours under ambient conditions. Hands can readily become contaminated after contact with such surfaces, and self-inoculation may lead to infection. Whereas washing your hands is crucial in preventing the spread of rhinovirus colds, proper disinfection of environmental surfaces may further reduce rhinovirus transmission. In this study, the authors compared the capacities of Lysol Disinfectant Spray, a bleach, a quaternary ammonium-based product, and a phenol-based product in interrupting the transfer of a type of rhinovirus from stainless steel disks to the finger pads of human volunteers. Among the findings were that the Lysol spray was able to reduce virus infectivity by > 99.99% after a contact of either 1 or 10 min, and no detectable virus was transferred to finger pads from Lysol-treated disks. The bleach reduced the virus titer by 99.7% after a contact time of 10 min, and again no virus was transferred from the disks treated with it.

Abstract 4

Author: Audera C, Patulny RV, Sander BH, Douglas RM

Title: Mega-dose vitamin C in treatment of the common cold: A randomised controlled trial

Journal: *Medical Journal of Australia.* 2001;175(7):359–362

The investigators were interested in studying the effect of large doses of vitamin C on the treatment of the common cold. They enlisted 400 volunteers to participate in an 18-month double-blind, randomized clinical trial with four intervention arms: vitamin C at daily doses of 0.03 g ("placebo"), 1 g, 3 g, or 3 g with additives ("Bio-C") taken at onset of a cold and for the following 2 days. They found no significant differences in any measure of cold duration or severity among the four medication groups. The investigators concluded that doses of vitamin C in excess of 1 g daily taken shortly after onset of a cold did not reduce the duration or severity of cold symptoms in adult volunteers when compared with a vitamin C dose less than the minimum recommended daily intake.

Abstract 5

Author: Khaw KT, Woodhouse P

Title: Interrelation of vitamin C, infection, haemostatic factors, and cardiovascular disease

Journal: *British Medical Journal.* 1995;310(6994):1559–1563

The two researchers hypothesized that the increase in fibrinogen concentration and respiratory infections in winter is related to seasonal variations in vitamin C status (assessed with serum ascorbate concentration). To test the hypothesis, they studied 96 people ages 65 to 74 years at intervals of 2 months over 1 year. The investigators found that average dietary intake of vitamin C varied from winter to summer. They also found that an increase in dietary vitamin C of 60 mg daily (about one orange) was associated with a decrease in fibrinogen concentrations of 0.15 g/1, equivalent (according to prospective studies) to a decline of approximately 10% in risk of ischemic heart disease. Based on this and other of their statistical results, the researchers concluded that the study findings support the hypothesis that vitamin C may protect against cardiovascular disease through an effect on hemostatic factors at least partly through the response to infection.

4. You are thinking of studying how to prevent school bullying. You go to ERIC to find out what is already known about the topic. You use these refining criteria: last six months; journal articles.

ANSWERS

1. Key words and other terms that can be used to find out about adults who are afraid of heights are acrophobia, agoraphobia, altitude, anxiety,

anxiety neuroses, arousal, awareness, behavior therapy, benzodiazepines, defense mechanism, desensitization, fear, fear of heights, internal-external control, neuropathy, panic, panic disorder, phobia, phobic disorders (diagnosis), phobic disorders (psychology) physiological correlates, set (psychology), threat, and vestibular apparatus.

2. Using PubMed, your search will result in nine citations and look something like this (as of July 2012).

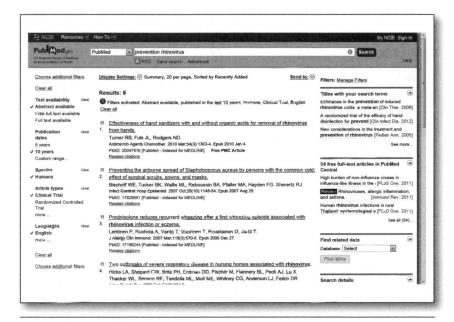

Source: US National Library of Medicine, Pubmed.gov

3. Abstracts 3, 4, and 5 are experiments and may be useful in the review. Abstract 1's information can be used to help interpret the review's findings. Because it collects no new information, it is not eligible for inclusion into the database that composes a literature review. Abstract 2 is a review of the literature; it may be a useful check on your review's content and conclusions.

4. Your preventing school bullying search of ERIC results in 10 articles (as of March 2013).

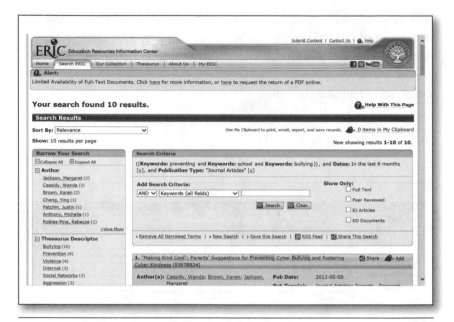

Source: U.S. Department of Education, Eric.ed.gov

ONLINE LITERATURE REVIEWS

For outstanding examples of stand-alone literature reviews, go to the Cochrane Collaboration Web site (http://www.cochrane.org).

The Cochrane Collaboration is an international nonprofit and independent organization, dedicated to making up-to-date, accurate information about the effects of health care readily available worldwide. It produces and disseminates systematic reviews of health care interventions and promotes the search for evidence in the form of clinical trials and other studies of interventions.

The major product of the collaboration is the *Cochrane Database of Systematic Reviews,* published quarterly as part of the Cochrane Library. Volunteer health care professionals do the reviews. They work in one of the many collaborative review groups with editorial teams overseeing the preparation and maintenance of the reviews, as well as application of the rigorous quality standards for which Cochrane Reviews have become known.

The following is a list of literature reviews available in their entirety online (as of July 2012. They have been selected to illustrate the range of topics, research questions, and research methods used to review the literature using a variety of bibliographic databases and other techniques. Some but not all reviews meet rigorous standards for high-quality information (see Chapters 2 and 3). Note that some of the reviews contain the word *meta-analysis* in their title. A meta-analysis (see Chapter 5) is a literature review that uses formal statistical techniques to sum up the results of similar but separate studies. The studies are similar in that they address the same research topic such as how to teach reading or how to prevent childhood obesity.

Bailey, E. J., Kruske, S. G., Morris, P. S., Cates, C. J., & Chang, A. B. (2008). Culture-specific programs for children and adults from minority groups who have asthma [Review]. *Cochrane Database of Systematic Reviews,* p. CD006580.

Cobner, R., & Hill, J. (2003). What works for whom? A critical review of treatments for children and adolescents [Review]. *Clinical Child Psychology & Psychiatry, 8,* 557–559. (found in PsycINFO)

Cooper, H., Robinson, J. C., & Patall, E. A. (2006). Does homework improve academic achievement? A synthesis of research, 1987–2003. *Review of Educational Research, 76*(1), 1–62. (found in Web of Science)

Cusick, L. (2002). Youth prostitution: A literature review. *Child Abuse Review, 11,* 230–251. (found in Sociological Abstracts)

Dennis, L. K., Beane Freeman, L. E., & VanBeek, M. J. (2003). Sunscreen use and the risk for melanoma: A quantitative review. *Annals of Internal Medicine, 139,* 966–978. (found in PubMed)

Diehl, K., Thiel, A., Zipfel, S., Mayer, J., Litaker, D. G., & Schneider, S. (2012). How healthy is the behavior of young athletes? A systematic literature review and meta-analyses [Review]. *Journal of Sports Science and Medicine, 11*(2), 201–220. (found in Web of Science)

Fink, A., Parhami, I., Rosenthal, R. J., Campos, M.D., Siani, A., & Fong, T. W. (2012). How transparent is behavioral intervention research on pathological gambling and other gambling-related disorders? A systematic literature review. *Addiction, 107*(11), 1915-1928. (found in PubMed)

Grabe, S., Ward, L. M., & Hyde, J. S. (2008). The role of the media in body image concerns among women: A meta-analysis of experimental and correlational studies. *Psychological Bulletin, 134,* 460–476. (found in PubMed and PsycINFO)

Graham, S., & Perin, D. (2007). What we know, what we still need to know: Teaching adolescents to write. *Scientific Studies of Reading, 11,* 313–335. (found in Web of Science)

Hoffler, T. N., & Leutner, D. (2007). Instructional animation versus static pictures: A meta-analysis. *Learning and Instruction, 17,* 722–738. (found in Web of Science)

Hofmann, S. G., & Smits, J. A. (2008). Cognitive-behavioral therapy for adult anxiety disorders: A meta-analysis of randomized placebo-controlled trials. *Journal of Clinical Psychiatry, 69,* 621–632. (found in PubMed)

Knorth, E. J., Harder, A. T., Zandberg, T., & Kendrick, A. J. (2008). Under one roof: A review and selective meta-analysis on the outcomes of residential child and youth care. *Children and Youth Services Review, 30,* 123–140. (found in Web of Science)

Lauer, P. A., Akiba, M., Wilkerson, S. B., Apthorp, H. S., Snow, D., & Martin-Glenn, M. L. (2006). Out-of-school-time programs: A meta-analysis of effects for at-risk students. *Review of Educational Research, 76,* 275–313. (found in Web of Science)

Lemstra, M., Neudorf, C., D'Arcy, C., Kunst, A., Warren, L. M., & Bennett, N. R. (2008). A systematic review of depressed mood and anxiety by SES in youth aged 10–15 years. *Canadian Journal of Public Health, 99*(2), 125–129. (found in PubMed)

Lundahl, B. W., Tollefson, D., Risser, H., & Lovejoy, M. C. (2008). A meta-analysis of father involvement in parent training. *Research on Social Work Practice, 18*(2), 97–106. (found in Web of Science)

Nigg, J. T., Lewis, K., Edinger, T., & Falk, M. (2012). Meta-analysis of attention-deficit/ hyperactivity disorder or attention-deficit/hyperactivity disorder symptoms, restriction diet, and synthetic food color additives [Article]. *Journal of the American Academy of Child and Adolescent Psychiatry, 51*(1), 86–97. doi: 10.1016/j .jaac.2011.10.015 (found in Web of Science and ERIC)

Reynolds, S., Wilson, C., Austin, J., & Hooper, L. (2012). Effects of psychotherapy for anxiety in children and adolescents: A meta-analytic review. *Clinical Psychology Review, 32*(4), 251–262. doi: 10.1016/j.cpr.2012.01.005 (found in PsycINFO)

Schroeder, C. M., Scott, T. P., Tolson, H., Huang, T. Y., & Lee, Y. H. (2007). A meta-analysis of national research: Effects of teaching strategies on student achievement in science in the United States. *Journal of Research in Science Teaching, 44,* 1436–1460. (found in Web of Science)

Shor, E., Roelfs, D. J., Bugyi, P., & Schwartz, J. E. (2012). Meta-analysis of marital dissolution and mortality: Reevaluating the intersection of gender and age. *Social Science & Medicine, 75*(1), 46–59. doi: 10.1016/j.socscimed.2012.03.010 (found in PsycINFO)

Siegenthaler, E., Munder, T., & Egger, M. (2012). Effect of preventive interventions in mentally ill parents on the mental health of the offspring: Systematic review and meta-analysis [Review]. *Journal of the American Academy of Child and Adolescent Psychiatry, 51*(1), 8–17. doi: 10.1016/j.jaac.2011.10.018 (found in Web of Science, ERIC, and PubMed)

Snook, B., Eastwood, J., Gendreau, P., Goggin, C., & Cullen, R. M. (2007). Taking stock of criminal profiling: A narrative review and meta-analysis. *Criminal Justice and Behavior, 34,* 437–453. (found in Web of Science)

Waters, E., de Silva-Sanigorski, A., Hall, B. J., Brown, T., Campbell, K. J., Gao, Y., Armstrong, R., Prosser, L., & Summerbell, C. D. (2011). Interventions for preventing obesity in children. *Cochrane Database of Systematic Reviews 2011, 12.* Retrieved from http://onlinelibrary.wiley.com/doi/10.1002/14651858.CD001871.pub3/full

Wood, S., & Mayo-Wilson, E. (2012). School-based mentoring for adolescents: A systematic review and meta-analysis [Review]. *Research on Social Work Practice, 22*(3), 257–269. doi: 10.1177/1049731511430836

SUGGESTED READINGS

Bero, L., & Rennie, D. (1995). The Cochrane Collaboration. *Journal of the American Medical Association, 274,* 1935–1938.

Girden, E. R., & Kabacoff, R. I. (2011). *Evaluating research articles from start to finish.* Thousand Oaks, CA: Sage.

Piotrowski, C., & Perdue, B. (2003). Benefits of multidatabase searching: A forensic case study. *Psychological Reports, 92,* 881–882.

Ridley, D. (2012). *The literature review: A step-by-step guide for students.* Thousand Oaks, CA: Sage.

NOTES

1.   Wisner, K. L., Gelenberg, A. J., Leonard, H., Zarin, D., & Frank, E. (1999). Pharmacologic treatment of depression during pregnancy [Review]. *Journal of the American Medical Association, 282,* 1264–1269.

2.   Lutters, M., & Vogt, N. (2003). Antibiotic duration for treating uncomplicated, symptomatic lower urinary tract infections in elderly women (Cochrane Review). In *The Cochrane Library,* Issue 4. (see http://www.cochrane.org)

✥ TWO ✥

SEARCHING AND SCREENING

The Practical Screen and Methodological Quality (Part 1—Research Design and Sampling)

═══════════ ⧽⧼ ═══════════

A Reader's Guide

Purpose of This Chapter

An important activity in the search for literature is to decide on criteria for including and excluding articles. The most efficient searches use two screens to select the studies that will be reviewed. The first screen is primarily practical. You use it to identify a broad range of potentially useful studies. This chapter explains how to use typical practical screening criteria such as a study's content, publication language, research setting and methods, and funding source, as well as the type of publication in which it appears.

The second screen is for methodological quality, and it is used to narrow the search by identifying the best available studies in terms of their adherence to methods that scientists and scholars rely on to gather sound evidence. Methodological quality refers to how well a study has been designed and implemented to achieve its objectives. Focusing on studies that have high quality is the only guarantee you have that the results of the review will be accurate.

The highest quality studies come closest to adhering to rigorous research standards. A useful way of thinking about research standards is in terms of the quality of study design and sampling, data collection, analysis, interpretation, and reporting. Study reports should provide sufficient information about their methods so that the reviewer has no trouble distinguishing high- from low-quality research. Among the questions the reviewer needs be able to answer are these: Is the research design internally and externally valid? Are the study's data sources reliable and valid? Are the analytic methods appropriate given the characteristics and quality of the study's data? Are the results meaningful in practical and statistical terms? Are the results presented in a cogent manner, describing the study's strengths and weaknesses?

An overview of the basic components of research design and sampling—two components of methodological quality—is given in this chapter. The next chapter explains data collection, analysis, and reporting.

Figure 2.1 illustrates the steps in conducting research literature reviews. The shaded portions are covered in this chapter, applying the practical and methodological screens to the search.

A literature search that has no restrictions may yield hundreds of candidate articles for review. It is unlikely, however, that you will want to review all of them because many will be irrelevant or poorly designed. Some articles will be published in a language you cannot read, for example, and others might focus on topics that are not on target. If you are interested in reviewing articles on how to prevent the common cold, for example, a search online will produce articles on viruses that cause colds, the psychological effects of having a cold, methods of treatment, and so on. Some articles might be useful, but others will not. Before beginning to review them all, you must sort through them to identify the ones that contain information on prevention.

Suppose you find 50 studies that focus on your general topic: Preventing colds. Even then, you cannot assume that you have finished your search. In all likelihood, some studies will be methodologically rigorous, deriving sound conclusions from valid evidence, whereas others will be methodologically weak. To ensure the accuracy of your review, you must continue the screening process so that you can correctly distinguish well-designed studies from poorly designed ones.

Efficient searches use two screens to sort out the relevant and strong studies from the others. The first screen is primarily practical. It is used to identify a broad range of articles that may be potentially usable in that they cover the topic of interest, are in a language you read, and are in a publication you respect and can obtain in a timely manner. The second screen is for quality, and it helps you narrow your search by identifying the best available studies. The best studies are not trying to sell you anything and use the methods that

Figure 2.1   Steps in Conducting Research Literature Reviews

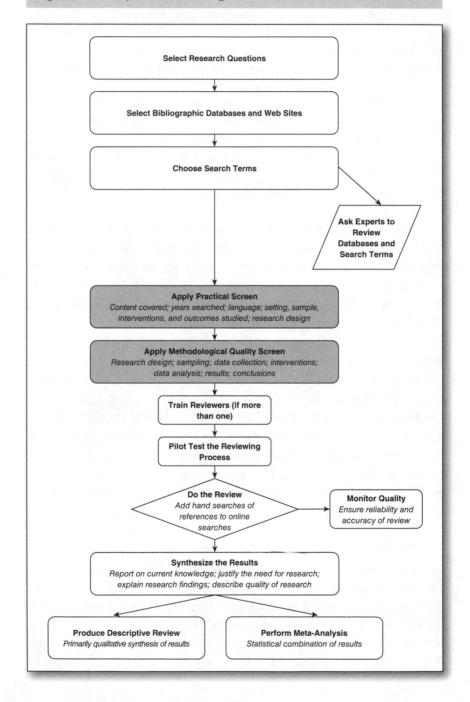

scientists and scholars rely on to gather sound evidence. Screening articles for methodological quality is essential in ensuring the accuracy of your review.

You must use both search screens—practical and methodological—to ensure the review's efficiency, relevance, and accuracy.

SEARCH SCREEN 1: THE PRACTICAL SCREEN

Examples of the variety of practical screening criteria that might be used to guide your search are illustrated below.

Including and Excluding Studies: Typical Practical Screening Criteria for Literature Review Searches

1. Publication language

   Example. Include only studies in English and Spanish.

2. Journal

   Example. Include all education journals. Exclude all sociology journals.

3. Author

   Example. Include all articles by Wendy Adams.

4. Setting

   Example. Include all studies that take place in community health settings. Exclude all studies that take place in community social service centers.

5. Participants or subjects

   Example. Include all men and women. Include all people who have a valid driver's license. Exclude all people who will not take the driving test in English or Spanish.

6. Program/intervention

   Example. Include all programs that are teacher led. Exclude all programs that are learner initiated.

7. Research design

   Example. Include only randomized trials/true experiments. Exclude studies without participant blinding.

8. Sampling

   Example. Include only studies that rely on randomly selected participants.

9. Date of publication

   Example. Include only studies published from January 1, 2005, to December 31, 2012.

10. Date of data collection

    Example. Include only studies that collected data from 2000 through 2012. Exclude studies that do not give dates of data collection.

11. Duration of data collection

    Example. Include only studies that collect data for 12 months or longer.

12. Content (topics, variables)

    Example. Include only studies that focus on primary prevention of illness. Exclude studies that focus on secondary or tertiary prevention. Exclude studies that focus on treatment.

13. Source of financial support

    Example. Include all privately supported studies. Exclude all studies receiving any government funds.

A literature review may use some or all types of practical screening criteria, as illustrated in these examples.

Practical Screening Criteria: Using Inclusion and Exclusion Criteria

Example 1. Social Functioning

To identify articles in English pertaining to measures of social functioning, we used three sources of information: The Oishi Social Functioning Bibliography (which cites 1,000 articles), PubMed (National Library of

Medicine), and PsycINFO (American Psychological Association). We limited candidate articles to those having the term *social functioning* in their titles. From these candidate articles, we selected only those that were published from 2008 to the present and that also described or used at least one questionnaire. We excluded letters, editorials, reviews, and articles that either were not written in English, French, Russian, Danish, or Spanish or dealt primarily with methodology or policy. We then reviewed the list of articles and restricted our selection to 15 prominent journals. Here is a summary of the inclusion and exclusion criteria:

Inclusion Criteria	Type
Term *social functioning* in titles	Content
Published from 2008 to the present	Publication date
Described or used at least one questionnaire	Content or instrument
English, French, Russian, Danish, or Spanish	Publication language
In 1 of 15 prominent journals (actual names given)	Journal
Exclusion Criteria	Type
Letters, editorials, review articles	Research design
Articles that deal with research design, measure development, or policy	Content

Example 2. Child Abuse and Neglect

We examined evaluations of programs to prevent child abuse and neglect conducted from 1990 through 2012. In our selection, we did not distinguish between types of abuse (such as physical or emotional) and neglect (such as emotional or medical), intensity, or frequency of occurrence. Only evaluations of programs that were family based, with program operations focused simultaneously on parents and children rather than just on parents, children, child care professionals, or the community, were included. We excluded studies that aimed to predict the causes and consequences of abuse or neglect or to appraise the effects of programs to treat children and families after abuse and neglect had been identified. We also excluded essays on abuse, cross-sectional studies, consensus statements, methodological research such as the development of a new measure of abuse, and studies that did not produce judgments of program effectiveness. Here is a summary of the inclusion and exclusion criteria:

Inclusion Criteria	Type
Evaluations of programs to prevent child abuse and neglect	Content
Conducted from 1990 through 2012	Duration of data collection
Family-based programs: focus on parents and families	Content
Exclusion Criteria	Type
Studies aiming to predict the causes and consequences of abuse or neglect	Content
Evaluations of programs to treat child abuse and neglect	Content
Essays on abuse, cross-sectional studies, consensus statements, and studies that do not produce judgments of effectiveness	Research design
Methodological research, such as the development of a new measure of abuse	Content

Search Screen 2: Methodological Quality Screening Criteria, Part 1—Research Design and Sampling

The second screen—for methodological quality—consists of setting standards for high-quality studies. The idea is that you should review only the studies that meet the selected (and justified) standards. In practice, this means that your search will be considerably narrowed.

Methodological quality refers to how well—scientifically—a study has been designed and implemented to achieve its objectives. The highest quality studies come closest to adhering to rigorous research standards. Only methodologically sound studies produce accurate results. Focusing on sound studies is the only way to ensure the accuracy of the review. Because of this, learning about research methods is an essential component of a research literature review.

To select high-quality studies, the literature reviewer should ask the following: (a) Is this study's research design internally and externally valid?

(b) Are the data sources used in the study reliable and valid? (c) Are the analytic methods appropriate given the characteristics and quality of the study's data? (d) Are the results meaningful in practical and statistical terms? As you will see from the discussion that follows, failure to provide satisfactory answers to some or all of these questions lessens a study's quality.

Criterion for Quality: Research Design

A study's research design refers to the way in which its subjects or participants—students, patients, and customers—are organized and measured. For instance, a study can be designed so that its participants are organized into two groups, one of which receives special treatment, but both are tested at least twice to find how they are.

Research designs are traditionally categorized as experimental or observational. In typical experimental studies, one or more groups of people participate in a new program or intervention (the "experiment"), and the researcher manipulates the environment to evaluate changes.

Experimental study designs typically involve two or more groups, at least one of which participates in an experiment while the other joins a control (or comparison) group, which does not take part in the experiment. The experimental group is given a new or untested, innovative program, intervention, or treatment. The control group is given an alternative. A group is any collective unit. Sometimes the unit is made up of individuals with a common experience, such as children who are in a reading program, people who fear heights, or scholarship winners. At other times, the unit is naturally occurring: a classroom, a business, or a hospital.

An example of an experimental research design might be one in which 100 teens are assigned at random to participate in a previously untried program to prevent high school dropout. The program includes work study classes and individual instruction to improve reading, writing, and computer skills. The progress of the students and their dropout rate are compared to another 100 teens who were randomly assigned to an alternative program. This program provides individual instruction but does not include work study.

Observational studies do not introduce new programs; they analyze already existing conditions and activities. An example of an observational study is one in which researchers analyze the school records of students to compare dropout rates between those who were in a prevention program and those who were not.

In general, experimental studies are considered more potent than observational designs. However, the use of experimental designs does not automatically guarantee a high-quality study, and it is important to learn about the characteristics of good research in order to make equitable and valid judgments.

Experimental Designs in Brief

Parallel Controls and Random Assignment: True Experiments. The groups in this design are created by first setting up eligibility criteria and then randomly assigning eligible *units* to one or more experimental and control groups. The groups can be observed and measured periodically. If the experimental group is observed to differ from the control group in a positive way on important variables (such as customer satisfaction, quality of life, health, and knowledge), the experiment is considered to be successful within certain predefined limits. The units that are randomly assigned may be individuals (such as Persons A, B, C, etc., or Teachers A, B, C, etc.) or clusters of individuals (such as schools, residential blocks, hospitals).

Random assignment (sometimes called randomization or random allocation) means that individuals or clusters of individuals are assigned by chance to the experimental or the control groups. With random assignment, the occurrence of previous events has no value in predicting future events. The alternative to randomization is regulation of the allocation process so that you can predict group assignment (such as assigning people admitted to a hospital on odd days of the month to the experimental group and those admitted on even days to the control group). A study with parallel controls and random assignment is illustrated next.

A Study with Parallel Controls and Random Assignment

Two reading programs were compared for students with reading difficulties. Over 4 years, half of all eligible children in each of 10 elementary schools were assigned at random to either Program A or Program B. Children were eligible if they were reading one or more grade levels below expectation as measured by the XYZ Reading Test. The design can be illustrated as follows:

Assigning Half of All Eligible Children in 10 Elementary Schools at Random to Program A or Program B

	Intervention Groups	
School	Program A	Program B
1 (100 children)	50	50
2 (60 children)	30	30
3 (120 children)	60	60
4 (90 children)	45	45
5 (100 children)	50	50
6 (90 children)	45	45
7 (70 children)	35	35
8 (150 children)	75	75
9 (150 children)	75	75
10 (100 children)	50	50

Random selection is different from random assignment. In some studies, the entire eligible population is chosen. In others, a sample or fraction of the population is chosen. If this fraction is selected randomly, you have random selection. If you next decide to randomly assign this selected sample into two or more groups, you also have random assignment, as illustrated below.

Random Selection and Random Assignment: Two Examples

1. In Study A, teens who volunteered to participate in an evaluation of an experimental Web-based history class were assigned at random to the experimental or a "control" program.

2. In Study B, a sample of teens was randomly selected from all who were eligible and then randomly assigned to the experimental or control program.

Comment. In the first study, teens were not selected at random but were chosen from a group of volunteers. Once chosen, however, they were assigned at random to the experimental or control program. In the second study, teens were randomly selected and randomly assigned. In general, random selection and random assignment are preferable to either alone.

Experimental study designs with randomly constituted parallel groups are the gold standards or the preferred designs when doing scientific research. They are sometimes referred to as *true experiments.* These designs—when implemented properly—can control for many errors or biases that may affect any experiment.

What are these errors or biases that lead to false conclusions? One of the most potentially damaging biases comes from the method of "selection." Selection bias is present when people who are initially different from one another and have differing prior risks for the outcome of interest are compared. Suppose a study is conducted after Schools 1 and 2 participate in a comparative test of two approaches to reading. The study results reveal that children in School 1's reading program—the control—score higher (better) on an attitude-to-reading inventory than do children in School 2—the experiment. Although the results may suggest a failed experiment, the two groups may have been different to begin with, even if they appeared to be similar. For instance, School 1's and 2's children may be alike in socioeconomic background, reading ability, and the competence of their reading teachers, but they may differ in other important ways. School 2, for example, may have a better library, a friendlier librarian, more resources to spend on extra program reading, a social system that reinforces reading, and so on. Less bias from the selection process would have resulted had students been randomly assigned into experimental and control groups regardless of school.

Biases can arise from unanticipated and unrecognized as well as recognized characteristics. Randomization is the only known way to control for unknown biases and to distribute them evenly among groups.

Designs using parallel controls and random assignment are more complex than other types of study designs. One issue that often arises in connection with these designs concerns the appropriate unit of randomization. Sometimes, for practical purposes, clusters (schools, companies), rather than individuals, are chosen for random assignment. When this happens, you cannot assume that the individuals forming the groups are comparable in the same way as they would have been had they been randomly chosen as individuals to be in the particular school or company. The reason is that if the researchers choose the assignment, they are in control, but if the individual participant or "subject" makes the selection, he or she is. After all, people go to certain schools, for example, because the schools meet the need of the individual and not of the experiment.

Other potential sources of bias include failure to adequately monitor the randomization process and to follow uniform procedures of randomization across all groups in the study. Training the people who do the randomizing and monitoring the quality of the process are essential, and the literature reviewer should be able to find these procedures discussed in the study.

In some randomized studies, the participants and investigators do not know which participants are in the experimental or the control groups: This is the double-blind experiment. When participants do not know, but investigators do, this is called the blinded trial. Some experts maintain that blinding is as important as randomization. Randomization, they say, eliminates influences at the start of a study but not the *confounders* that occur during the course of the study. For instance, confounding can occur if participants get extra attention or the control group catches on to the experiment. The extra attention and changes in the control group may alter the outcomes of a study. Blinding is often difficult to achieve in social experimentation, so the wary reviewer should pay special attention to the biases that may have occurred in randomized controlled studies without blinding.

Despite its scientific virtues, you cannot assume that randomization alone guarantees that a study has produced "truth." At the minimum, valid study results also depend on accurate data collection and appropriate statistical analysis and interpretation.

For examples of randomized controlled trials, go to the following sources:

Baird, S. J., Garfein, R. S., McIntosh, C. T., & Ozler, B. (2012). Effect of a cash transfer programme for schooling on prevalence of HIV and herpes simplex type 2 in Malawi: A cluster randomised trial. *Lancet, 379*(9823), 1320–1329. doi: 10.1016/s0140-6736(11)61709-1

Buller, M. K., Kane, I. L., Martin, R. C., Grese, A. J., Cutter, G. R., Saba, L. M., et al. (2008). Randomized trial evaluating computer-based sun safety education for children in elementary school. *Journal of Cancer Education, 23,* 74–79.

Butler, R. W., Copeland, D. R., Fairclough, D. L., Mulhern, R. K., Katz, E. R., Kazak, A. E., et al. (2008). A multicenter, randomized clinical trial of a cognitive remediation program for childhood survivors of a pediatric malignancy. *Journal of Consulting and Clinical Psychology, 76,* 367–378.

DuMont, K., Mitchell-Herzfeld, S., Greene, R., Lee, E., Lowenfels, A., Rodriguez, M., et al. (2008). Healthy Families New York (HFNY) randomized trial: Effects on early child abuse and neglect. *Child Abuse & Neglect, 32,* 295–315.

Fagan, J. (2008). Randomized study of a prebirth coparenting intervention with adolescent and young fathers. *Family Relations, 57,* 309–323.

Johnson, J. E., Friedmann, P. D., Green, T. C., Harrington, M., & Taxman, F. S. (2011). Gender and treatment response in substance use treatment-mandated parolees. *Journal of Substance Abuse Treatment, 40*(3), 313–321. doi: 10.1016/j.jsat.2010.11.013

Nance, D. C. (2012). Pains, joys, and secrets: Nurse-led group therapy for older adults with depression. *Issues in Mental Health Nursing, 33*(2), 89–95. doi: 10.3109/01612840.2011.624258

Poduska, J. M., Kellam, S. G., Wang, W., Brown, C. H., Ialongo, N. S., & Toyinbo, P. (2008). Impact of the Good Behavior Game, a universal classroom-based behavior intervention, on young adult service use for problems with emotions, behavior, or drugs or alcohol. *Drug and Alcohol Dependence, 95,* S29–S44.

Rdesinski, R. E., Melnick, A. L., Creach, E. D., Cozzens, J., & Carney, P. A. (2008). The costs of recruitment and retention of women from community-based programs into a randomized controlled contraceptive study. *Journal of Health Care for the Poor and Underserved, 19,* 639–651.

Swart, L., van Niekerk, A., Seedat, M., & Jordaan, E. (2008). Paraprofessional home visitation program to prevent childhood unintentional injuries in low-income communities: A cluster randomized controlled trial. *Injury Prevention, 14*(3), 164–169.

Thornton, J. D., Alejandro-Rodriguez, M., Leon, J. B., Albert, J. M., Baldeon, E. L., De Jesus, L. M., et al. (2012). Effect of an iPod video intervention on consent to donate organs: A randomized trial. *Annals of Internal Medicine, 156*(7), 483–490. doi: 10.1059/0003-4819-156-7-201204030-00004

Parallel Controls without Random Assignment. Nonrandomized, parallel controls (quasi-experimental designs or nonequivalent control groups design) come about when you have at least two already existing groups, one of which is designated experimental. In education, the researcher might choose two comparable classrooms or schools and designate onc as experimental. In community-based research, the researcher might use two similar communities. Researchers aim for groups that are as similar as possible so that they can be compared fairly or without bias. Unfortunately, the researchers can never be sure the groups are comparable. It is unlikely that the two groups would be as similar as they would if the researcher had assigned them through a random lottery. Here is an illustration.

Parallel Controls but No Random Assignment

A nonrandomized trial was used to test a program to reduce the use of antipsychotic drugs in nursing homes. The program was based on behavioral techniques to manage behavior problems and encourage gradual antipsychotic drug withdrawal. Two rural community nursing homes with elevated antipsychotic use were in the experimental group, and two other comparable homes were selected as parallel controls. Residents in both groups of homes had comparable demographic characteristics and functional status, and each group had a baseline rate of 29 days of antipsychotic use per 100 days of nursing home residence.

The above example uses a type of quasi-experimental design called a nonequivalent control groups design. Other quasi-experimental designs include the time-series design and its variations.

Parallel control designs without randomization are easier and less costly to implement than experimental designs with randomization, and many researchers use them. But these designs increase the likelihood that external factors will bias the results. Because of this, they are sometimes called *quasi-experimental* designs. A typical bias associated with nonrandom assignment is selection or membership bias.

Membership bias refers to the characteristics that members of groups share simply because they are in the group. The idea is that preexisting groups are usually not assembled haphazardly: They come together precisely because they share similar values, attitudes, behavior, or social and health status. Examples of groups with shared characteristics are people who live in the same neighborhood (who are likely to be similar in their incomes), children who have the same teacher (who may share similar abilities), patients who see a particular physician (who may have a particular medical problem), prisoners at a minimum-security facility (who have committed a certain level of crime), and prisoners at a maximum-security facility (who also have committed a certain level of crime and one that differs from those of prisoners in a minimum-security facility). Only random assignment can guarantee the limits within which two groups are equivalent from the point of view of all variables that may influence a study's outcomes.

Membership bias can seriously challenge a study's accuracy. When researchers use parallel controls without random assignment, you should look to see if they have administered a premeasure to determine the equivalence of the groups on potentially important characteristics at the study's start. In the study described above, the researchers demonstrate the equivalence of the groups by reporting that residents in each of the two homes had comparable demographic characteristics, functional status, and use of antipsychotics.

Statistical methods (e.g., propensity, instrumental variables methods, and regression discontinuity) are available to "control" for the influence of confounding variables when random assignment is not used. A variable that is more likely to be present in one group of subjects than in the comparison group and that is related to the outcome of interest and confuses or confounds the results is called a confounding variable. As a rule, however, it is better to control for confounders before the researchers collect data—that is, as part of design and sampling—than afterward, during analysis. You should review the design, sampling, and statistical analysis sections of the article to find out if the researchers adequately dealt with confounding.

For examples of nonrandomized controlled trails or quasi-experimental studies, go to the following sources:

Corcoran, J. (2006). A comparison group study of solution-focused therapy versus "treatment- as-usual" for behavior problems in children. *Journal of Social Service Research, 33,* 69–81.

Cross, T. P., Jones, L. M., Walsh, W. A., Simone, M., & Kolko, D. (2007). Child forensic interviewing in Children's Advocacy Centers: Empirical data on a practice model. *Child Abuse & Neglect, 31,* 1031–1052.

Gatto, N. M., Ventura, E. E., Cook, L. T., Gyllenhammer, L. E., & Davis, J. N. (2012). LA Sprouts: A garden-based nutrition intervention pilot program influences motivation and preferences for fruits and vegetables in Latino youth [Article]. *Journal of the Academy of Nutrition and Dietetics, 112*(6), 913–920. doi: 10.1016/j.jand.2012.01.014

Hébert, R., Raîche, M., Dubois, M. F., Gueye, N. R., Dobuc, N., Tousignant, M., & Grp, P. (2010). Impact of PRISMA, a coordination-type integrated service delivery system for frail older people in Quebec (Canada): A quasi-experimental study [Article]. *Journals of Gerontology Series B-Psychological Sciences and Social Sciences, 65*(1), 107–118. doi: 10.1093/geronb/gbp027

Kutnick, P., Ota, C., & Berdondini, L. (2008). Improving the effects of group working in classrooms with young school-aged children: Facilitating attainment, interaction and classroom activity. *Learning and Instruction, 18,* 83–95.

Orthner, D. K., Cook, P., Sabah, Y., & Rosenfeld, J. (2006). Organizational learning: A cross-national pilot-test of effectiveness in children's services. *Evaluation and Program Planning, 29,* 70–78.

Pascual-Leone, A., Bierman, R., Arnold, R., & Stasiak, E. (2011). Emotion-focused therapy for incarcerated offenders of intimate partner violence: A 3-year outcome using a new whole-sample matching method [Article]. *Psychotherapy Research,* *21*(3), 331–347. doi: 10.1080/10503307.2011.572092

Rice, V. H., Weglicki, L. S., Templin, T., Jamil, H., & Hammad, A. (2010). Intervention effects on tobacco use in Arab and non-Arab American adolescents [Article]. *Addictive Behaviors, 35*(1), 46–48. doi: 10.1016/j.addbeh.2009.07.005

Struyven, K., Dochy, F., & Janssens, S. (2008). The effects of hands-on experience on students' preferences for assessment methods. *Journal of Teacher Education, 59,* 69–88.

Self-Controls

A design with self-controls uses a group of participants to serve as its own comparison. Suppose, for example, students were surveyed three times: at the beginning of the year to find out their attitudes toward community service, immediately after their participation in a 1-year course to find out the extent to which their attitude changed, and at the end of 2 years to ascertain if the change is sustained. This three-measurement strategy describes a design using the students as their own control. In the example, the survey measures the students once before and twice after the intervention (a new course).

Self-controlled designs are extremely weak because they are prone to many biases. Participants may become excited about taking part in an experiment; they may mature physically, emotionally, and intellectually; or historical events can intervene. For example, suppose a study reveals that the students in a 2-year test of a school-based intervention acquire important attitudes and behaviors and retain them over time. This desirable result may be due to the new course or to the characteristics of the students who, from the start, may have been motivated to learn and have become even more excited by being in an experimental program. Another possibility is that over the 2-year intervention period, students may have matured intellectually, and this development rather than the program is responsible for the learning. Also, historical or external events may have occurred to cloud the effects of the new course. For example, suppose that during the year, an inspired teacher gives several stimulating lectures to the students. The students' outstanding performance on subsequent tests may be due as much or more to the lectures as to the program.

The addition of a control group is necessary to strengthen self-controlled designs, as shown next.

Combined Self-Control and Parallel Control Design to Evaluate the Impact of Education and Legislation on Children's Use of Bicycle Helmets

An anonymous questionnaire regarding use of bicycle helmets was sent twice to nearly 3,000 children in three counties. The first mailing took place 3 months before an educational campaign in County 1 and 3 months before the passage of legislation requiring helmets and an education campaign in County 2. The second mailing took place 9 months after completion of the education and combined education-legislation. Two surveys (9 months apart) were also conducted in County 3, the control. County 3 had neither education nor legislation pertaining to the use of bicycle helmets. The table and associated text summarize the results.

Percentage of Children Reporting Helmet Use "Always" or "Usually"

	Before Intervention	After Intervention
County 1: Education only	8	13[a]
County 2: Education and legislation	11	37[b]
County 3: No intervention	7	8

Note: The percentages are small and do not add up to 100% because they represent just the proportion of children answering "always" or "usually." Other responses (such as "rarely") constituted the other choices.

a. $p < .01$. This means that the observed result (always or usually reporting helmet use) will occur by chance 1 in 100 times. The p or p value is the probability that an observed result (or result of a statistical test) is due to chance.

b. $p < .0001$. This means that the observed result will occur by chance 1 in 10,000 times.

Note. More information about p values and other statistical terms can be found in Chapter 3.

Findings. The proportion of children who reported that they "always" or "usually" wore a helmet increased significantly ($p < .0001$) from 11% before to 37% in County 2 (education and legislation) and 8% to 13% ($p < .01$) in County 1 (education only). The increase of 1% in County 3 was not statistically significant.

Comment. Education alone and education combined with legislation were relatively effective: Either one or both increase the proportion of children reporting helmet use. The education may have taught children to give the socially acceptable responses on the survey, but other studies in the literature suggest that single education programs alone have not usually encouraged children to give desirable responses to survey questions. The fact that the control group did not improve suggests that County 1's and 2's efforts were responsible for the improvements. The addition of the control group adds credibility to the study results.

Historical Controls or Existing Data

Studies that use historical controls rely on data that are available from an existing database. These data are sometimes called "norms" to refer to the fact they are the reference points. They are historical because they were collected in the past.

Historical controls include established norms such as scores on standardized tests (e.g., the SATs and GREs), the results of studies conducted in the past, and vital statistics such as birth and death rates. These data substitute for the data that would come from a parallel control.

Suppose you are reviewing the literature to find out how your state or province compares with the rest of the country in its provision of routine school-based mental health services. Your state has just completed a survey of its schools. You come across Table 2.1 in a report.

The people who prepared the table have used historical controls in the form of an existing database (National Survey of Children's Mental Health Services, 2003) as a reference against which to compare the results of the more recent survey. (The statistical methods for comparing the results are not included in this example.)

Historical controls are convenient; their main source of bias is the potential lack of comparability between the group on whom the data were originally collected and the group of concern in the study. In the example given in the table, the reviewer has to determine if children in the state have different needs or resources compared with the rest of the county. If so, then the comparison group is not appropriate.

The validity of the comparisons between historical controls and current groups may also be compromised if the data come from two different time periods because of rapid social changes. In the example in Table 2.1, the reviewer might fault the researcher for using data that are 10 (or more) years old, particularly if evidence shows that mental health services, needs, and resources have changed markedly from over the data collection period.

When reviewing the literature, ask the following: Is the choice of historical control explained and justified? Are the normative data reliable, valid, and appropriate?

Table 2.1   Percentages of School Children in a Hypothetical State (HS) and Country (HC) Who Have Access to Routine School-Based Mental Health Services

	≤10 Years (%)		10 to 14 Years (%)		15 to 17 Years (%)	
	HS	HC	HS	HC	HS	HC
All children	89.9	97.2	92.3	84.5	89.5	90.8
Family income						
Under $25,000	83.7	82.4	86.7	86.3	87.6	88.8
$25,000 to $50,000	95.7	92.7	91.3	92.5	86.5	88.3
$51,000 to $75,000	95.3	91.3	96.1	94.6	90.1	89.4
Greater than $75,000	95.3	94.4	97.7	96.5	96.7	94.7

Sources: National Survey of Children's Mental Services (2003) and State Survey of Children's Mental Health Services (1998).

OBSERVATIONAL DESIGNS IN BRIEF

Cohort Designs

A *cohort* is a group of people who have something in common and who remain part of a study group over an extended period of time. In public health research, cohort studies are used to describe and predict the risk factors for a disease and the disease's cause, incidence, natural history, and prognosis. Cohort studies may be *prospective* or *retrospective*. With a prospective design, the direction of inquiry is forward in time, whereas with a retrospective design, the direction is backward in time.

Prospective Cohort Designs

Does a High-Fiber Diet Prevent Colon Cancer?

A team of researchers was interested in finding out if a high-fiber diet prevents colon cancer. They mailed out questionnaires to a sample of registered nurses (the cohort) asking them about their diet and other risk factors and received over 121,000 completed responses. Every 2 years for two decades, they sent out questionnaires to update their information and to ask the nurses about the occurrence of any diseases, including colon cancer. The researchers confirmed the nurses' report of disease by examining their medical records. The statistical analysis of the data showed that dietary fiber intake did not prevent colon cancer. Nurses who consumed the least amount of dietary fiber did not differ from nurses who consumed the most in rates of colon cancer.

This is a very brief description of one small component of the Nurses' Health Study, a large multiyear cohort study. With rigorous cohort designs, potential *predictive* factors (such as diet) are measured before an *outcome* (such as colon cancer) occurs. Over a long time period and with multiple and frequent valid measures, the researcher may be able to infer that the factor is (or is not) a cause of the outcome.

Another example of a prospective cohort study involves the study of criminal careers.

Do Criminal Career Patterns Differ Across Race and by Sex?

Researchers analyzed data from individuals (the cohort) who participated in the Providence sample of the National Collaborative Perinatal Project. They focused on patterns of prevalence, frequency, chronicity, and specialization in violence for the entire cohort, as well as for samples stratified by race, sex, and race together with sex. In addition, demographic and juvenile offending characteristics were used to predict adult offender status. The researchers found that three variables significantly predicted adult offender status. Males and non-Whites were significantly more likely than females and Whites to be registered as adult offenders. Of the two juvenile offending indicators, only one, chronic offending, significantly predicted adult offender status. Having a violent arrest as a juvenile did not significantly predict adult offender status.

Question: Which were the predictor(s) in this study? Which were the outcomes?

High-quality prospective or *longitudinal* studies are expensive to conduct, especially if the investigator is concerned with outcomes that are relatively rare or hard to predict. Studying rare and unpredictable outcomes requires large samples and numerous measures. Also, researchers who do prospective cohort studies have to be on guard against loss of subjects over time or attrition. For instance, longitudinal studies of children are often beset by attrition because over time, they lose interest, move far away, change their names, and so on. If a large number of people drop out of a study, the sample that remains may be very different from the one that left. The remaining sample may be more motivated or less mobile than those who left, for example, and these factors may be related in unpredictable ways to any observed outcomes.

When reviewing prospective cohort studies, make sure that the researchers address how they handled loss to follow-up or attrition. Ask the following: How large a problem was attrition? Were losses to follow-up handled in the analysis? Were the study's findings affected by the losses?

For examples of prospective cohort studies, go to the following:

Brown, C. S., & Lloyd, K. (2008). OPRISK: A structured checklist assessing security needs for mentally disordered offenders referred to high security psychiatric hospital. *Criminal Behaviour and Mental Health, 18,* 190–202.

Chauhan, P., & Widom, C. S. (2012). Childhood maltreatment and illicit drug use in middle adulthood: The role of neighborhood characteristics. *Development and Psychopathology, 24*(Special Issue 03), 723–738. doi: 10.1017/S0954579412000338

Fuchs, C. S., Giovannucci, E. L., Colditz, G. A., Hunter, D. J., Stampfer, M. J., Rosner, B., et al. (1999). Dietary fiber and the risk of colorectal cancer and adenoma in women. *New England Journal of Medicine, 340,* 169–176.

Kemp, P. A., Neale, J., & Robertson, M. (2006). Homelessness among problem drug users: Prevalence, risk factors and trigger events. *Health & Social Care in the Community, 14,* 319–328.

Kerr, T., Hogg, R. S., Yip, B., Tyndall, M. W., Montaner, J., & Wood, E. (2008). Validity of self-reported adherence among injection drug users. *Journal of the International Association of Physicians in AIDS Care, 7*(4), 157–159.

Kuyper, L. M., Palepu, A., Kerr, T., Li, K., Miller, C. L., Spittal, P. M., et al. (2005). Factors associated with sex-trade involvement among female injection drug users in a Canadian setting. *Addiction Research & Theory, 13*(2), 193–199.

Piquero, A. R., & Buka, S. L. (2002). Linking juvenile and adult patterns of criminal activity in the Providence cohort of the National Collaborative Perinatal Project. *Journal of Criminal Justice, 30,* 259–272.

Pletcher, M. J., Vittinghoff, E., Kalhan, R., Richman, J., Safford, M., Sidney, S., Lin, F., & Kertesz, S. (2012). Association between marijuana exposure and pulmonary function over 20 years. *JAMA: The Journal of the American Medical Association, 307*(2), 173–181. doi: 10.1001/jama.2011.1961

White, H. R., & Widom, C. S. (2003). Does childhood victimization increase the risk of early death? A 25-year prospective study. *Child Abuse & Neglect, 27,* 841–853.

Because of the difficulties and expense of implementing prospective cohort designs, many cohort designs reported in the literature tend to be retrospective. An example retrospective cohort design is illustrated as follows.

Retrospective Cohort Design

Does a Relationship Exist Between Family History and Diagnosis of Breast Cancer?

The investigators searched a hospital's database of diagnoses between 2000 and 2004 and found 250 women who had a diagnosis of cancer in situ. These 250 women are the cohort. The investigators reviewed these 250 patients' medical records to find out about their family's medical history and about other factors that might be associated with the disease. The data collected by the researchers enabled them to study the relationship between family history and other variables and the occurrence of cancer in this sample of 250.

What Are the Possible Causes of Xenophobia in German Youth?

Using available data from a large, ongoing study of youths from East and West Berlin, trends of change in adolescent xenophobia were analyzed. The study's database contained the results of two surveys: The Self-Interested Survey and the Self-Esteem Scale. Two main hypotheses were tested—namely, that self-interest and low self-esteem are the driving forces behind xenophobia among 13- to 16-year-olds.

Retrospective cohort designs have the same strengths as prospective designs. Like prospective designs, retrospective designs can establish that a predictor variable (such as self-esteem) precedes an outcome (such as xenophobia). Also, because data are collected before the outcomes are known, the measurement of variables that might predict the outcome (such as self-esteem) cannot be biased by prior knowledge of which people are likely to develop the problem (such as xenophobia). Retrospective cohort studies are usually less expensive to do than prospective studies because they rely on existing data. But the results may not be as convincing because the existing data on which the investigator depends may not include the subjects and information that the investigator might prefer if he or she had done the original study. When you review a retrospective cohort study, ask the following: How typical or representative is the sample? Is the investigation of the cohort inclusive? Did the analysis include all pertinent variables?

For an example of retrospective cohort studies, go to the following:

Boehnke, K., Hagan, J., & Hefler, G. (1998). On the development of xenophobia in Germany: The adolescent years. *Journal of Social Issues* [Special issue: Political development: Youth growing up in a global community], *54*, 585–602.

Edith, H. H., Pierik, F. H., de Kluizenaar, Y., Willemsen, S. P., Hofman, A., van Ratingen, S., W., et al. (2012). Air pollution exposure during pregnancy, ultrasound measures of fetal growth, and adverse birth outcomes: A prospective cohort study. *Environmental Health Perspectives, 120*(1), 150–156. doi: 10.1289/ehp.1003316

Harper, S., Rushani, D., & Kaufman, J. S. (2012). Trends in the black-white life expectancy gap, 2003-2008. *JAMA: The Journal of the American Medical Association, 307*(21), 2257–2259. doi: 10.1001/jama.2012.5059

Hoge, C. W., Auchterlonie, J. L, & Milliken, C. S. (2006). Mental health problems, use of mental health services, and attrition from military service after returning from deployment to Iraq or Afghanistan. *JAMA: The Journal of the American Medical Association, 295*(9), 1023–1032. doi: 10.1001/jama.295.9.1023

Lee, S. J., Taylor, C. A., & Bellamy, J. L. (2012). Paternal depression and risk for child neglect in father-involved families of young children [Article]. *Child Abuse & Neglect, 36*(5), 461–469. doi: 10.1016/j.chiabu.2012.04.002

Santos, I. S., Matijasevich, A., & Domingues, M. R. (2012). Maternal caffeine consumption and infant nighttime waking: Prospective cohort study. *Pediatrics, 129*(5), 860–868. doi: 10.1542/peds.2011-1773

Case Control Designs

Case control designs are generally retrospective. They are used to explain why a phenomenon currently exists by comparing the histories of two different groups, one of which is involved in the phenomenon. For example, a case control design might be used to help understand the social, demographic, and attitudinal variables that distinguish people who at the present time have been identified with frequent headaches from those who do not have frequent headaches.

The cases in case control designs are individuals who have been chosen on the basis of some characteristic or outcome (such as frequent headaches). The controls are individuals without the characteristic or outcome. The histories of cases and controls are analyzed and compared in an attempt to uncover one or more characteristics present in the cases and not in the controls.

How can researchers avoid having one group decidedly different from the other, say, healthier or smarter? Some methods include randomly selecting the controls, using several controls, and carefully matching controls and cases on important variables.

The Case Control Design in Two Studies

The Role of Alcohol in Boating Deaths

Alcohol is increasingly recognized as a factor in many boating fatalities, but the association between alcohol consumption and mortality among boaters has not been well quantified. This study aimed to determine the association of alcohol use with passengers' and operators' estimated relative risk of dying while boating. To do this, the researchers carried out a case control study of recreational boating deaths among persons aged 18 years or older from 1990 to 1998 in Maryland and North Carolina ($n = 221$). They compared the cases with control interviews obtained from a multistage probability sample of boaters from the same locations at which the deaths occurred in each state from 1997 to 1999 ($n = 3,943$).

Knee Arthritis and Japanese Women

This study investigated the relationship between knee osteoarthritis (OA) and constitutional factors (e.g., weight), history of joint injuries, and occupational factors using a case control study among women in Japan.

The study covered three health districts in Japan. Cases were women 45 years of age and older who were diagnosed with knee OA by orthopedic physicians using radiography. Controls were selected randomly from the general population and were individually matched to each case for age, sex, and residential district. Subjects were interviewed using structured questionnaires to determine medical history, including history of joint injury, physical activity, socioeconomic factors, and occupation. Height and weight were measured.

In the first study, a complex random sampling scheme was employed to minimize bias among control subjects and maximize their comparability with cases (e.g., deaths took place in the same location). In the second study, the controls were selected randomly and then were matched to each case for age, sex, and residential districts.

Epidemiologists and other health workers often use case control designs to provide insight into the causes and consequences of disease and other health problems. Reviewers of these studies should be on the lookout for certain methodological problems, however. First, cases and controls are often chosen from two separate populations. Because of this, systematic differences (such as motivation and cultural beliefs) may exist between or among the groups that are difficult to anticipate, measure, or control, and these differences may influence the study's results.

Another potential problem with case control designs is that the data often come from people's recall of events, such as asking women to discuss the history of their physical activity or asking boaters about their drinking habits. Memory is often unreliable, and if so, the results of a study that depends on memory may result in misleading information.

For examples of case control studies, go to the following:

Belardinelli, C., Hatch, J. P., Olvera, R. L., Fonseca, M., Caetano, S. C., Nicoletti, M., et al. (2008). Family environment patterns in families with bipolar children. *Journal of Affective Disorders, 107*(1–3), 299–305.

Bookle, M., & Webber, M. (2011). Ethnicity and access to an inner city home treatment service: A case-control study. *Health & Social Care in the Community, 19*(3), 280–288. doi: 10.1111/j.1365-2524.2010.00980.x

Davis, C., Levitan, R. D., Carter, J., Kaplan, A. S., Reid, C., Curtis, C., et al. (2008). Personality and eating behaviors: A case-control study of binge eating disorder. *International Journal of Eating Disorders, 41*, 243–250.

Hall, S. S., Arron, K., Sloneem, J., & Oliver, C. (2008). Health and sleep problems in cornelia de lange syndrome: A case control study. *Journal of Intellectual Disability Research, 52*, 458–468.

Menendez, C. C., Nachreiner, N. M., Gerberich, S. G., Ryan, A. D., Erkal, S., McGovern, P. M., Church, T. R., Mongin, S. J., & Feda, D. M. (2012). Risk of physical assault against school educators with histories of occupational and other violence: A case-control study. *Work, 42*(1), 39–46.

Smith, G. S., Keyl, P. M., Hadley, J. A., Bartley, C. L., Foss, R. D., Tolbert, W. G.,
    et al. (2001). Drinking and recreational boating fatalities: A population-based
    case-control study. *Journal of the American Medical Association, 286,*
    2974–2980.
Yoshimura, N., Nishioka, S., Kinoshita, H., Hori, N., Nishioka, T., Ryujin, M., et al.
    (2004). Risk factors for knee osteoarthritis in Japanese women: Heavy weight,
    previous joint injuries, and occupational activities. *Journal of Rheumatology,
    31*(1), 157–162.

A NOTE ON OTHER DESIGNS AND STUDIES: CROSS-SECTIONAL SURVEYS AND CONSENSUS STATEMENTS

Cross-Sectional Surveys

Cross-sectional designs result in a portrait of one or many groups at one period of time. These designs are frequently associated with mail and other self-administered survey questionnaires and face-to-face and telephone interviews. In fact, cross-sectional studies are sometimes called survey or descriptive designs. The following are three illustrative uses of cross-sectional designs.

Cross-Sectional Designs

1. Refugees are interviewed to find out their immediate fears and aspirations.

2. A survey is mailed to consumers to identify perceptions of the quality of the goods and services received when ordering by catalog.

3. A community participates in a Web survey to find out its needs for youth services.

Cross-sectional surveys are used to describe a study's sample and provide baseline information at the start of an experiment. The study's sample may consist of individuals or institutions such as businesses, schools, and hospitals. A researcher who conducts a Web survey with 500 small businesses to find out their maternity leave policies is doing a cross-sectional study.

Baseline information consists of demographic data (age, gender, income, education, health) and statistics on variables such as current knowledge, attitudes, and behaviors. A researcher may, however, look for relationships between demographic data and other variables. For instance, a cross-sectional survey of knowledge of current events among middle school children might study the relationship between gender (one baseline variable) and knowledge of current events (another baseline variable).

The major limitation of cross-sectional studies is that on their own and without follow-up, they provide no information on causality: They only provide information on events at a single, fixed point in time. For example, suppose a researcher finds that girls have less knowledge of current events than do boys. The researcher cannot conclude that being female somehow causes less knowledge of current events. The researcher can only be sure that in *this* survey, girls had less knowledge than boys.

To illustrate the point further, suppose you are doing a literature review on community-based exercise programs. You are specifically interested in learning about the relationship between age and exercise. Does exercise decrease with age? In your search of the literature, you find the following report.

A Report of a Cross-Sectional Survey of Exercise Habits

In March of this year, Researcher A surveyed a sample of 1,500 people between the ages of 30 and 70 to find out about their exercise habits. One of the questions he asked participants was, "How much do you exercise on a typical day?" Researcher A divided his sample into two groups: People 45 years of age and younger and people 46 years and older. Researcher A's data analysis revealed that the amount of daily exercise reported by the two groups differed, with the younger group reporting 15 minutes more exercise on a typical day.

Based on this summary, does amount of exercise decline with age? The answer is that you cannot get the answer from Researcher A's report. The decline seen in a cross-sectional study like this one can actually represent a decline in exercise with increasing age, or it may reflect the oddities of this particular sample. The younger people in this study may be especially sports minded, whereas the older people may be particularly anti-exercise. As a reviewer, you need to figure out which of the two explanations is better. One way you can do this is to search the literature to find out which conclusions are supported by other studies. Does the literature generally sustain the idea that amount of exercise always declines with age? After all, in some communities, the amount of exercise done by older people may actually increase because with retirement or part-time work, older adults may have more time to exercise than do younger people.

Suppose you are interested in finding out how parents of children with Tourette's disorder and parents of children with asthma compare in their mental health and burden of caregiving. Can you get the information you need from the following cross-sectional survey?

A Cross-Sectional Survey of Two Groups of Parents

Researchers examined the mental health and caregiver burden in parents of children with Tourette's disorder compared with parents of children with asthma. They surveyed parents at Tourette's disorder and pediatric asthma hospital outpatient clinics. The survey consisted of measures of parent mental health (General Health Questionnaire [GHQ]-28) and caregiver burden (Child and Adolescent Impact Assessment). Of the parents of children with Tourette's, 76.9% had mental health distress on the GHQ-28, compared with 34.6% of the parents of children with asthma; this effect remained significant after taking into account demographic variables (such as age and education). Parents of children with Tourette's also experienced greater caregiver burden.

It is difficult to tell from the example if the differences in mental health found by the researchers are due to the nature of Tourette parents' caregiving burden or to something else entirely. It is possible, for example, that the particular group of Tourette parents might have significant mental health problems regardless of their children's illness. The reviewer needs more information about the two study samples and how they were selected in order to make a decision as to the validity of the researchers' findings.

For examples of cross-sectional studies, go to the following:

Belardinelli, C., Hatch, J. P., Olvera, R. L., Fonseca, M., Caetano, S. C., Nicoletti, M., et al. (2008). Family environment patterns in families with bipolar children. *Journal of Affective Disorders, 107*(1–3), 299–305.

Carmona, C. G. H., Barros, R. S., Tobar, J. R., Canobra, V. H., & Montequín, E. A. (2008). Family functioning of out-of-treatment cocaine base paste and cocaine hydrochloride users. *Addictive Behaviors, 33,* 866–879.

Cooper, C., Robertson, M. M., & Livingston, G. (2003). Psychological morbidity and caregiver burden in parents of children with Tourette's disorder and psychiatric comorbidity. *Journal of the American Academy of Child & Adolescent Psychiatry, 42,* 1370–1375.

Davis, C., Levitan, R. D., Carter, J., Kaplan, A. S., Reid, C., Curtis, C., et al. (2008). Personality and eating behaviors: A case-control study of binge eating disorder. *International Journal of Eating Disorders, 41,* 243–250.

Hall, S. S., Arron, K., Sloneem, J., & Oliver, C. (2008). Health and sleep problems in cornelia de lange syndrome: A case control study. *Journal of Intellectual Disability Research, 52,* 458–468.

Joice, S., Jones, M., & Johnston, M. (2012). Stress of caring and nurses' beliefs in the stroke rehabilitation environment: A cross-sectional study. *International Journal of Therapy & Rehabilitation, 19*(4), 209–216.

Kypri, K., Bell, M. L., Hay, G. C., & Baxter, J. (2008). Alcohol outlet density and university student drinking: A national study. *Addiction, 103,* 1131–1138.

Meijer, J. H., Dekker, N., Koeter, M. W., Quee, P. J., Van Beveren, N. J., & Meijer, C. J. (2012). Cannabis and cognitive performance in psychosis: A cross-sectional study in patients with non-affective psychotic illness and their unaffected siblings. *Psychological Medicine, 42*(4), 705–716. doi: 10.1017/s0033291711001656

Negriff, S., Fung, M. T., & Trickett, P. K. (2008). Self-rated pubertal development, depressive symptoms and delinquency: Measurement issues and moderation by gender and maltreatment. *Journal of Youth and Adolescence, 37,* 736–746.

Schwarzer, R., & Hallum, S. (2008). Perceived teacher self-efficacy as a predictor of job stress and burnout. *Applied Psychology: An International Review, 57* (Suppl. 1), 152–171.

Consensus Statements

Consensus statements are common in health and medicine and provide guidance to physicians and patients on how to identify and care for dozens of problems, including knee replacement, epilepsy, and cataracts. A group or panel of knowledgeable individuals issues consensus statements, and they do so because the available literature on that topic is incomplete or contradictory. Consensus panels generally agree that the best way to get information is through controlled experimentation. But good study data are not always immediately available.

The best consensus statements result from a consideration of the world's literature in combination with group process methods known to make maximum use of participants' expertise. The number of participants in most consensus development activities ranges from 9 to 14. The most famous are the National Institutes of Health (NIH) Consensus Statements (http://consensus.nih.gov).

Reviewers of the literature are often tempted to include consensus statements to justify the need for a study or its conclusions. Consensus statements are observational studies, however, and are prey to many of the same limitations as observational studies are.

Books

Many books contain excellent literature reviews, and their bibliographies are a gold mine for other reviewers. Books are also essential guides to understanding theory and for helping you to validate the need for your study, confirm your choice of literature, and certify (or contradict) its findings. By definition, however, literature reviews are based on an analysis of the original studies. Original studies allow the reviewer to report, "Jones and Smith *found. . . .*" With books you must report, "Jones and Smith *say. . . .*"

Internal and External Validity

A study design with external validity produces results that apply to the study's target population. An externally valid survey of the preferences of airline passengers over 45 years of age means that the findings apply to all airline passengers of that age.

A design is internally valid if it is free from nonrandom error or bias. A study design must be internally valid in order to be externally valid. One of the most important questions to ask when reviewing the literature is, Does this study's design have internal validity? The following is a checklist of the influences on a study that threaten its internal validity.

Internal Invalidity: A Checklist of Potential Threats to a Study's Accuracy

✓   *Maturation*

Maturation refers to changes within individuals that result from natural, biological, or psychological development. For example, in a 5-year study of a preventive health education program for high school students, the students may mature intellectually and emotionally, and this new maturity may be more important than the program in producing changes in health behavior.

✓ *Selection*

Selection refers to how people were chosen for a study and, if they participate in an experiment, how they were assigned to groups. Selection bias is minimized when every eligible person or unit has an equal, nonzero chance of being included.

✓ *History*

Historical events may occur that can bias the study's results. For example, suppose a national campaign has been created to encourage people to make use of preventive health care services. If a change in health insurance laws favoring reimbursement for preventive health care occurs at the same time as the campaign, it may be difficult to separate the effects of the campaign from the effects of increased access to care that have been created by more favorable reimbursement for health care providers.

✓ *Instrumentation*

Unless the measures used to collect data are dependable, you cannot be sure that the findings are accurate. For example, in a pretest, posttest, or self-controlled design, an easier measure after an intervention or program than before one will erroneously favor the intervention.

✓ *Statistical regression*

Suppose people are chosen for an intervention to foster tolerance. The basis for selection, say, was their extreme views, as measured by a survey. A second administration of the survey (without any intervention) may appear to suggest that the views were somehow softened, but in fact, the results may be a statistical artifact. This is called regression to the mean.

✓ *Attrition (loss to follow-up)*

Attrition is another word for loss of data such as occurs when participants do not complete all or parts of a survey. People may not complete study activities because they move away, become ill or bored, and so on. Sometimes participants who continue to provide complete data throughout a long study are different from those who do not, and this difference biases the findings.

Risks to external validity are most often the consequence of the way in which participants or respondents are selected and assigned. For example, respondents in an experimental situation may answer survey questions atypically because they know they are in a special experiment; this is called the "Hawthorne" effect. External validity is also a risk just because respondents are tested, surveyed, or observed. They may become alert to the kinds of behaviors that are expected or favored. Sources of external invalidity are included in the following checklist.

External Invalidity: A Checklist of Risks to Avoid

✓ *Reactive effects of testing*

A measure given before an intervention can sensitize participants to its aims. Suppose two groups of junior high school students are eligible to participate in a program to teach ethics. Say that the first group is surveyed regarding its perspectives on selected ethics issues and then shown a film about young people from different backgrounds faced with ethical dilemmas. Suppose that the second group of students is just shown the film. It would not be surprising if the first group performed better on a postmeasure if only because the group was sensitized to the purpose of the movie by the questions on the "premeasure."

✓ *Interactive effects of selection*

This threat occurs when an intervention or program and the participants are a unique mixture—one that may not be found elsewhere. Suppose a school volunteers to participate in an experimental program to improve the quality of students' leisure time activities. The characteristics of the school (some of which may be related to the fact that it volunteered for the experiment) may interact with the program so that the two together are unique; the particular blend of school and intervention can limit the applicability of the findings.

✓ *Reactive effects of innovation*

Sometimes the environment of an experiment is so artificial that all who participate are aware that something special is going on and behave uncharacteristically.

✓   *Multiple-program interference*

It is sometimes difficult to isolate the effects of an experimental intervention because of the possibility that participants are in other complementary activities or programs.

The following examples illustrate how internal and external validity are affected in two different study designs.

How the Choice of Research Design Affects Internal and External Validity

1. Parallel Controls Without Random Assignment

Description. The Work and Stress Program is a yearlong program to help reduce on-the-job stress. Eligible people can enroll in one of two variations of the program. To find out if participants are satisfied with the quality of the program, both groups complete an in-depth questionnaire at the end of the year, and the results are compared.

Comment. The internal validity is potentially marred by the fact that the participants in the groups may be different from one another at the beginning of the program. More "stressed" persons may choose one program over the other, for example. Also, because of initial differences, the attrition, or loss to follow-up, rate may be affected. The failure to create randomly constituted groups will jeopardize the study's external validity by the interactive effects of selection.

2. Parallel Controls With Randomization

Description. Children's Defense Trust commissioned an evaluation of three different interventions to improve school performance. Eligible children were randomly assigned to one of the three interventions, baseline data were collected, and a 3-year investigation was made of effectiveness and efficiency. At the end of the 3 years, the children were examined to determine their functioning on a number of variables, including school performance and behavior at home and at school. The children were also interviewed extensively throughout the study.

Comment. This design is internally valid. Because children were randomly assigned to each intervention, any sources of change that might compete with the intervention's impact will affect all three groups equally. To improve external validity, the findings from a study of other children will be compared with those from the Children's Defense Trust. This additional comparison does not guarantee that the results will hold for a third group of children. Another consideration is that school administrators and staff may not spend as much money as usual because they know the study involves studying efficiency (reactive effects of innovation). Finally, we do not know if and how baseline data collection affected children's performance and interviews (interaction between testing and the intervention).

CRITERION FOR QUALITY: SAMPLING

What Is a Sample?

A *sample* is a portion or subset of a larger group called a population.

The target population consists of the institutions, persons, problems, and systems to which or to whom a study's findings are to be applied or *generalized.* Consider these two target populations and samples.

Two Target Populations and Two Samples

1. Target population: All teacher training programs in the state

Program. Continuous Quality Improvement: An intervention to monitor and change the quality of teacher training. One index of quality is the performance of students on statewide reading and math tests.

Sample. Five teacher training institutions were selected to try out the Quality Improvement experiment. After 1 year, for all participating teacher trainees, a 10% sample of student performance in reading and math was evaluated.

Comment. The target for this study is all teacher training programs in the state. Five will be selected for a Continuous Quality Improvement program. To appraise the program's quality, the researcher sampled 10% of students to assess their performance in reading and math. The findings were applied to all teacher training programs in the state.

2. Target population: All students needing remediation in reading

Program. Options for Learning

Sample. Five schools in three counties; within each school, 15 classes; for each class, at least two to five students who need remediation in reading.

Comment. Students who need assistance in reading were the targets of the program. The researchers selected five schools in three counties and, within them, 15 classes with two to five students in each. The findings were applied to all students who need special aid in reading.

Inclusion and Exclusion Criteria or Eligibility of Participants

A sample is a constituent of a larger population to which a study's findings will be applied. If a study plans to investigate the impact of a counseling program on children's attitudes toward school, for example, and not all students in need of more favorable attitudes are to be included in the program, then the researcher has to decide on the types of students who will be the focus of the study. Will the research concentrate on students of a specific age? With particular achievement levels? With poor attendance records?

From the literature reviewer's perspective, one mark of methodological quality is evidence of explicit inclusion and exclusion criteria. Failure to be explicit means that the reviewer will find it practically impossible to determine who was included and excluded from the study and for whom the findings are appropriate. Claims made by researchers regarding the applicability of their study's findings to groups of people or places can be evaluated only within the context of the subjects or participants who were eligible to be in a study and who actually participated.

The next example contains hypothetical inclusion and exclusion criteria for an evaluation of such a program to foster children's favorable attitudes toward school.

Inclusion and Exclusion Criteria for a Study of the Impact of a Program to Foster Favorable Student Attitudes to School

Inclusion

- All students attending schools in the ZIP codes listed below (not included in this example) who are currently in the sixth through ninth grade

- Students who speak English or Spanish
- Students who have participated in the E.T. (Eliminate Truancy) program

Exclusion

- All students who are currently incarcerated

Comment. The researcher set explicit criteria for the sample of students who are included in the study and for whom its findings are appropriate. The sample includes children in the sixth through ninth grade who speak English and Spanish, live within the confines of certain ZIP codes, and have participated in the Eliminate Truancy (E.T.) program. The findings are not applicable to students who meet just some of the criteria; for example, they are in the sixth grade, live in one of the specified ZIP codes, speak Spanish, but have NOT participated in the E.T. program.

Methods of Sampling

Sampling methods are usually divided into two types. The first is called *random* or *probability sampling,* and it is considered the best way to ensure the validity of any inferences made about a program's effectiveness and its generalizability. In probability sampling, every member of the target population has a known probability of being included in the sample. Probability or random sampling methods sometimes require knowledge of probability statistics; many statistical software programs have random-sampling capabilities, but their use is not meant for the statistically challenged.

A second type of sampling method produces a *convenience sample.* A convenience sample consists of participants who are selected because they are available. In convenience sampling, some members of the target population have a chance of being chosen, but others do not because they are not present when the sample is assembled. As a result, the data collected from a convenience sample may not be applicable to the target group at all. (The people who show up may differ from those who do not.) For example, suppose a researcher who is concerned with evaluating a college's student health service decided to interview 100 students who came for assistance during the week of December 26 to January 1. Suppose that 100 students are interviewed. The problem is that the end of December in some parts of the world is associated with respiratory viruses and skiing accidents; moreover, many schools are closed during that week and students are not around. Thus, the resulting data could very well be biased because the survey excluded many students simply because they were not on campus (and if they were ill, did not receive care or received care elsewhere).

Simple Random Sampling

In simple random sampling, every subject or unit has an equal chance of being selected. Because of this equality of opportunity, random samples are considered relatively unbiased. Typical ways of selecting a simple random sample include using a table of random numbers or a computer-generated list of random numbers and applying them to lists of prospective participants.

Suppose a researcher wanted to use a table and had the names of 20 psychologists from which 10 were to be selected at random. The list of names is called the sampling frame. First, the researcher would assign a number to each name, 1 to 20 (e.g., Adams = 1; Baker = 2; Thomas = 20). Then using a table of random numbers, which can be found online (enter table of random numbers or digits) and in many statistics books, the researcher would choose the first 10 digits between 1 and 20. Or a list of 10 numbers between 1 and 20 can be generated using any one of the most commonly available statistical programs.

Systematic Sampling

Suppose a researcher had a list with the names of 3,000 high school seniors from which a sample of 500 was to be selected. In systematic sampling, 3,000 would be divided by 500 to yield 6, and every sixth name would be selected. An alternative would be to select a number at random, say, by tossing dice. Suppose a toss came up with the number 5. Then, the fifth name would be selected first, then the 10th, 15th, and so on until 500 names were selected.

Systematic sampling should not be used if repetition is a natural component of the sampling frame or list from which the sample is to be drawn. For example, if the frame is a list of names, those beginning with certain letters of the alphabet might get excluded because, for certain ethnicities, they appear infrequently.

Stratified Sampling

A stratified random sample is one in which the population is divided into subgroups or "strata," and a random sample is then selected from each group. For example, in a program to teach students problem-solving skills, a researcher might choose to sample students of differing age, achievement, and self-confidence. Age, achievement, and self-confidence are the strata.

The strata or subgroups are chosen because the researcher provides evidence that they are related to the dependent variable or outcome measure—in this case, problem-solving skills. That is, the researcher provides the reviewer with convincing data—from high-quality literature and expert opinion—that age, general achievement, and perceptions of self-confidence influence ability to problem solve.

If the researcher neglects to use stratification in the choice of a sample, the results may be confounded. Suppose the literature suggests that women of varying ages react differently to a certain type of health initiative. If the researcher fails to stratify by age, good and poor performance may be averaged among the women participating in the initiative, and no effect will be seen—even if one or more groups benefited.

When stratification is not used, statistical techniques (such as analysis of covariance and regression) may be applied retrospectively (after the data have already been collected) to correct for confounders ("covariates") of the dependent variables or outcomes. In general, it is better to anticipate confounding variables by sampling prospectively than to correct for them by analysis, retrospectively. The reason is that statistical corrections require very strict assumptions about the nature of the data, assumptions for which the sampling plan may not have been designed. With few exceptions, using statistical corrections afterward results in a loss of power or ability to detect true differences.

Cluster Sampling

Clusters are naturally occurring groups such as schools, clinics, community-based service organizations, cities, states, and so on. In cluster sampling, the population is divided into batches. The batches can be randomly selected and assigned, and their constituents can be randomly selected and assigned. For example, suppose that 10 counties are trying out a new program to improve voter registration; the control program is the traditional program. With random cluster sampling, each county is a cluster, and each can be selected and assigned at random to the new or traditional program.

Convenience Sampling

Convenience samples are those for which the probability of selection is unknown. Researchers use convenience samples because they are easy to get. This means that some people have no chance at all of being selected, simply because they are not around to be chosen. These samples are considered biased, or not representative of the target population, unless proven otherwise (through statistical methods, for example).

THE SAMPLING UNIT

A major concern in sampling is the potential discrepancy between the "unit" to be sampled and the unit that is analyzed statistically. For instance, suppose a group of researchers is interested in finding out about patient satisfaction in a medical organization that has five large clinics. The researchers survey 6,000 patients in a clinic in the far north and 5,000 in a clinic in the far south. On the basis of the results in both clinics, the researchers report that patients in the medical organization are extremely satisfied with their medical care. The findings show, for instance, that of the 11,000, nearly 98% state that their care is as good as or better than any care they have ever received. The medical care organization is very pleased with these findings.

The literature reviewer has to be careful with the conclusion of studies that do not address discrepancies between who is sampled and whose data are analyzed. In the above example, two clinics were sampled (the sampling unit), but data were analyzed for 11,000 patients (the analysis unit). Because only two of five clinics were in the sample, you cannot be sure that the two clinics are not different from the remaining three and that you have a sample size of 2 and not of 11,000. A better strategy, but one that is much more difficult to implement, might have been to sample 11,000 persons across all five clinics.

Statistical methods are available for "correcting" for the discrepancy between units of sampling and analysis. When appropriate, examine if and how discrepancies between sampling and analysis units are handled. Because the analysis methods used to correct for clustering are complex, you may need statistical consultation.

THE SIZE OF THE SAMPLE

The size of the sample is important for several reasons. Small samples may not be able to include the mix of people or programs that should be included in a study and may be unable to detect an effect even if one would have taken place with more people. A study's ability to detect an effect is its **power.** A **power analysis** is a statistical method of identifying a sample size that is large enough to detect the effect, if one actually exists. A most commonly used research design is one in which two randomly assigned groups are compared to find out if differences exist between them. "Does Program A differ from Program B in its ability to improve satisfaction? Quality of life? Reading? Math? Art? Mental health? Social functioning?" is a fairly standard research question. To answer the question accurately, the researcher has to design the study so that a sufficient number of subjects are in each program group so that if a difference is actually present, it will be uncovered. Conversely, if there is no difference between the two groups, the researcher does not want to conclude falsely that there is one.

Statistical methods are available for researchers to identify a sample that is large enough to detect actual effects. The power of an experimental study is its ability to detect a true difference—in other words, to detect a difference of a given size (say, 10%) if the difference actually exists. Many published articles do not include their power calculations, so if differences are not observed, the problem may have been that the sample was not large enough to detect a difference among groups, even if one may have been present.

RESPONSE RATE

The response rate is the number who are measured or Response Rate observed or who responded to a survey (numerator) divided by the number of eligible respondents (denominator):

$$\text{Response Rate} = \frac{\text{Number who respond}}{\text{Eligible to respond}}$$

All studies aim for a high response rate. No standard exists, however, to assist the literature reviewer in deciding whether the aim was achieved and, if not, the effect on the study's outcomes.

Consider two examples. In the first, 50% of eligible persons complete all items on a health survey. In the second, 100% of eligible persons respond, but they fail to complete about 50% of the items on the survey.

Nonresponse: Subjects and Items

1. The National State Health Interview is completed by 50% of all who are eligible. Health officials conclude that the 50% who do not participate probably differ from participants in their health needs and demographic characteristics.

2. According to statistical calculations, the Commission on Refugee Affairs (CORA) needs a sample of 100 for their mailed survey. Based on the results of previous mailings, a refusal rate of 20% to 25% is anticipated. Just in case, 125 eligible people are sent a survey. One hundred twenty persons respond, but on average, they answer fewer than half of all questions.

In the first case described above, 50% of eligible state residents do not complete the interview. These nonrespondents may be very different in their health needs, incomes, and education than the 50% who do respond. When nonrespondents and respondents differ on important factors, this is called nonresponse bias. Nonresponse bias may seriously impair a study's generalizability (external validity) because the findings, which were expected to apply to a relatively broad group, are now applicable just to the persons who responded or agreed to participate. Reviewers should be on the alert for studies that do not explain the consequences of nonresponse. Questions such as these should be answered: Of those who were eligible, how many participated? What was the reason for the nonresponse? How do responders compare to nonresponders? How is the study's internal and external validity affected by the nonresponse?

In addition to person nonresponse, item nonresponse may introduce bias. Item nonresponse occurs when respondents do not complete all items on a survey or test. This type of bias comes about when respondents do not know the answers to certain questions or refuse to answer them because they cannot (e.g., they do not understand the questions) or believe them to be sensitive, embarrassing, or irrelevant.

Statistical methods may be used to correct for nonresponse to the entire survey or to just some items. One method involves "weighting." Suppose a survey wants to compare younger (younger than 25 years) and older (26 years and older) college students' career goals. A review of school records reveals that younger students are 40% of the population. Although all 40% are given a survey to complete, only 20% do so. Using statistical methods, the 20% response rate can be weighted to become the equivalent of 40%. The accuracy of the result depends on the younger respondents being similar in their answers to the nonrespondents and different in their answers to the older respondents.

Another method of correcting for nonresponse is called imputation. With imputation, values are assigned for the missing response, using the responses to other items as supplementary information. Scientifically sound studies explain in detail how missing data are handled and the effects of missing data on the findings.

The following checklist can be used when reviewing a study's presentation and quality as it pertains to research design and sampling. The list is probably too extensive to use for any single literature review, and so you must decide which questions to answer on a case-by-case basis.

A Checklist for Evaluating the Presentation
and Quality of Study Design and Sampling

- ✓ If more than one group is included in the study, are the participants randomly assigned to each?

- ✓ Are participants measured over time? If so, is the number of observations explained? Justified?

- ✓ If observations or measures are made over time, are the choice and effects of the time period explained?

- ✓ Are any of the participants "blinded" to the group—experimental or control—to which they belong?

- ✓ If historical controls are used, is their selection explained? Justified?

- ✓ Are the effects on internal validity of choice, equivalence, and participation of the sample subjects explained?

- ✓ Are the effects on external validity (generalizability) of choice, equivalence, and participation of the subjects explained?

- ✓ If a sample is used, are the subjects randomly selected?

✓ If the unit sampled (e.g., students) is not the population of main concern (e.g., teachers are), is this addressed in the analysis or discussion?

✓ If a sample is used with a nonrandom sampling method, is evidence given regarding whether they are similar to the target population (from which they were chosen) or to other groups in the study?

✓ If groups are not equivalent at baseline, is this problem addressed in analysis or interpretation?

✓ Are criteria given for including subjects?

✓ Are criteria given for excluding subjects?

✓ Is the sample size justified (say, with a power calculation)?

✓ Is information given on the size and characteristics of the target population?

✓ If stratified sampling is used, is the choice of strata justified?

✓ Is information given on the number and characteristics of subjects in the target population who are eligible to participate in the study?

✓ Is information given on the number and characteristics of subjects who are eligible and who also agree to participate?

✓ Is information given on the number and characteristics of subjects who are eligible but refuse to participate?

✓ Is information given on the number and characteristics of subjects who dropped out or were lost to follow-up before completing all elements of data collection?

✓ Is information given on the number and characteristics of subjects who completed all elements of data collection?

✓ Is information given on the number and characteristics of subjects on whom some data are missing?

✓ Are reasons given for missing data?

✓ Are reasons given why individuals or groups dropped out?

SUMMARY OF KEY POINTS

An efficient literature search is always filtered through two screens. The first screen is primarily practical. It is used to identify studies that are potentially pertinent in that they cover the topic, are in a language you read, and appear in a publication you respect. The second screen is for methodological quality, which is used to identify the best available studies in terms of their adherence to the methods that scientists and scholars rely on to gather sound evidence. You must use both screens to ensure the review's relevance and accuracy.

- Typical practical criteria for literature review searches include

  Publication language

  Journal

  Author

  Setting

  Participants

  Type of program or intervention

  Research design

  Sampling

  Date of publication

  Date of data collection

  Duration of data collection

  Content (topics, variables)

  Source of financial support

- Methodological quality refers to how well—scientifically—a study has been designed and implemented to achieve its objectives. The highest quality studies adhere to rigorous research standards.
- A study's research design refers to the way in which its subjects or constituents—students, patients, and customers—are organized and observed. Research designs are traditionally categorized as experimental or observational.
- Typical experimental designs include the following:

Parallel controls in which groups are assigned randomly or the true experiment. Parallel means that each group is assembled at the same time. When 500 students are randomly assigned to an experimental group while, at the same time, 500 are assigned to a control group, you have parallel controls (each group is assembled at the same time) with random assignment. This design is also called a simple randomized controlled trial or true experiment.

Parallel controls in which participants are not randomly assigned to groups or the quasi-experiment. These are called nonrandomized controlled trials, quasi-experiments, or nonequivalent controls. When children are assigned to an experimental after-school program because they live in City A, and another group is assigned to a control program because they live in City B, you have a quasi-experiment or nonrandomized trial.

Self-control. These require premeasures (also called pretests) and post-measures (also called posttests) and are also called longitudinal or before-after or pretest-posttest designs. For instance, a study is longitudinal if employees in a fitness program are given a series of physical examinations before participation in a new health promotion program and 6 months, 1 year, and 2 years after participation.

Historical controls. These use "normative data" against which to compare a group. Normative data are historical because they come from already existing databases. For instance, a researcher who evaluates a program to improve employees' blood pressure levels and uses standard tables of normal blood pressure to monitor improvement is conducting a study that uses historical controls.

- Observational designs produce information on groups and phenomena that already exist. Researchers who do observational studies have "less control" than do researchers who conduct experimental studies. Because of this, observational designs are considered less rigorous than experimental research designs. Typical observational designs include the following:

Cohorts. These designs provide data about changes in a specific population. Suppose a survey of the aspirations of athletes participating in the Olympics is given in 2000, 2004, and 2008. This is a cohort design, and the cohort is 2000 Olympians.

Case controls. These studies help explain a current phenomenon. At least two groups are included. When you survey the medical records of a sample of people with heart disease and a sample without the disease to find out about the similarities and differences in past illnesses, you have used a case control design.

Cross-sections. These provide descriptive or survey data at one fixed point in time. A survey of American voters' current choices is an example of a cross-sectional research design.

- A study design is internally valid if it is free from nonrandom error or bias. A study design must be internally valid to be externally valid and to produce accurate findings. One of the most important questions to ask when reviewing the literature is this: Does this study's design have internal validity? Threats to internal validity include the following:

  ✓ **Maturation.** Maturation refers to changes within individuals that result from natural, biological, or psychological development.

  ✓ **Selection.** Selection refers to how people were chosen for the study and, if they participated in an experiment, how they were assigned to groups.

  ✓ **History.** Historical events are extraneous forces that occur while the study is in operation and may interfere with its implementation and outcomes.

  ✓ **Instrumentation.** Unless the measures used to collect data are dependable or reliable, the findings are unlikely to be accurate.

  ✓ **Statistical regression.** A tendency of very high or low values to move toward the mean or average: A statistical artifact.

  ✓ **Attrition.** This is another word for loss of data such as occurs when participants do not complete all or parts of the study's data collection instruments.

- A study design with external validity produces results that apply to the study's target population.
- Threats to external validity are most often the consequence of the way in which participants or respondents are selected and assigned. For example, respondents in an experimental situation may answer questions atypically because they know they are in a special experiment. External validity is also at risk just because respondents are tested,

surveyed, or observed. They may become alert to the kinds of behaviors that are expected or favored. Threats to external validity include the following:

- ✓ **Reactive effects of testing.** A premeasure can sensitize participants to the aims of an intervention.

- ✓ **Interactive effects of selection.** This occurs when an intervention and the participants are a unique mixture—one that may not be found elsewhere.

- ✓ **Reactive effects of innovation.** Sometimes the environment of an experiment is so artificial that all who participate are aware that something special is going on and behave uncharacteristically.

- ✓ **Multiple-program interference.** It is sometimes difficult to isolate the effects of an experimental intervention because of the possibility that participants are in other complementary activities or programs.

- Sampling methods are usually divided into two types. The first is called probability sampling, and it is considered the best way to ensure the validity of any inferences made about a program's effectiveness and its generalizability. In probability sampling, every member of the target population has a known probability of being included in the sample. Few studies use true probability sampling. The second type of sample is the convenience sample in which participants are selected because they are available. In convenience sampling, some members of the target population have a chance of being chosen, but others do not. As a result, the data that are collected from a convenience sample may not be applicable to the target group at all.

- Types of sampling include the following:

Simple random sampling. In simple random sampling, every subject or unit has an equal chance of being selected. Because of this equality of opportunity, random samples are considered relatively unbiased.

Systematic sampling. Suppose a researcher had a list with the names of 3,000 high school seniors from which a sample of 500 was to be selected. In systematic sampling, 3,000 would be divided by 500 to yield 6, and every sixth name would be selected.

Stratified sampling. A stratified random sample is one in which the population is divided into subgroups or "strata," and a random sample is then selected from each group.

Cluster sampling. A cluster is a naturally occurring group such as schools, clinics, community-based service organizations, cities, states, and so on. In cluster sampling, the population is divided into batches. The batches can be randomly selected and assigned, and their constituents can be randomly selected and assigned.

Convenience samples. Convenience samples are those for which the probability of selection is unknown. Researchers use convenience samples because they are easy to get. This means that some people have no chance at all of being selected, simply because they are not around to be chosen. These samples are considered biased or not representative of the target population, unless proven otherwise (through statistical methods, for example).

- A study's ability to detect an effect if it is present is its power. A power analysis is a statistical method of identifying a sample size that is large enough to detect the effect, if one actually exists.
- The response rate is the number who respond (numerator) divided by the number of eligible respondents (denominator):

$$\text{Response Rate} = \frac{\text{Number who respond}}{\text{Number eligible to respond}}$$

EXERCISES

1. The Community Family Center had 40 separate counseling groups, each with about 30 participants. The director of the center conducts and reports on an experiment to improve attendance rates at the sessions. Random selection of individuals from all group members for the experiment was impossible; such selection would have created friction and disturbed the integrity of some of the groups. Instead, a design was used in which five of the groups—150 people— were randomly selected to take part in the experiment, and five continued to

receive traditional counseling. Every 3 months, the director compares the attendance of all persons in the experimental group with those in the control group. Compare and comment on the sampling and analysis units.

    a. Which method of sampling is used?

    b. Compare and comment on the units of sampling and analysis.

2. The Medical Group developed an interactive computer-based educational intervention to prevent strokes. A study was conducted to compare the computer intervention with the traditional method that consisted of written handouts routinely given to all persons between 45 and 75 years of age. The study was experimental, with parallel controls. Of 310 eligible persons, 140 were between 45 and 60 years old, and 62 of these were men. The remaining 170 were between 61 and 75 years, and 80 of these were men. The researchers randomly selected 40 persons from each of the four subgroups and randomly assigned every other person to the computer intervention and the remainder to the control (written materials).

    a. Which sampling method is used?

    b. Which eligibility criteria do you think may have applied?

    c. Draw the sampling plan.

3. Two hundred teen counselors signed up for a continuing education program. Only 50, however, participated in an evaluation of the program's impact. Each participant was assigned a number from 001 to 200 and, using a table, 50 names were selected by moving down columns of three-digit random numbers and taking the first 50 numbers within the range 001 to 200.

    a. Which sampling method is used?

    b. What is the response rate?

4. What is the research design in the following studies? What are the threats to internal and external validity?

Study A. The ABC MicroLink Company experimented with a program to provide its employees with options for caring for their older parents. Human resources staff interviewed all employees to find out how much they learned from the program and if they were planning to use its content.

Study B. Teens in the ALERT program voluntarily joined one of three 1-month rehabilitation programs. Data were collected on teens' knowledge and self-confidence before and after participation in each program.

ANSWERS

1a. Cluster sampling

1b. The sampling unit was a "group," so there were five units or groups. The analysis compared average attendance among 150 persons in the experiment and 150 in the control. A problem with the accuracy of the results may arise if one or more of the groups has a unique identity (e.g., more cohesive, more cooperative, more knowledgeable).

2a. Stratified random sampling

2b. Must be between 45 and 75 years of age. Must be willing to use interactive computer for educational purposes.

2c. Sampling plan

The Population

	Age	
	45–60	*61–75*
Men	62	80
Women	78	90

The Sample

	Age	
	45–60	*61–75*
Men	40	40
Women	40	40

3a. Simple random sampling

3b. 50/200 or 25%

4. *Study A.* Cross-sectional design. *The internal validity* of cross-sectional designs may be affected by nearly all possible threats. Historical events (such as new legislation regarding the care of older parents), for example, may occur at the same time as the program, and

these may be as or more influential than the program. Selection may threaten internal validity because of the nature of the sample that participates and completes all study activities. Because of the perilous state of internal validity in cross-sectional designs, you cannot count on them to produce externally valid results. *External validity* may be influenced by the reactive effects of innovation.

Study B. Cohort design. Selection is a possible risk to *internal validity* because participants in the two groups may have been different from one another at the beginning of the program. For example, more self-confident teens may choose one program over the other. Also, attrition may be different between the two groups. Risks to *external validity* include the reactive effects of innovation, interactive effects of selection, and, possibly, multiple-program interference.

SUGGESTED READINGS

Campbell, D. T., & Stanley, J. C. (1963). *Experimental and quasi-experimental design for research.* Chicago: Rand-McNally.

Cohen, J. (1988). *Statistical power analysis for the behavioral sciences* (2nd ed.). Hillsdale, NJ: Lawrence Erlbaum.

Cook, D. C., & Campbell, D. T. (1979). *Quasi-experimentation: Design and analysis issues for field settings.* Boston: Houghton Mifflin.

Creswell, J. W. (2008). *Research design: Qualitative, quantitative, and mixed methods approaches* (3rd ed.). Thousand Oaks, CA: Sage.

De Vaus, D. (2002). *Research design in social research.* Thousand Oaks, CA: Sage.

Fink A. (2008). *Practicing research: Discovering evidence that matters.* Thousand Oaks, CA: Sage.

Fink, A. (2012). *Evidence-based public health.* Thousand Oaks, CA: Sage.

Henry, G. T. (1990). *Practical sampling.* Newbury Park, CA: Sage.

Hulley, S. B., Cummings, S. R., Browner, W. S., Grady, D., Hearst, N., & Newman, T. B. (Eds.). (2006). *Designing clinical research* (2nd ed., chaps. 5 and 6). Philadelphia: Lippincott, Williams & Wilkins.

McIntyre, A. (2008). *Participatory action research.* Thousand Oaks, CA: Sage.

Riegelman, R. K., & Hirsch, R. P. (2004). *Studying a study and testing a test: How to read the health science literature.* Boston: Little, Brown.

For sample size software, go to your favorite search engine and type in *sample size calculator.*

☆ THREE ☆

SEARCHING AND SCREENING

Methodological Quality (Part 2—Data Collection, Interventions, Analysis, Results, and Conclusions)

═══════════ ʚ✿ɞ ═══════════

A Reader's Guide

Purpose of This Chapter

A literature search may uncover hundreds of studies on any given topic, but only some—possibly just a few—will be methodologically rigorous enough to furnish trustworthy information. A study that has methodological rigor relies on valid data collection, appropriate statistical analysis, accurate reporting of results, and justified interpretations and conclusions.

The chapter defines and gives examples of valid and reliable data collection and identifies standards for evaluating the appropriateness of a study's statistical and/or qualitative analysis. The chapter also identifies techniques for determining if the reported results of data collection and analysis are directly linked to a study's objectives and if the conclusions follow from the results. Because you will be reviewing studies that include interventions or programs, the chapter provides criteria for evaluating how adequately they are described.

Some studies mix their methods. Mixed-method research uses qualitative and statistical or quantitative methods in the same study. The chapter discusses qualitative and mixed-method research and provides guidance in evaluating how transparently they report their objectives, methods, findings, and conclusions.

Figure 3.1 shows the steps in conducting a research literature search. This chapter deals with the shaded area: Applying the methodological screen to a study's data collection, interventions, analysis, results, and conclusions.

DATA COLLECTION AND DATA SOURCES: METHODS AND MEASURES

Data collection is the soul of a study. The validity or "truth" of all research depends on accurate data. As a literature reviewer, one of your primary responsibilities is to evaluate the quality of a study's data. Ask the following of each study you review: What methods were used to collect data? Did the data come from credible and relevant sources? Are the data demonstrably reliable and valid?

Figure 3.1   Steps in Conducting a Research Literature Search

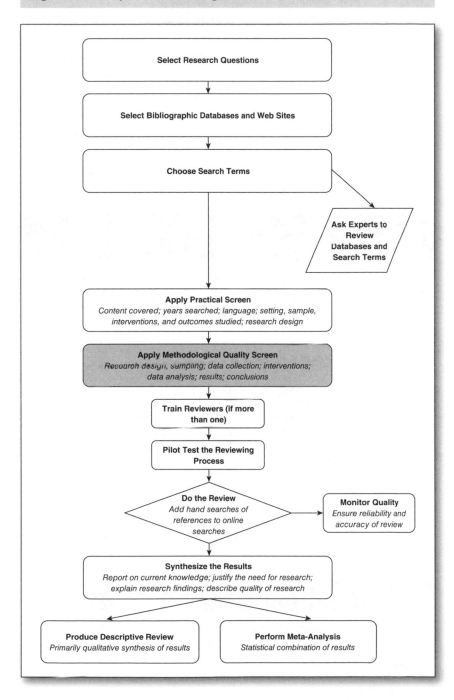

Researchers use a variety of methods to collect data. These include administering achievement tests, survey questionnaires, and face-to-face and telephone interviews; analyzing large databases (such as a school's enrollment data) or vital statistics (such as infant mortality rates); observing individuals and groups; reviewing the literature and personal, medical, financial, and other statistical records; performing physical examinations and laboratory tests; and using simulations and clinical scenarios or performance tests. A reviewer must learn to evaluate the characteristics of these methods and assess their validity for each study reviewed. The validity of a data collection method refers to its accuracy.

Consider the options for data collection in the following two studies.

Study 1. Quality of Medical Care and Children With Asthma

Question. Has participation in ACTO (Asthmatic Children Take Over) resulted in a statistically and clinically meaningful improvement in quality of care for experimental compared with control asthmatic children?

Data Collection Needs	Potential Data Sources and Measures
1. Identifying children for the experimental and control groups	1. Physical examinations, medical record reviews, surveys of health care practitioners and patients
2. Measuring quality of medical care	2. Medical record reviews, surveys of health care practitioners and patients

Study 2. Quality of Life

Question. When compared with the traditional program, does participation in the Center for Healthy Aging improve older persons' quality of life by expanding their social contacts?

Data Collection Needs	Potential Data Sources
Data Collection Needs	*Potential Data Sources*
1. Identifying older persons for the experimental and control groups	1. Lists of names or ID codes of participants in the experimental and control groups
2. Measuring quality of life, especially social contact	2. Surveys of participants to ask about nature and extent of social contacts; surveys of their families, friends, and health care providers; reviews of diaries kept by patients; observations of participants' weekly activities

Study 1 is concerned with "quality of care," and Study 2 is interested in "quality of life." These are the *outcome* or *dependent variables*. In both studies, the researchers are concerned with the effects of particular programs or interventions (ACTO and Center for Healthy Aging) on these variables. The interventions are called *predictor* or *independent variables*. A variable is simply a factor or a characteristic of interest in a study with differing values for different subjects. A predictor variable is a factor (such as program participation, age, education, current physical and mental health status) that may affect the outcome.

Answering the question in Study 1 pertaining to quality of care and asthmatic children requires completion of at least two tasks: Identifying children with asthma and assigning them to the experimental and control groups. Children with asthma can be identified through physical examinations, medical record reviews, or surveys of health care practitioners and patients. Data to measure quality of care for asthma can come from medical records reviews or surveying health care practitioners.

For the second study, a review of sampling logs containing lists of names and identification numbers can be used to identify persons for the experimental and control groups. To measure social contact, the researcher can survey and observe participants, ask them to keep records or diaries of their activities, and survey participants' friends, families, and health care providers.

No single method for collecting data is inherently better or valid than another. The choice of which type to use depends on a study's needs and resources. For instance, a researcher who wants to compare the views of people in several countries may rely on an Internet survey rather than on a mailed questionnaire. In studies of people who may have difficulty reading or seeing, researchers may use interviews rather than self-administered surveys including online surveys or mailed questionnaires.

Data collection methods are often chosen as much for their practicality as their quality. For example, suppose you are interested in learning about quality of life, and you review two studies to find out about it. The first study relies on face-to-face interviews because the investigators are convinced that interviews by skilled staff members are the best method for getting personal information. Furthermore, the investigators have the resources to train their staff to do the interviews and are satisfied with their data.

The second quality-of-life study takes another approach and relies on self-administered survey questionnaires administered via e-mail and "snail mail." The researchers in the second study assert that people are most honest when answering questions privately. A major factor in their choice of data collection method, however, was that self-administered surveys are often less expensive to do than interviews. Which method is better? Interviews or self-administered surveys? Actually, from this limited information, you cannot tell. The deciding factor for the literature reviewer when critically examining a study's data collection is not the method or measures but, rather, whether the measure provides *reliable* and *valid* information.

Reliability

A reliable data collection method is one that is relatively free from "measurement error." Because of this error, individuals' obtained scores are different from their true scores (which can only be obtained from perfect measures). The measures are surveys, tests, medical record reviews, observation, physical examinations, and so on. What causes this error? In some cases, the error results from the measure itself: It may be difficult to understand or poorly administered. For example, a self-administered questionnaire will produce unreliable results if its reading level is too high for the people who are to complete it. If the reading level is on target, but the directions are unclear, the measure will be unreliable anyway. But even with simplified language and clear directions, measurement error is still possible because it can also come directly from people. For example, if persons in a dentist's waiting room are asked to complete a questionnaire, and they are especially anxious or fatigued, their obtained scores are likely to differ from their true scores.

Reliability is often divided into four categories: Test-retest reliability, equivalence, homogeneity, and inter- and intrarater reliability.

Test-retest reliability refers to a high correlation between scores from time to time. Suppose students' behavior in the playground is observed twice: First in April and a second time in May. If the survey is reliable, and no special program or intervention to change behavior is introduced, on average, we expect behavior to remain the same. The major conceptual difficulty in establishing test-retest reliability is in determining how much time is permissible between the first and second administration. If too much time elapses, external events (people mature and learn) might influence responses for the second administration. If too little time passes, the respondents may remember and simply repeat their answers or behavior from the first administration. From the literature reviewer's perspective, an explanation and justification by the study authors of the interval between reliability tests is always desirable.

Equivalence or *alternate-form reliability* refers to the extent to which two assessments measure the same concepts at the same level of difficulty. Suppose students are given an achievement test before participating in a new computer skills class and then again 2 months after completing it. Unless the two tests are of equal difficulty, better performance after the second administration can represent performance on an easier test rather than improved learning. In reviewing studies that use pre- and posttesting or self-control research designs, look for evidence of the equivalence of measures. Also, because this approach to reliability requires two administrations, check for an explanation and discussion of the appropriateness of the interval between them.

As an alternative to establishing equivalence between two forms of the same measure, researchers sometimes compute a split-half reliability. To do this requires dividing a measure into two equal halves (or alternate forms) and obtaining the correlation between the two halves. Problems arise if the two halves vary in difficulty; however, because only one administration is required, at least the concern over the duration of intervals between testing is eliminated.

Homogeneity refers to the extent to which all items or questions assess the same skill, characteristic, or quality. Sometimes, this type of reliability is referred to as internal consistency. A Cronbach's coefficient alpha, which is basically the average of all the correlations between each item and the total score, is often calculated to determine the extent of homogeneity. A correlation is a measure of the linear relationship between two measurements made on the same subjects. For instance, you can calculate the correlation between height and weight or between years in school and numbers of books read for pleasure each month. Correlations range from +1 (perfect positive correlation) to –1 (perfect negative correlation). A correlation of 0 means no relationship. Researchers might report a homogeneity test if they wanted to find out the extent to which the items on a student satisfaction questionnaire correlate with one another.

When reviewing the literature, look for definitions of all key variables and evidence that the questions or items used to measure the variable are consistent in their assessment of the variable.

Interrater reliability refers to the extent to which two or more individuals agree on their measurement of an item. Suppose two individuals were sent to a prenatal care clinic to observe waiting times, the appearance of the waiting and examination rooms, and the general atmosphere. If the observers agreed perfectly on all items, then interrater reliability would be perfect. Interrater reliability is enhanced by training data collectors, providing them with a guide for recording their observations, and monitoring the quality of the data collection over time. *Intrarater reliability* refers to a single individual's consistency of measurement over time, and this, too, can be enhanced by training, monitoring, and education.

Agreement among raters and for a single rater over time for an agree-disagree situation is often computed using a statistic called kappa (κ). In your role as reviewer, look for higher (e.g., above 0.60) rather than lower kappas for each study measure of importance. (For more on kappa, see Chapter 4.)

Validity

Validity refers to the degree to which a measure assesses what it purports to measure. For example, a test that asks students to *recall* information will be considered an invalid measure of their ability to *apply* information. Similarly, an attitude survey will not be considered valid unless you can prove that people who are identified as having a positive attitude on the basis of their responses to the survey are different in some observable way from people who are identified as having a negative attitude.

Content validity refers to the extent to which a measure thoroughly and appropriately assesses the skills or characteristics it is intended to measure. For example, a researcher who is interested in developing a measure of mental health has to first define the concept (What is mental health? What are the defining characteristics of mental health?) and next find a measure that adequately assesses all aspects of the definition. Because of the complexity of the task, the literature is often consulted either for a model or conceptual framework from which a definition can be derived. It is not uncommon in establishing content validity to see a statement such as, "We used XYZ Cognitive Theory to select items on mental health, and we adapted the ABC Role Model Paradigm for questions about social relations."

Face validity refers to how a measure appears on the surface: Does it seem to ask all the needed questions? Does it use the appropriate language and language level to do so? Face validity, unlike content validity, does not rely on established theory for support.

Criterion validity is made up of two subcategories: Predictive validity and concurrent validity.

Predictive validity refers to the extent to which a measure forecasts future performance. A graduate school entry examination that predicts who will do well in graduate school (as measured, for example, by grades) has predictive validity.

Concurrent validity is demonstrated when two assessments agree or a new measure compares favorably with one that is already considered valid. For example, to establish the concurrent validity of a new aptitude test, the researcher can administer the new and the older validated measure to the same group of examinees and compare the scores. Or the researcher can administer the new test to the examinees and then compare the scores to experts' judgment of students' aptitude. A high correlation between the new test scores and the criterion measure's—the older validated test—means the new test has concurrent validity. Establishing concurrent validity is useful when a new measure is created that claims to be shorter, cheaper, or fairer than an older one.

Construct validity is established experimentally to demonstrate that a measure distinguishes between people who do and do not have certain characteristics. For example, a researcher who claims constructive validity for a measure of competent teaching will have to prove that teachers who do well on the measure are more competent than teachers who do poorly.

Construct validity is commonly established in at least two ways:

1. The researcher hypothesizes that the new measure correlates with one or more measures of a similar characteristic (convergent validity) and does not correlate with measures of dissimilar characteristics

(discriminant validity). For example, a researcher who is validating a new quality-of-life measure might posit that it is highly correlated ("converges") with another quality-of-life measure, a measure of functioning, and a measure of health status. At the same time, the researcher would hypothesize that the new measure does not correlate with (it "discriminates" against) selected measures of social desirability (the tendency to answer questions so as to present yourself in a more positive light) and of hostility.

2. The researcher hypothesizes that the measure can distinguish one group from another on some important variable. For example, a measure of compassion should be able to demonstrate that people who are high scorers are compassionate and that people who are low scorers are unfeeling. This requires translating a theory of compassionate behavior into measurable terms, identifying people who are compassionate and who are unfeeling (according to the theory), and proving that the measure consistently and correctly distinguishes between the two groups.

To evaluate the reliability and validity of a study's data collection, use this checklist.

A Checklist to Use in Evaluating Reliability and Validity of Data Collection

- Are the data collection methods adequately described?
- Define all key variables.
- Provide information on measure type, content, length.
- Explain and justify intervals between administrations.

The researcher should define all key variables and provide information on the type of measure (e.g., test, survey), its content, and its length. If a measure is administered more than once (e.g., before and after) an intervention, check to see that the length of time between administrations is explained and that its potential effect on test-retest reliability is discussed.

✓ *Is the measure reliable?*

Look for evidence that data collection measures have internal consistency or test-retest reliability. Check to see if data are provided on intrarater reliability (if just one observer is involved in the study) or for interrater reliability (if two or more observers are involved).

If a data collection measure is used to get demographic information, such as age, gender, and ethnicity, reliability is not as important a concept as validity (i.e., getting an accurate answer). Ask: Is this the best way to ask these questions with this study's population? In other words, have the questions been answered correctly by other people with a similar reading level, in this part of the country, in this age group, and so on?

✓ *Is the measure valid?*

Carefully review the data on validity presented in the study's report. If a measure was specifically developed for the current study, what evidence do the researchers provide that it accurately measures the variables of concern? If the measure is adapted from another measure, do the researchers offer proof that the current study population is sufficiently like the validation population in important characteristics (e.g., reading level, knowledge, severity of illness, etc.)? Sometimes the researchers will cite a reference to a measure without describing its appropriateness to the current study. In this case, you may have to get the original article to check on the original validation sample.

✓ *Do the researchers explain the consequences of using measures with compromised reliability and validity?*

You may find studies that do not discuss the reliability and validity of their measures. Without such information, the literature reviewer cannot tell if the study's findings are true or false. How much confidence do these researchers have in their findings? Do they justify their confidence by comparing their results with other studies with similar populations? How confident are you in their explanations?

INTERVENTIONS AND PROGRAMS: REVIEWING THE RESEARCH LITERATURE TO FIND OUT WHAT WORKS

Many studies involve experimenting with and evaluating the effectiveness of interventions or programs. A literature review of effectiveness studies or outcomes research—also called program evaluation—provides data on "what works" in solving important societal problems. For example, a public health department may want to support an outreach program to attract young mothers to prenatal care. Rather than create a new program, the health department may conduct a review of the reports of existing prenatal care outreach interventions to find out which ones are effective, the specific populations (e.g., younger women, high-risk women) for which they are effective, the settings in which they take place (e.g., community health settings, schools, churches), and the costs of implementation. On the basis of the results, the health department can then decide on whether to adopt the effective interventions, adapt them to meet local needs, or create a new program.

Researchers, program planners, consumers, and policy makers are interested in the outcomes of these studies so as to make informed decisions about interventions that should be supported and implemented because evidence already exists that they are effective. An intervention is a systematic effort to achieve preplanned objectives such as advancing knowledge and changing behaviors, attitudes, and practices. Interventions may be educational (e.g., a reading program), medical (e.g., an operation) or heath related (e.g., a prenatal care outreach program or a new health care delivery system), psychosocial (e.g., family support sessions), or work related (e.g., a work-study program). They may involve a whole nation (e.g., Medicare) or a relatively few people in a single office, school, or hospital.

Studies in which programs are tested and evaluated differ from other research studies in that they focus on the outcomes and impact of purposely created interventions and not natural history. The literature reviewer can make an assessment of the quality of this type of study only if the researchers clearly describe the planned intervention and provide evidence that the intervention that was planned was implemented in a standardized manner across all experimental settings.

Compare these two versions of a program description. Which is better? Is anything missing?

Two Versions of a Program Description

Objective. To evaluate the effectiveness of a teacher-delivered curriculum in favorably modifying high school students' knowledge, beliefs, and self-confidence in relation to health-promoting activities (such as paying attention to diet and exercise and getting regular dental checkups).

Description 1

The curriculum focuses on conveying facts about health promotion, fostering theoretically derived beliefs favorable to health promotion, and teaching skills necessary for the successful performance of health-promoting behaviors.

Description 2

The curriculum consists of six one-class-period lessons, implemented on consecutive days. The first two lessons focus on conveying the correct facts about health promotion and disease prevention, including the merits of diet, exercise, and psychosocial health and directing students to appropriate resources based on personal needs. The middle two lessons focus on clarifying students' personal values pertaining to involvement in risky health behaviors and helping them (using role-play rehearsal) with the negotiation skills necessary to promote health behaviors. The final two lessons focus on helping students obtain negotiation skills for consistently applying health behaviors. A manual has been developed to help classroom teachers implement the curriculum. This manual is the result of implementation studies developed for all eight national tests of the curriculum throughout the country. (See the manual's appendix for details of teacher training sessions that can be used to standardize curriculum administration.)

The second description provides detailed information and is clearer than the first. Among the important pieces of information contained within the description are the number of lessons and their content. The reference to implementation studies, resulting in a teacher's manual with lessons for curriculum administration, suggests that the program's operations were standardized during experimentation and that these standard formats can also be employed in practice. The second description also provides information on the program's setting: A classroom. Neither description covers the control or comparison program—if one was used. Evaluations involving control groups should also include descriptions of the alternative interventions. Finally, neither the first nor the second description tells you the costs of implementation.

The following is a checklist for use in deciding on the quality of the descriptions of the programs or interventions that are the focus of evaluation research.

A Checklist for Appraising the Quality of
Program/Intervention Descriptions

✓ Are specific program objectives provided for the experimental program? The control?

✓ Is the content clearly described for the experimental group? The control? Where can the reviewer gain access to a detailed version (online? Directly from the researchers?)

✓ Is the program based on a theory (of learning? Of behavior change?)

✓ Is adequate information provided on whether the experimental program was implemented as planned in all experimental sites?

✓ Is adequate information given regarding how to implement (e.g., through training) the experimental program in nonexperimental sites?

✓ Is sufficient information provided on the settings in which the program and its evaluation were tested?

✓ Is sufficient information provided on the program's participants?

✓ Where can evidence of effectiveness be found?

DATA ANALYSIS: STATISTICAL METHODS IN THE RESEARCH LITERATURE

A literature reviewer should acquire a basic understanding of statistics and learn how to read and interpret statistical results in text and in tables and figures. These skills will help you evaluate the quality of each study's analysis, results, and conclusions.

Statistical methods are clearly among the most technical of the reviewers' needed skills. Do not assume that you can adequately evaluate the literature without knowledge of how researchers analyze data. In case of doubt, a statistics text and/or an expert should be consulted.

Statistical Methods and What to Look For: An Overview

To help the reviewer check on the quality of the statistical analysis, it often helps to understand the process used by researchers in selecting analytic techniques. The article should describe and justify each method as well as the statistical program used in the analysis. Unusual or new methods must be referenced so that the reviewer can learn more about them. Many prominent journals rely on statisticians to evaluate the quality of their published reports. However, many journals do not have special reviewers, assuming they are peer reviewed at all.

To select the most suitable analysis for a research study, the researcher-analyst will have answered these four questions.

Questions Answered in Selecting Statistical Methods

1. Which independent and dependent variables are contained within the study's main research questions?

2. Are the data that measure the independent and the dependent variables categorical (e.g., number of males and number of females), ordinal (e.g., high, medium, low), or continuous (e.g., an average of 4.8 on a 5-point scale)?

3. What statistical methods may be used to answer the research question, given the number (1 or more than 1) and characteristics (categorical, continuous) of the independent and dependent variables?

4. Do the data meet all the assumptions of the statistical tests (e.g., is the sample size sufficient? Are the data "normally distributed"?)?

Independent and Dependent Variables

A first step in selecting a statistical method is to identify the type of data that result from measuring each independent or predictor variable and each dependent or outcome variable. A variable is a measurable characteristic that varies in the population. Weight is a variable, and all persons weighing 60 kilograms have the same numerical weight. Satisfaction is also a variable. In this case, however, the numerical scale has to be devised and rules must be created for its interpretation. For example, in Study A, employee satisfaction may be measured on a scale of 1 to 100, with 1 corresponding to the very lowest satisfaction and 100 to the very highest. In Study B, employee satisfaction may be measured by proxy by counting the proportion of employees who stay with the company for 3 or more years, and if the number equals a preset standard, then satisfaction is considered high.

Independent variables are so called because they are independent of any intervention. They are used to explain or predict outcomes (the dependent variable), which are dependent on the outcomes of the intervention. Typical independent variables include group membership (experimental and control) and demographic characteristics (such as age, gender, education, income) as illustrated below.

The terms *independent* and *predictor* variables, like the terms *dependent* and *outcome* variables, are a function of which discipline you study. Researchers in health and medicine often use *predictor* and *outcome,* whereas other disciplines use *independent* and *dependent.* For most of this discussion, the terms *independent* and *dependent* are used.

Examples of Independent Variables

Question. How do men and women compare in their rates of heart disease?

Independent variable: Gender (men, women)

Question. Who benefits most from participation in Outward Boundaries? Boys or girls? Children 13 years of age and younger or 14 and older?

Independent variables: Gender (boys, girls) and age (13 years of age and younger, 14 and older)

Question. How do participants in new Program A and traditional Program B compare in their ability to complete work-related tasks?

Independent variables: Participation (Programs A and B)

Dependent variables: "Outcomes" such as skills, attitudes, knowledge, efficiency, and quality of teaching and learning

Examples of Dependent Variables

Question. How do men and women compare in their rates of heart disease?

Dependent variable: Rates of heart disease

Question. Who benefits most from participation in Outward Boundaries? Boys or girls? Children 13 years of age and younger or 14 and older?

Dependent variable: Benefit

Question. How do participants in Programs A and B compare in their attendance and ability to complete work-related tasks?

Dependent variables: Attendance, ability to complete work-related tasks

Data are collected to measure both the independent and dependent variables. The following is an example of the connection between study questions, independent and dependent variables, and data collection.

Independent and Dependent Variables and Data Collection

Question. Is there a difference in literature-reviewing skills between participants in Programs A and B? Participants in Program A have joined a new program, and the difference should be positive and in their favor.

Independent variable: Participation versus no participation in a new program

Data collection measure: Attendance logs

Dependent variable: Literature-reviewing skills

Data collection measure: Performance test

Measurement Scales and Their Data

The data in any study can come from three different types of measurement scales. These are termed *categorical, ordinal,* and *continuous.* In turn, the data they produce are called categorical, ordinal, and continuous data.

Categorical Scales. Categorical scales produce data that fit into categories.

1. What is your gender? *(Circle one)*

   Male 1

   Female 2

2. Name the statistical method. *(Circle one)*

   Chi-square 1

   ANOVA 2

Typically, categorical data are described as percentages and proportions (50 of 100, or 50% of the sample was male). The measure used to describe the center of their distribution is the mode, or the number of observations that appears most frequently.

Ordinal Scales. If an inherent order exists among categories, the data are said to be obtained from an ordinal scale:

How much education have you completed? *(Circle one)*

Never finished high school 1

High school graduate, but no college 2

Some college 3

College graduate 4

Ordinal scales are used to ask questions that call for ratings of how you feel (*excellent, very good, good, fair, poor, very poor*), whether you agree (*strongly agree, agree, disagree, strongly disagree*), and your opinion regarding the probability that something is present (*definitely present, probably present, probably not present, definitely not present*). They are also used for data on variables whose characteristics can be arranged or ordered by class (such as *high, medium,* and *low*), quality (e.g., *highly positive, positive, negative, strongly negative*), and degree (such as *very conservative, somewhat conservative, somewhat liberal, very liberal*).

Percentages and proportions are used to describe ordinal data, and the center of the distribution is often expressed as the median, or the observation that divides the distribution into two halves. For instance, with ordinal data, statements are made such as, "Fifteen percent of Alta Vista's nursing home residents are moderately demented" and "The median nursing home director has 12 or more years' experience in long-term care." The median is equal to the 50th percentile, and so the latter statement means that 50% of nursing home directors have 12 or more years' experience and 50% have less than 12 or more years' experience.

Continuous Scales. When differences between numbers have a meaning on a numerical scale, they are called continuous. For example, age is a continuous variable, and so are weight and length of survival with a disease.

Scores on tests and other measures are usually continuous. For example, a score of 90 may be considered higher than a score of 50 on a 100-item achievement test. But is a score of 25 half the achievement of a score of 50? Sometimes yes, sometimes no. Furthermore, in some studies, lower numerical scores may actually be better (e.g., a lower weight for a given height). Because the meaning of a score is not always apparent, the researcher owes the reviewer an explanation of all scoring systems. If one is not forthcoming, the reviewer cannot adequately evaluate the meaning of the study's results.

Means and standard deviations are used to summarize the values of continuous measures. Sometimes, ordinal data are analyzed as if they were numerical. For instance, if on a 5-point scale, six people assign a rating of 3 and four people assign a rating of 2, then the average rating is 2.6. The calculation is as follows: Six people's ratings of 3 (6×3) plus four people's ratings of 2 (4×2) = 26 divided by 10 persons = 2.6.

Statistical and Practical Significance

Researchers often use statistical methods to determine if meaningful or *significant* differences exist between groups. If they do, you will find a statement such as, "The differences between the experimental and control programs were statistically significant ($p < .01$)." The $p < .01$ or p value is a statistic that (for all practical purposes) is used to explain whether a measured difference is due to an intervention rather than to chance.

In the example shown in Table 3.1, a commonly used statistical method, the *t* test, is used to compare two groups: Students in the WORK-FIND program and students in a control group (no program). The results are presented in a table that is similar to one that you are likely to find in standard research reports.

The table shows (in the Measures column) that the dependent variables are knowledge, attitudes, performance, and confidence. Students in both programs are compared in terms of these measures before and after the program. The question is this: Are the differences significant when you compare the magnitude of changes before and after in the WORK-FIND group with those in the no-program group? The table shows with an asterisk that the magnitude of differences was statistically significant for two variables: Knowledge and performance. Because of these significant findings, the researcher will conclude that WORK-FIND rather than chance is likely to be responsible for the difference.

Statisticians test the hypothesis that no differences exist between groups. This is called the *null hypothesis.* They then choose a level of significance and the value the test statistic must obtain to be significant. The level of significance—called alpha—is set in advance as .05, .01, or .001. Their final step involves performing calculations to determine if the test statistic—the p value—is less than alpha. If it is, and the null hypothesis is not confirmed, it will be rejected in favor of an alternative—namely, that a difference does exist. Ideally, the difference is one that supports the effectiveness of the experimental program. When the null is rejected in favor of an alternative, then the differences are said to be statistically significant. (More information on tests of statistical significance can be found in the statistics texts recommended at the end of this chapter.)

Statistical significance is not the same as practical significance, and this may have an important bearing on the reviewer's use of a particular study. The following illustrates the difference between statistical and practical significance.

Table 3.1 Before and After Mean Scores (Standard Deviations) and Net Change Scores for WORK-FIND and a No-Program Group (N = 500 Students)

Measures	WORK-FIND Students		No-Program Students		Net Difference	t	p
	Before	After	Before	After			
Knowledge	75.6 (11.8)	85.5 (8.8)	78.8 (10.9)	81.2 (9.6)	7.5	8.9	.0001*
Attitudes	2.5 (1.1)	2.1 (1.0)	2.5 (1.1)	2.3 (1.1)	0.15	1.5	.14
Performance	3.5 (0.7)	3.8 (0.7)	3.7 (10.7)	3.8 (0.7)	0.19	4.7	.0001*
Confidence	4.4 (0.6)	4.5 (0.6)	4.4 (0.6)	4.4 (0.6)	0.09	1.2	.22

*Statistically significant.

Statistical and Practical Significance

Question. Do students improve in their knowledge of how to interpret food label information when choosing snacks? Improvement will be demonstrated by a statistically significant difference in knowledge between participating and nonparticipating students. The difference in scores must be at least 15 points. If a 15-point difference is found, participants will be studied for 2 years to determine the extent to which the knowledge is retained. The scores must be maintained (no significant differences) over the 2-year period.

Measurements: Knowledge is measured on a 25-item test.

Analysis: A *t* test will be used to compare the two groups of students in their knowledge. Scores will be computed a second time, and a *t* test will be used to compare the average or mean differences over time.

In this example, tests of statistical significance are called for twice: To compare participating and nonparticipating students at one point in time and to compare the same participants' scores over time. In addition, the stipulation is that for the scores to have educational or practical meaning, a 15-point difference between participants and nonparticipants must be obtained and sustained. With experience, researchers have found that in a number of situations, statistical significance is sometimes insufficient evidence of an intervention's effectiveness. With very large samples, for example, very small differences in numerical values (such as scores on an achievement test) can be statistically significant but have little practical meaning. In the example above, the standard includes a 15-point difference in test scores. If the difference between scores is statistically significant but only 10 points, then the program will not be considered educationally significant.

The difference between practical and statistical significance is a very important one to consider when reviewing literature that evaluates programs and interventions. You may review a study whose investigator concludes that an intervention is effective because of statistically significant differences in scores over time. However, if you, the reviewer, closely examine the data provided by the investigator, you may find that the differences in scores are small, say, one or two points. Remember: If samples are very large, or the measures from which the scores are derived are of marginal validity, then as a reviewer, you should be wary of accepting statistical differences.

Good statistical practice has come to mean reporting actual values (e.g., averages, standard deviations, proportions) and not just the results of statistical tests. When statistical tests are used, the actual p values should be reported (e.g., $p = .03$ rather than $p < .05$). The merits of using actual values can be seen in that without them, a finding of $p = .06$ may be viewed as "not significant," whereas a finding of $p = .05$ will be. Conventional p values are $p < .001$, $.01$, and $.05$.

Confidence Intervals

Confidence intervals (often together with significance tests) are standard practice in describing the relationships between and among groups. A confidence interval (CI) is derived from sample data and has a given probability (such as 95%) that the unknown true value is located within the interval. Why do you need an interval? Because the point value (such as an average score) is probably not entirely accurate due to the errors that result from imperfect sampling, measurement error, and faulty research designs. Statisticians say that it is probably more accurate to provide a range of values.

Using any standard method found in a statistics text, for example, the 95% confidence interval (95% CI) of an 8 percentage-point difference between groups might come out to be between 3% and 13%. A 95% CI means that about 95% of all such intervals will include the unknown true difference and 5% will not. Suppose the smallest practical difference the researcher expects is 15%, but he or she obtains an 8% difference ($p = .03$). Although statistically significant, the difference is not meaningful in practical terms, according to the researcher's own standards.

Table 3.2 shows the use of 95% confidence intervals to compare the means of three programs. The table shows that for Program A, 95% of all intervals will contain the true mean, which is between 7.6654 and 14.3346; for Program B, 95% of all intervals between 4.1675 and 12.1182 will contain the true mean, and so on. These intervals can be plotted on a graph. If the means do not overlap, differences exist. If the mean of one group is contained in the interval of the second, differences do not exist. If the intervals overlap but not the means, you cannot tell if differences exist. Look at Figure 3.2.

Table 3.2   Comparison of Three Programs

Program	Mean	Standard Deviation	95% CI for Mean
A	11.0000	3.6056	7.6654 to 14.3346
B	8.1429	4.2984	4.1675 to 12.1182
C	16.4286	3.1547	13.5109 to 19.3462
Total	11.8571	4.9828	9.5890 to 14.1253

Figure 3.2   Graph of a Comparison of the Confidence Intervals for the Mean Outcomes of Three Programs

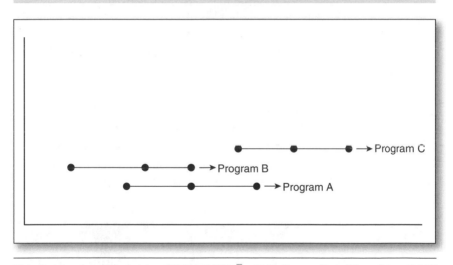

Note: Program A confidence interval 7.67 to 14.33, $\overline{X} = 11.00$; Program B confidence interval: 4.17 to 12.12, $\overline{X} = 8.14$; Program C confidence interval: 13.51 to 19.35, $\overline{X} = 16.43$.

Program B's mean score is within Program A's confidence interval. Program C's interval overlaps only slightly with Program A's.

Differences in the means can be seen, and you can reject the null (that the means are the same). The confidence interval and p are related. In fact, if you test the differences using an analysis of variance, you will find that the p value is .002: A statistically significant difference.

Which Analytic Method Is Best?

No analytic method is best. Some are more appropriate than others, so when you review a study's analytic quality, you must determine the appropriateness of the method.

Choosing an analytic method to find the answer to a study question depends on the following:

- Whether data on the independent variable come from a categorical, ordinal, or numerical scale
- The number of independent variables
- Whether data on the dependent variable come from a categorical, ordinal, or numerical scale
- The number of dependent variables
- Whether the design, sampling, and quality of the data meet the assumptions of the statistical method (The use of many statistical methods requires your data to meet certain preexisting conditions—assumptions. These often include the size of the sample and the "shape" of the distribution of responses.)

The literature reviewer cannot adequately evaluate a study's methods unless the research questions (or hypotheses or objectives) and methods are explained. The following example illustrates the relationships a reviewer should look for among study questions, research design, independent and dependent variables, research design and sample, types of measures, and data analysis.

Example: Evaluating Study Data Analysis: Illustrative Connections Among Questions, Designs, Samples, Measures, and Analysis

Question. Is the quality of day care satisfactory? Satisfactory means a statistically significant difference in quality of day care favoring program versus control program participants.

Independent variable: Group membership (participants versus controls)

Design: An experimental design with parallel controls

Sampling: Eligible participants are assigned at random to an experimental and control group; 150 participants are in each group (a statistically derived sample size).

Dependent variable: Quality of day care

Measures and types of data: Group membership (categorical); quality of day care (numerical data: data are from the DAYCARES Questionnaire, a 100-point survey in which higher scores mean better quality)

Analysis: A two-sample independent groups *t* test

Justification for the analysis: This particular *t* test is appropriate when the independent variable is measured on a categorical scale and the dependent variable is measured on a numerical scale. In this case, the assumptions of a *t* test are met. These assumptions are that each group has a sample size of at least 30, both groups' size is about equal, the two groups are independent (an assumption that is met most easily with a strong evaluation design and a high-quality data collection effort), and the data are normally distributed. A normal distribution is a continuous set of data that is bell shaped with half the area to the left of the mean and half to the right. If one of the assumptions of the *t* test is seriously violated, other analytic methods should be used, such as the Wilcoxon rank-sum test, also called the Mann-Whitney *U* test. This test makes no assumption about the normality of the distribution. (For more information, see the appropriate references at the end of the chapter.)

Although no definitive rules can be set for analyzing all data, Table 3.3 is a general guide to the selection of some commonly used data-analytic methods. (Statistical calculations are not covered in this book.) The guide is presented here to give the reviewer insights into the kinds of information to look for in evaluating the appropriateness of a study's data-analytic methods. When reviewing complex studies or studies in publications of uncertain quality, statistical consultation may be necessary.

For simplicity, the guide omits ordinal variables. When independent variables are measured on an ordinal scale, statisticians often treat them as if they are categorical. For example, a study whose aim is to predict the outcomes of participation in a program for patients with good, fair, or poor functional status can regard good, fair, and poor (ordinal, independent variables) as categorical. When dependent variables are measured on an ordinal scale, they are habitually treated as if they were continuous. For example, if the dependent variable in a nutrition program is the length of time a diet is maintained (less than 3 months, between 3 and 6 months, and more than 6 months) by men and women with differing motivations to diet, the dependent, ordinal variable can, for the sake of the analysis, be treated as continuous.

Check (in a statistics text or computer manual or call in a consultant) that the analysis used in each study you review meets the assumptions of each statistical analysis. The assumptions may include the 130 characteristics of the sample (e.g., "normally" distributed—that is, conforming to a symmetric, bell-shaped probability distribution) or the size of the sample. (Normal distributions are discussed in the statistics texts referenced at the end of this chapter.)

Use the following checklist when examining the quality of a study's data analysis.

A Checklist for Evaluating a Study's Data Analysis

✓ Do the researchers:

✓ provide information on the "flow" of participants? Specifically, do the researchers provide data on the number of study participants

✓ Are research questions clearly stated?

✓ Are the independent (predictor) variables defined? Are the dependent (outcome) variables defined?

✓ Do the researchers explain the type of data (e.g., continuous, categorical) obtained from measures of the independent and dependent variables?

✓ Are statistical methods adequately described?

✓ Is a reference provided for the statistical program used to analyze the data?

✓ Are statistical methods justified?

✓ Is the purpose of the analysis clear?

✓ Are scoring systems described?

✓ Are potential confounders adequately controlled for in the analysis?

✓ Are analytic specifications of the independent and dependent variables consistent with the evaluation questions or hypotheses under study?

✓ Is the unit of analysis specified clearly?

✓ If statistical tests are used to determine differences, is practical significance discussed?

✓ If statistical tests are used to determine differences, is the actual p value given?

✓ If the study is concerned with differences among groups, are confidence limits given describing the magnitude of any observed differences?

Table 3.3 Guide to the Selection of Data-Analytic Methods

Sample Study Questions	Type of Data: Independent Variable	Type of Data: Dependent Variable	Potential Analytic Method
For study questions with one independent and one dependent variable:			
Do participants in the experimental and control groups differ in their use or failure to use mental health services?	Categorical: Group (experimental and control)	Categorical: Use of mental health services (used services or did not)	Chi-square, Fisher's exact test, relative risk (risk ratio), odds ratio
How do the experimental and control groups compare in their skills (measured by their numerical scores on the Skills Survey)?	Categorical: Group (experimental and control)	Continuous (skills scores)	Independent samples t test
How do electricians in the United States, Canada, and England compare in their attitudes (measured by their numerical scores on the Skills Survey)?	Categorical (more than two values: United States, Canada, and England)	Continuous (skills scores)	One-way ANOVA (uses the F test)
Do high numerical scores on the Skills Survey predict high numerical scores on the Knowledge Test?	Categorical (skills scores)	Continuous (knowledge scores)	Regression (when neither variable is independent nor dependent, use correlation)

(Continued)

Table 3.3 (Continued)

Sample Study Questions	Type of Data: Independent Variable	Type of Data: Dependent Variable	Potential Analytic Method
For questions with two or more independent variables:			
Do men and women in the experimental and control programs differ in whether they attended at least one parent-teacher conference?	Categorical (gender, group)	Categorical (attended or did not attend at least one parent-teacher conference)	Log-linear
Do men and women with differing scores on the Knowledge Test differ in whether they attended at least one parent-teacher conference?	Categorical (gender) and continuous (knowledge scores)	Categorical (attended or did not attend at least one parent-teacher conference)	Logistic regression
How do men and women in the experimental and control programs compare in their attitudes (measured by their numerical scores on the Attitude Survey)?	Categorical (gender and group)	Continuous (attitude scores)	Analysis of variance (ANOVA)
How are age and income and years living in the community related to attitudes (measured by numerical scores on the Attitude Survey)?	Continuous (age and income and years living in the community)	Continuous (attitude scores)	Multiple regression
How do men and women in the experimental and control programs compare in their attitudes (measured by their numerical scores on the Attitude Survey) when their level of education is controlled?	Categorical (gender and group) with confounding factors (such as education)	Continuous (attitude scores)	Analysis of covariance (ANCOVA)

Sample Study Questions	Type of Data: Independent Variable	Type of Data: Dependent Variable	Potential Analytic Method
For questions with two or more independent and dependent variables:			
How do men and women in the experimental and control programs compare in their numerical attitude and knowledge scores?	Categorical (gender and group)	Continuous (scores on two measures: Attitudes and knowledge)	Multivariate analysis of variance (MANOVA)

The Results

A study's results are the findings that pertain to its objectives, questions, or hypotheses. For example, if a main study question asks if students' knowledge improves after participation in a new school program, make certain that the researcher presents an answer to that question.

Watch for study results that gloss over negative findings. Negative findings are those that suggest that a remedy is ineffective or that a treatment is harmful. Also be wary of studies that gloss over findings for the main sample (e.g., persons 45 years of age and older) and, instead, provide results on subgroups (men and women 45 years of age and older who own their own home). If the subgroups were not selected for the study from the start according to prespecified eligibility criteria, the findings may be inaccurate. Some researchers continue to analyze data until they find something that looks "interesting." For example, suppose that the overall analysis of a school program finds that students' knowledge does not improve; researchers may continue to analyze data until they find at least one subgroup for whom the program was successful. When such unplanned findings are presented, make certain that the authors describe the findings for these subgroups as preliminary.

When evaluating the quality and usefulness of results, examine whether the study's authors give response rates for each group and that they also describe the study participants' relevant demographic and other characteristics (such as their health or educational status). When sampling is used, evaluate whether the researcher provides data that compare the eligible sample who agreed to participate in the study with those who are eligible but refused, did not complete the entire program, or did not provide complete data on all measures. Make certain that no inconsistencies exist between the author's text and the tables or figures used to justify the text.

Here is a checklist for evaluating the presentation of study results.

A Checklist for Evaluating Presentation of a Study's Results

Do the researchers:

✓ provide information on the "flow" of participants? Specifically, do the researchers provide data on the number of study participants

   o evaluated for potential enrollment?
   o randomly (or conveniently) assigned to groups?
   o who received the program as assigned for each study group?
   o who completed treatment as assigned, by study group?
   o who completed follow-up as planned, by study group?
   o included in main analysis, by study group?

✓ Describe deviations from study as planned, together with reasons.

✓ Dates defining the periods of recruitment and follow-up

✓ Baseline or initial characteristics of each group (e.g., demographic characteristics); any characteristics that can influence outcomes in the particular study (e.g., motivation, literacy level)

✓ For each outcome, a summary of results for each group of participants. Look for how large an effect is present and how confident one can be about the effect (e.g., 95% confidence interval).

Conclusions

A study's conclusions must come directly from the data collected by the study. Look at these examples of READ, a high school reading curriculum, and a fitness program at DevSoft.

Conclusions: On What Should They Be Based?

Program: READ

READ, an innovative reading curriculum for high schools, was introduced into all 12th-grade classes in Aberdeen City. About 5,642 (90%) of all 12th graders completed the 2-year program. Success was measured by standardized reading achievement tests, use of the library, and surveys of students, teachers, and parents. Nearly 50% of the 5,642 students improved their reading achievement scores in an educationally meaningful way. Library use was up by 45% in the first year and by 62% in the second. When asked how satisfied they were with participation, 92% of students, 89% of teachers, and 94% of parents said they were very or extremely satisfied.

Poor conclusion. We conclude that READ is an effective curriculum for high school students.

Better conclusion. We conclude that READ is an effective curriculum for 12th graders in Aberdeen City high schools.

Comment. The information provided in the study description allows only an inference about program effectiveness that pertains to the study's included participants: 12th graders at Aberdeen City High. No firm conclusions can be drawn about 12th graders in other city schools (resources may differ), nor can conclusions be drawn about students in other grades.

Program: Fitness for DevSoft

After participation in a 1-year fitness program involving counseling in diet, exercise, and psychosocial well-being, employees at DevSoft were observed for an additional 6-month period. We found that nearly all employees in the program continued their healthful practices for the 6 months.

Poor conclusion. Our researchers concluded that we should adopt the program as part of DevSoft's ongoing employee health activities, especially since fitness programs at InterPlace and SystemsNet have also been proven effective.

Better conclusion. Preliminary results suggest that the fitness program is effective. Because 6 months is probably not enough time to monitor the persistence of behavior changes associated with new diets, exercise regimens, and other therapies, we recommend continued observation over a 2-year period. Systems Net, using a very similar program, found that to sustain behavior change, close monitoring was essential.

Comment. An important component of any research activity is enough observation time to document sustained effects. The first set of researchers was too hasty to conclude that the fitness program was effective; data from other studies indicate that the 6-month period was not sufficient to observe sustained behavior change.

All good studies include a discussion of their limitations and their influence on the conclusions. Check to make sure all limitations are discussed. Studies may be limited because they could not enroll the ideal sample, implement the best design, or collect perfectly valid data. Ask: Are all limitations discussed? How do the limitations affect the validity of the findings?

It is often a good idea for researchers to compare their study's results with other investigators' findings. As the reviewer, you should examine the nature of the comparisons to determine if the conditions under which both studies (the one you are reviewing and the comparison study) were performed are similar. For example, ask these questions: Are the study objectives and methods equivalent? How about the sample and setting? It is also important to check to see if an editorial or letters to the editor of the publication in which the study appears challenge the study's methods or conclusions.

Here is a checklist for evaluating the presentation of a study's conclusions.

A Checklist for Evaluating the Presentation of a Study's Conclusions

✓ Do researchers provide a brief synopsis of the findings?

✓ Do they provide an explanation of why the findings occurred as they did?

✓ Are the conclusions based on the study's data in that findings are applied only to the sample, setting, and programs included in the research?

✓ Do the researchers compare the study's relevant findings to those from other studies and, whenever possible, include a systematic review that combines the results with the results of other, relevant studies?

✓ Are the limitations of design, sampling, data collection, and so on described?

✓ To what extent do the limitations prohibit you from having confidence in the conclusions?

✓ Do the researchers provide information to summarize the implications of their work or make recommendations as to how to advance the field?

Reviewing Qualitative Research: A Special Note

Qualitative researchers study human or social problems in their natural settings and attempt to make sense of these problems in terms of the meanings people bring to them. The results of qualitative research are often presented as a detailed, complex, and holistic picture or story.

Qualitative research is naturalistic and interpretive, involving the studied use of a variety of empirical materials such as case studies, personal experience, life stories, interviews, observations, and historical and visual texts. Oriented primarily toward exploration, discovery, and induction, this type of research often results in individuals' own accounts of their attitudes, motivations, and behavior.

Qualitative research, which tends to focus on "the story," is often contrasted with quantitative research, which tends to focus on "the numbers." In actual fact, qualitative research uses numbers, and quantitative research (which usually means experimental research) uses stories. When reviewing the literature, you should not focus on whether a study is qualitative or quantitative but concentrate instead on its accuracy and the value of its findings.

As a reviewer, you are likely to encounter qualitative studies when you examine the literature on topics that do not lend themselves to quantification for methodological or ethical reasons. The following are examples of the types of qualitative studies you might encounter.

Sample Studies Associated With Qualitative Research

- Studies of the feelings and behaviors of persons who are unable to participate in traditional experiments and surveys

  Examples. Young children, persons who do not speak the investigator's primary language or are from a different culture, persons who cannot read and cannot complete self-administered questionnaires, those who are seriously mentally ill, the very young, terminally ill patients

- Studies of the feelings and behaviors of persons who are unwilling to participate in traditional experiments

  Examples. Street people, substance abusers, persons who participate in illegal or socially unacceptable activities

- Studies that attempt to document and understand the activities and progress of emerging institutions or groups

  Examples. Newly created schools, educational systems, and health care organizations; social, economic, and political phenomena, including people's reactions to and participation in political movements and life-style choices

- Studies investigating how to supplement traditional research methods

  Examples. To find out which problems and questions are important and should be addressed by future research to generate research questions and hypotheses; to add depth, meaning, and detail to statistical findings; to find out how persons think, feel, or behave when standardized measures are not yet available

- Studies that collect data when traditional research methods may raise ethical questions

  Examples. Studies in which randomization cannot take place because the intervention or treatment is thought extremely likely to be effective and so an alternative is not possible, studies of persons with medical or learning disabilities who cannot sign informed consent forms, the very young, the frail elderly

- Studies of a single individual, society, culture, or phenomenon

  Examples. A biography of a social or political leader, a report on the social and health beliefs of a defined cultural group, an investigation of the components of a caring nurse-patient interaction, research into the coping mechanisms of survivors of incest

Qualitative research, like other types of research, aims to tell it like it is—that is, to provide valid information. How can you tell if a qualitative study is high quality? Do you need to have different standards from the ones you use to evaluate experimental research? The good news is that many standards used to evaluate the quality of experiments can be applied to qualitative research. For example, you can expect the best qualitative studies to meet these standards:

- Specific research questions
- Defined and justified sample
- Valid data collection
- Appropriate analytic methods
- Interpretations based on the data

The main differences between qualitative and other methods can be found in the areas of research design, the use of an inductive and descriptive approach, and the narrative style of the report. Qualitative studies tend to rely on single settings and relatively small samples from which in-depth information is collected. For example, for a review of the literature on homeless children, you might find an article reporting on 25 children's perceptions of living in a single shelter for homeless families. A study claiming to be experimental that relied only on a sample size of 25 would not pass the reviewer's quality screen. But studies on topics such as homelessness face inherent methodological difficulties (e.g., assembling large samples) and ethical problems (e.g., obtaining informed consent from children's families). The reviewer of such studies must decide whether the importance and singularity of the information that might result from the research outweigh the limitations associated with small sample sizes and weak—from the experimental point of view—research design.

The following checklist of criteria for quality can be used to evaluate the presentation and quality of qualitative research.

*A Checklist for Evaluating the Presentation
and Quality of Qualitative Research*

✓   **The data collection methods must be reliable and valid and accompanied by supporting evidence of their accuracy.**

Obtaining reliable and valid data may mean collecting data from many sources and from several independent researchers. Ask: If multiple researchers are used, what methods are used to determine if they agree on an observation? How are disagreements resolved? Are the results shown to the study's participants? External reviewers?

Qualitative researchers use techniques such as *participant observations* in which they become actual participants in the group or organization being studied. They may live in the community being studied, for instance. This closeness enables researchers to get an inside view of the group's context and objectives but may also reduce objectivity. Training and practice in observation can enhance objectivity. Ask: Do observers receive training? Is their inter-rater reliability monitored? If observers disagree, who mediates among them? If observations are compromised, what is done? If interviews are conducted, do the researchers describe the methods used to record data (e.g., tape recorders, video cameras, handwritten or computerized notes)? Are interviewers trained? Is their quality monitored?

✓ **The study should contain proof of a rigorous research design.**

Although qualitative researchers do not manipulate their research setting, techniques such as *triangulation* are available to strengthen the study design. Triangulation refers to reliance on a combination of several methods, including quantitative as well as qualitative strategies. Examples include using multiple data sources, researchers, or research methods and reliance on several perspectives, theories, or traditions of inquiry to interpret a single set of data.

✓ **Sound sampling methods should be explicit.**

Qualitative studies usually rely on sites and subjects that are available and accessible. Convenience samples may not be the best choice, however. Ask: Do the researchers explain and justify the sample? What methods are used to bolster the link between the characteristics of the sample and its size and any groups to whom the researchers want the findings to apply? Do the researchers obtain the consent of the participants in a formal way?

✓ **The researchers should describe their traditions of inquiry and research perspectives.**

Qualitative research has several traditions or approaches to investigation, and each has its own assumptions and procedures that will affect the authors' assumptions, style, and interpretations. One example is the use of phenomenological inquiry (a method used by psychologists), which focuses on the experience of a phenomenon for particular people. The phenomenon may be an emotion, a relationship, a job, an organization, or a culture. Another common approach, the ethnographic, comes from anthropology and focuses on the study of the traditions and mores of cultures. Other traditionally used methods of inquiry include biography, case study, and grounded theory (from sociology). Ask: Do researchers describe their methods of inquiry? Do they clarify their biases or perspectives?

Not all qualitative research adheres strictly to a method of inquiry, but all researchers bring a perspective to their studies. These perspectives may be religious, legal, ethical, clinical, political, economic, and so on.

✓   **The analysis methods must be carefully explained.**

Qualitative research produces enormous amounts of data. Listening to 5 hours of recorded conversation can be a daunting task and produce voluminous notes. Ask: Do the researchers describe who did the listening? Were listeners trained? Which categories were used to organize the data? How were the categories chosen? Are they reliable and valid? That is, is evidence provided that at least two researchers agree on the categories? Do the researchers offer proof that they have accounted for all collected data, including information from *outliers,* or cases that do not "fit" in? What do the researchers do to guard against the risk of giving great weight to high status or more articulate informants? What do they do about missing data? Are rival explanations considered? Are the study's limitations discussed?

The following is a selected list of qualitative research studies of varying degrees of quality. You may want to evaluate each using the above criteria.

Qualitative Research Studies

Bastiaens, H., Van Royen, P., Pavlic, D. R., Raposo, V., & Baker, R. (2007). Older people's preferences for involvement in their own care: A qualitative study in primary health care in 11 European countries. *Patient Education and Counseling, 68*(1), 33–42.

Buse, C. E. (2010). Escaping the ageing body? Computer technologies and embodiment in later life [Article]. *Ageing & Society, 30,* 987–1009. doi: 10.1017/s0144686x10000164

Hungerland, B., Liebel, M., Liesecke, A., & Wihstutz, A. (2007). Paths to participatory autonomy—The meanings of work for children in Germany. *Childhood—A Global Journal of Child Research, 14,* 257–277.

Loke, A. Y., Wan, M. L. E., & Hayter, M. (2012). The lived experience of women victims of intimate partner violence. *Journal of Clinical Nursing, 21*(15–16), 2336-2346. doi: 10.1111/j.1365-2702.2012.04159.x

Mikal, J. P., & Grace, K. (2012). Against abstinence-only education abroad: Viewing Internet use during study abroad as a possible experience enhancement [Article]. *Journal of Studies in International Education, 16*(3), 287–306. doi: 10.1177/1028315311423108

Motley, C. M., & Craig-Henderson, K. M. (2007). Epithet or endearment? Examining reactions among those of the African diaspora to an ethnic epithet. *Journal of Black Studies, 37,* 944–963.

Ng, W., & Roberts, J. (2007). "Helping the family": The mediating role of outside directors in ethnic Chinese family firms. *Human Relations, 60,* 285–314.

Ploeg, J., De Witt, L., Hutchison, B., Hayward, L., & Grayson, K. (2008). Evaluation of a research mentorship program in community care. *Evaluation and Program Planning, 31,* 22–33.

Roshita, A., Schubert, E., & Whittaker, M. (2012). Child-care and feeding practices of urban middle class working and non-working Indonesian mothers: A qualitative study of the socio-economic and cultural environment [Article]. *Maternal and Child Nutrition, 8*(3), 299–314. doi: 10.1111/j.1740-8709.2011.00298.x

SmithBattle, L. (2007). "I wanna have a good future"—Teen mothers' rise in educational aspirations, competing demands, and limited school support. *Youth & Society, 38,* 348–371.

Tod, A. M., Lusambili, A., Homer, C., Abbott, J., Cooke, J. M., Stocks, A. J., & McDaid, K. A. (2012). Understanding factors influencing vulnerable older people keeping warm and well in winter: A qualitative study using social marketing techniques. *BMJ Open, 2*(4). doi: 10.1136/bmjopen-2012-000922

Townson, L., Macauley, S., Harkness, E., Docherty, A., Dias, J., Eardley, M., et al. (2007). Research project on advocacy and autism. *Disability & Society, 22,* 523–536.

Vincent, C., Braun, A., & Ball, S. J. (2008). Childcare, choice and social class: Caring for young children in the UK. *Critical Social Policy, 28,* 5–26.

Walker, A., & Hutton, D. M. (2006). The application of the psychological contract to workplace safety. *Journal of Safety Research, 37,* 433–441.

Reviewing Mixed Methods Research

Mixed methods researchers collect, analyze, and integrate qualitative and statistical or quantitative data into a single study. Researchers use mixed methods to assist them in understanding an experimental study's findings or to incorporate users' perspectives in the development and evaluation of a program, service, or policy. The next two examples illustrate these common reasons for mixed methods research.

Example 1: Mixed Methods to Better Understand Experimental Results

The investigators found that experimental group participants reported significantly more discomfort with study participation than control group participants. This finding surprised the study team. To help them understand the findings, the team convened three focus groups and asked them about the discomfort's causes.

Example 2: Mixed Methods to Incorporate User Perspectives into Program Development

The study's main purpose was to develop online education to improve people's use of Web-based health information. The investigators convened five focus groups and conducted in-depth interviews with 15 people to identify preferences for learning. They asked participants questions about the value of audio and video. Using the information from the groups and interviews, the investigators developed the education and observed its usability and in a small sample. Once they had evidence that the education was probably ready for use in a larger population, they evaluated its effectiveness by using statistical methods to compare the knowledge, self-efficacy, and Internet use among two groups, one of which received the new education while the other used an already existing online program.

Mixed methods research reviewers have a daunting task. They must review the reliability and validity of each method's application to the research questions and also appraise if and how well the findings were combined to yield accurate and relevant results and conclusions.

The following is a selected list of mixed methods research studies.

Biasutti, M., & El-Deghaidy, H. (2012). Using Wiki in teacher education: Impact on knowledge management processes and student satisfaction. *Computers & Education, 59*(3), 861–872.

Christ, T., Arya, P., & Chiu, M. M. (2012). Collaborative peer video analysis. *Journal of Literacy Research, 44*(2), 171–199.

Coles, E., Themessl-Huber, M., & Freeman, R. (2012). Investigating community-based health and health promotion for homeless people: A mixed methods review. *Health Education Research, 27*(4), 624–644. doi: 10.1093/her/cys065

DeCuir-Gunby, J. T., Marshall, P. L., & McCulloch, A. W. (2012). Using mixed methods to analyze video data. *Journal of Mixed Methods Research, 6*(3), 199–216. doi: 10.1177/1558689811421174

Hussaini, K., Hamm, E., & Means, T. (2012, December 11). Using community-based participatory mixed methods research to understand preconception health in African American communities of Arizona. *Maternal and Child Health Journal.* doi: 10.1007/s10995-012-1206-5

Marczinski, C. A., & Stamates, A. L. (2012). Artificial sweeteners versus regular mixers increase breath alcohol concentrations in male and female social drinkers. *Alcoholism: Clinical and Experimental Research.* doi: 10.1111/acer.12039

McEwen, A., Hackshaw, L., Jones, L., Laverty, L., Amos, A., & Robinson, J. (2012). Evaluation of a programme to increase referrals to stop-smoking services using Children's Centres and smoke-free families schemes. *Addiction, 107*(2), 8–17.

Tan, S. B., Williams, A. F., & Morris, M. E. (2012). Experiences of caregivers of people with Parkinson's disease in Singapore: A qualitative analysis. *Journal of Clinical Nursing, 21*(15–16), 2235–2246.

Ungar, M., & Liebenberg, L. (2011). Assessing resilience across cultures using mixed methods: Construction of the child and youth resilience measure. *Journal of Mixed Methods Research, 5*(2), 126–149. doi: 10.1177/1558689811400607

Yu, S. (2012). College students' justification for digital piracy: A mixed methods study. *Journal of Mixed Methods Research, 6*(4), 364–378.

Zander, K., Stolz, H., & Hamm, U. (2013). Promising ethical arguments for product differentiation in the organic food sector. A mixed methods research approach. *Appetite, 62*, 133–142. doi: 10.1016/j.appet.2012.11.015

SUMMARY OF KEY POINTS

- Researchers collect data by administering achievement tests, survey questionnaires, and face-to-face and telephone interviews; analyzing large databases or vital statistics; observing individuals and groups; reviewing the literature and personal, medical, financial, and other statistical records; performing physical examinations and laboratory tests; and using simulations and clinical scenarios or performance tests.

- No single method of collecting data is inherently better or has more quality than another. Usually, data collection methods are chosen for their practicality as well as for their quality. For the literature reviewer, the deciding factor in determining the quality of a study's data collection is not the method itself but whether it provides reliable and valid information.

- A reliable data collection method is one that is relatively free from "measurement error." Because of this error, individuals' obtained scores are different from their true scores. Types of reliability include the following:

Test-retest reliability. A measure has test-retest reliability if the correlation between scores from time to time is high. The major conceptual difficulty in establishing test-retest reliability is in determining how much time is permissible between the first and second administration. If too much time elapses, external events might influence responses for the second administration; if too little time passes, the respondents may remember and simply repeat their answers from the first administration.

Equivalence or alternate-form reliability. This type refers to the extent to which two assessments measure the same concepts at the same level of difficulty. As an alternative to establishing equivalence between two forms of the same measure, researchers sometimes compute a split-half reliability. To do this requires dividing a measure into two equal halves (or alternate forms) and obtaining the correlation between the two halves.

Homogeneity. This kind of reliability refers to the extent to which all items or questions assess the same skill, characteristic, or quality. Sometimes this type of reliability is referred to as internal consistency. Cronbach's coefficient alpha, which is basically the average of all the correlations between each item and the total score, is often calculated to determine the extent of homogeneity.

Interrater. This type of reliability refers to the extent to which two or more individuals agree.

Intrarater. This type reliability refers to a single individual's consistency of measurement, and this, too, can be enhanced by training, monitoring, and continuous education.

- Validity refers to the degree to which a measure assesses what it purports to measure. At least four types of validity are commonly discussed.

Content validity refers to the extent to which a measure thoroughly and appropriately assesses the skills or characteristics it is intended to measure.

Face validity refers to how a measure appears on the surface: Does it seem to ask all the needed questions? Does it use the appropriate language and language level to do so? Face validity, unlike content validity, does not rely on established theory for support.

Criterion validity is made up of two subcategories: Predictive validity and concurrent validity. Predictive validity refers to the extent to which a measure forecasts future performance. Concurrent validity is demonstrated when two assessments agree or a new measure is compared favorably with one that is already considered valid.

Construct validity is established experimentally to demonstrate that a measure distinguishes between people who do and do not have certain characteristics.

- The appropriateness of each data-analytic method depends on whether the independent variable is measured on a categorical, ordinal, or numerical scale; the number of independent variables; whether the dependent variable is measured on a categorical, ordinal, or numerical scale; the number of dependent variables; and whether the quality and characteristics of the data meet the assumptions of the statistical method.
- Watch for study results that gloss over negative findings.
- Be wary of studies that gloss over findings for the main sample and, instead, provide results on subgroups.
- Check that a study's conclusions come directly from the data collected by the study's researcher.
- Check to make certain that the study's methodological limitations are discussed so that you can judge how much confidence to place in the findings.
- Check editorials and letters to the editor of the publication in which the study appears to make certain that major methods and conclusions are not being challenged.
- Qualitative research takes place in natural social settings rather than in the controlled environments associated with experimental research. Oriented primarily toward exploration, as well as discovery and induction, this type of research often results in individuals' own accounts of their attitudes, motivations, and behavior.
- When reviewing the literature, you should not focus on whether a study is qualitative or quantitative but concentrate instead on its accuracy and the value of its findings.

- The following checklist can be used to evaluate the presentation and quality of qualitative research. The checklist should be regarded as a supplement to the usual criteria for evaluating the quality and value of a study.

  ✓ The researchers should describe their traditions of inquiry.

  ✓ The data collection methods must be reliable and valid and accompanied by supporting evidence of their accuracy.

  ✓ The study should contain proof of a rigorous research design.

  ✓ Sound sampling methods should be explicit.

  ✓ The analysis methods must be carefully explained.

- Mixed methods is a type of research characterized by collecting, analyzing, and integrating qualitative and statistical or quantitative data into a single study. Two common uses for mixed methods are to assist researchers in better understanding an experimental or quantitative study's findings and to incorporate users' perspectives into the development and evaluation of a program, service, or policy.

EXERCISES

1. Read the following excerpts from study reports and tell which concepts of reliability and validity are covered.

   a. The self-administered questionnaire was adapted with minor revisions from the Student Health Risk Questionnaire, which is designed to investigate knowledge, attitudes, behaviors, and other cognitive variables regarding HIV and AIDS among high school students. Four behavior scales measured sexual activity (four questions in each scale) and needle use (five questions). Twenty-three items determined a scale of factual knowledge regarding AIDS. Cognitive variables derived from the health belief model and social learning theory were employed to examine personal beliefs and social norms (12 questions).

   b. More than 150 financial records were reviewed by a single reviewer with expertise in this area; a subset of 35 records was reviewed by a second blinded expert to assess the validity of the review. Rates of agreement for single items ranged from 81% ($\kappa = .77$, $p < .001$) to 100% ($\kappa = 1, p < .001$).

    c. Group A and Group B supervisors were given a 22-question quiz testing literature review principles derived from the UCLA guidelines. The quiz was not scored in a blinded manner, but each test was scored twice.

2. Look at Table 3.A and evaluate the adequacy of the write-up of results that comes after.

Write-Up of Results

Table 3.A presents the before and after means and the observed net change scores for each of the eight survey measures for the 500 Program WORK-FIND and comparison students. Significant effects favoring Program WORK-FIND were observed for five of the eight measures: Knowledge, beliefs about benefits, beliefs about standards, self-reliance, and risk-taking behaviors. Based on the information, Program WORK-FIND is effective.

Table 3.A   Before and After Mean Scores (Standard Deviations) and Net Change Scores, by Program Group (500 Students)

Measures	WORK-FIND Students		No-Program Students		Net Difference	t	p
	Before	After	Before	After			
Knowledge	75.6 (11.8)	85.5 (8.8)	78.8 (10.9)	81.2 (9.6)	7.5	8.9	.0001*
Beliefs							
Goals	2.5 (1.1)	2.1 (1.0)	2.5 (1.1)	2.3 (1.1)	−0.15	1.5	.14
Benefits	3.5 (0.7)	3.8 (0.7)	3.7 (10.7)	3.8 (0.7)	0.19	4.7	.0001*
Barriers	4.4 (0.6)	4.5 (0.6)	4.4 (0.6)	4.4 (0.6)	0.09	1.2	.22
Values	5.4 (0.9)	5.5 (0.8)	5.5 (0.9)	5.5 (0.9)	0.09	0.7	.50
Standards	2.8 (0.6)	2.9 (0.6)	2.8 (0.6)	2.8 (0.6)	0.12	3.0	.003*
Self-reliance	3.7 (0.7)	3.9 (0.7)	3.7 (0.7)	3.8 (0.7)	0.10	2.2	.03*
Risk-taking behavior	1.5 (2.5)	1.3 (2.3)	1.0 (2.0)	1.3 (2.4)	−0.48	2.8	.006*

*Statistically significant.

ANSWERS

1a. Content validity because the measure is based on a number of theoretical constructs (e.g., the health belief model and social learning theory).

1b. Interrater reliability because agreement is correlated between scorers. If we also assume that each expert's ratings are true, then we have concurrent validity. Kappa (κ) is a statistic used to adjust for agreements that could have arisen by chance alone.

1c. Test-retest reliability because each test is scored twice.

2. Before you evaluate the report of results, based on the table, first answer these questions:

   a. What do the columns represent? In this example, the columns give data on the mean scores and standard deviations (in parentheses) for WORK-FIND and no-program students before and after the program. The net difference in scores and the t statistic and p value are also shown.

   b. What do the rows represent? In this case, the rows show the specific variables that are measured—for example, knowledge and goals.

   c. Are any data statistically or otherwise significant? In this case, knowledge, benefits, self-reliance, and risk-taking behavior are statistically significant, as indicated by the asterisk. (To be significant, differences must be attributable to a planned intervention, such as Program WORK-FIND, rather than to chance or historical occurrences, such as changes in vocational education that are unrelated to Program WORK-FIND.) Statistical significance is often interpreted to mean a result that happens by chance less than once in 20 times, with a p value less than or equal to .05. A p value is the probability of obtaining the results of a statistical test by chance.

   The write-up is fair—until the last sentence. The last sentence states that Program WORK-FIND is effective, but the table does not offer enough information for us to come to this conclusion. Suppose the standard for effectiveness is that Program WORK-FIND must be favored in six or seven (rather than five) of the measures. In that case, of course, the last sentence of the write-up would be false. The last sentence would also be false if the five measures that were favored were much less important than any one of the three that were not.

SUGGESTED READINGS

American Psychological Association. (2012). *Standards for educational and psychological testing.* Washington, DC: APA. Retrieved from http://www.apa.org/science/programs/testing/standards.aspx

Braitman, L. (1991). Confidence intervals assess both clinical and statistical significance. *Annals of Internal Medicine, 114,* 515–517.

Creswell, J. W. (2007). *Qualitative inquiry and research design.* Thousand Oaks, CA: Sage.

Denzin, N., & Lincoln, Y. (2011). *The SAGE handbook of qualitative research.* Thousand Oaks, CA: Sage.

Des Jarlais, D. C., Lyles, C., & Crepaz, N. (2004). Improving the reporting quality of nonrandomized evaluations of behavioral and public health interventions: The TREND statement. *American Journal of Public Health, 94*(3), 361–366. Retrieved 2012 from http://www.cdc.gov/trendstatement/

Fink, A. (2008). *Evaluating research: Discovering evidence that matters.* Thousand Oaks, CA: Sage.

Fink, A. (2011*). Evidence-based public health practice.* Thousand Oaks, CA: Sage.

Flick, U. (2008). *Designing qualitative research.* Thousand Oaks, CA: Sage.

Flick, U. (2008). *Managing quality in qualitative research.* Thousand Oaks, CA: Sage.

Furr, M. R., & Bacharach, V. R. (2007). *Psychometrics: An introduction.* Thousand Oaks, CA: Sage.

Goodwin, L. D., & Leech, N. L. (2003). The meaning of validity in the new standards for educational and psychological testing: Implications for measurement courses. *Measurement & Evaluation in Counseling & Development, 36,* 181–192.

Gregory, R. J. (2004). *Psychological testing: History, principles, and applications.* Needham Heights, MA: Allyn & Bacon.

Guyatt, G. H., Oxman, A. D., Schünemann, H. J., Tugwell, P., & Knottnerus, A. (2011). GRADE guidelines: A new series of articles in the Journal of Clinical Epidemiology. *Journal of Clinical Epidemiology, 64*(4), 380–382. doi: 10.1016/j.jclinepi.2010.09.011

Litwin, M. (2003). *How to assess and interpret survey psychometric.* Thousand Oaks, CA: Sage.

Lohr, K. N. (2004). Rating the strength of scientific evidence: Relevance for quality improvement programs. *International Journal of Quality in Health Care, 16*(1), 9–18. doi: 10.1093/intqhc/mzh005

Marchall, C., & Rossman, G. (2010). *Designing qualitative research*. Thousand Oaks, CA: Sage.

McIntire, S. A. (2006). *Foundations of psychological testing: A practical approach*. Thousand Oaks, CA: Sage.

McIntyre, A. (2008). *Participatory action research*. Thousand Oaks, CA: Sage.

Miles, M. B., & Huberman, A. M. (1994). *Qualitative data analysis: An expanded sourcebook* (2nd ed.). Thousand Oaks, CA: Sage.

Moustakas, C. (1994). *Phenomenological research methods*. Thousand Oaks, CA: Sage.

Patton, M. Q. (1987). *How to use qualitative methods in evaluation*. Newbury Park, CA: Sage.

Patton, M. Q. (1997). *Utilization-focused evaluation: The new century text* (3rd ed.). Thousand Oaks, CA: Sage.

Salkind, N. J. (2004). *Statistics for people who (think they) hate statistics* (2nd ed.). Thousand Oaks, CA: Sage.

Salkind, N. J. (2007). *Statistics for people who (think they) hate statistics* (3rd ed.). Thousand Oaks, CA: Sage.

Sandelowski, M., & Barroso, J. (2003). Toward a metasynthesis of qualitative findings on motherhood in HIV-positive women. *Research in Nursing & Health, 26,* 153–170.

Savall, H., Zardet, V., Bonner, M., & Peron, M. (2008). The emergence of implicit criteria actually used by reviewers of qualitative research articles: Case of a European journal. *Organizational Research Methods, 11,* 510–540.

Siegel, S. (1956). *Nonparametric statistics for the behavioral sciences*. New York: McGraw-Hill.

Silverman, D., & Marvasti, A. (2008). *Qualitative research: A comprehensive guide*. Thousand Oaks, CA: Sage.

Strauss, A., & Corbin, C. (1990). *Basics of qualitative research: Grounded theory procedures and techniques*. Newbury Park, CA: Sage.

West, S., King, V., Carey, T. S., Carey, T., & Lohr, K. (2002). *Systems to rate the strength of the evidence*. Rockville, MD: Agency for Healthcare Research and Quality, Department of Health and Human Services.

Yin, R. K. (1994). *Case study research design and methods* (2nd ed.). Thousand Oaks, CA: Sage.

⸙ FOUR ⸙

DOING THE REVIEW

A Reader's Guide Chapter

A Reader's Guide

Purpose of This Chapter

Literature reviews are data-gathering activities. This chapter explains how to ensure that the information you collect from the literature is accurate and comprehensive. Although literature reviews may be conducted by a single person, two or more reviewers can improve reliability. This chapter provides details on how to ensure a reliable and high-quality review by training and supervising multiple reviewers. Pilot testing is also discussed because reviews should be done only after first practicing.

Regardless of the number of reviewers, a standard method should be developed to help pinpoint the information to be extracted from each study. This chapter explains how to develop and use reproducible literature review abstraction forms. Formal checklists, such as CONSORT and TREND, are also discussed. These checklists guide reviewers so that they focus their review on agreed-upon standards for transparent and accurate reporting.

Figure 4.1 shows the steps involved in conducting a research literature review. This chapter covers the shaded portions of the figure: Train the reviewers, pilot test the reviewing process, do the review, and monitor its quality.

TYPES OF INFORMATION: METHODS AND CONTENT

A literature review is a method of collecting information to answer research questions or find out what is known about a particular topic. In all probability, you want the information to be correct, comprehensive, and unbiased. To achieve this aim, you conduct a research review. This type of review depends on scientifically conducted research projects or studies.

A study's validity depends on the rigor of its methods, including research design, sampling, data collection, and analysis. Other factors that may affect a study's validity include the researchers' affiliation, the date and source of publication, and the origins of financial support. A study's content is its substance, and it consists of its objectives, participants, settings, interventions, results, and conclusions.

Read these instructions to a reviewer for collecting data on the methods and content of studies of the determinants and consequences of alcohol misuse in older people.

Figure 4.1 Steps Involved in Conducting a Research Literature Review

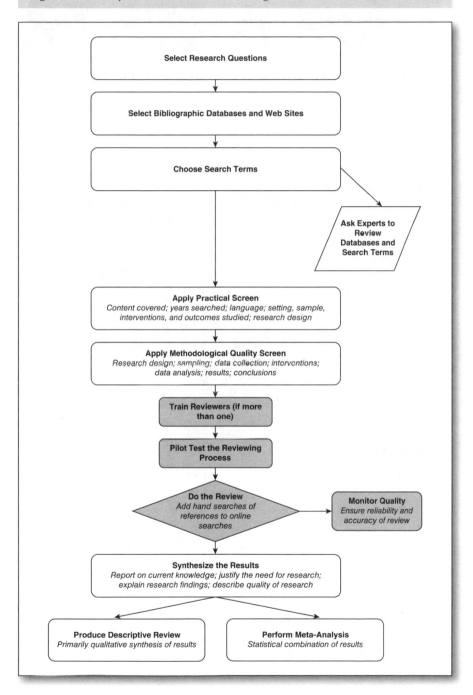

**Reviewing the Research Literature: Examples
of Types of Information Collection for a Study of
Alcohol Misuse in Older People**

Type 1: Data on Methods and Other Factors Affecting Quality

For each study, tell if

- Major variables and terms are defined; these include alcoholism, heavy drinking, problem drinking, alcohol abuse, alcohol dependence, and alcohol-related problems.
- Psychometric evidence (such as reliability statistics) is offered to demonstrate that the instrument used to study alcoholism, heavy drinking, problem drinking, alcohol abuse, alcohol dependence, and alcohol-related problems is pertinent to persons 65 years or older.
- The study data are collected prospectively.
- The sample is obtained randomly from a specifically defined population, or the entire eligible population is chosen.
- The choice of sample size is explained.
- The adequacy of the response rate is discussed.
- Information is offered that is specifically pertinent to alcohol-related problems of older persons.
- The researchers provide psychometric evidence for the validity of the data sources used for the main variables (e.g., social isolation, health status).

Type 2: Data on Content

For each study, describe or give

- Study objectives: The hoped-for specific outcomes or expectations of the study
- Definitions of main variables (such as health status and quality of life)
- Settings: The locales in which the study was conducted (such as in a doctor's office or senior service center)
- Intervention or program: The main objectives, activities, and structural or organizational characteristics of the program or intervention
- Research design: Experimental or observational; if experimental, controlled or not

- Sample size and composition: How many participants are in each setting; group (e.g., experimental and control, male and female)
- Measures for main variables: How each variable (e.g., satisfaction) is measured (e.g., the ABC Satisfaction Survey—Online Version)
- Conclusions: In authors' own words: What the study's findings suggest about

  Determinants of alcohol misuse

  Consequences of alcohol misuse
- Source of data (journal and year of publication)
- Source of financial support

It is almost always important to review methods *and* content. A review of methodological quality without reference to content may be important to researchers who want to improve the quality of a field's research methods, but reviewers are often concerned primarily with content. A review of content without an understanding of its methodological quality, however, may very well lead the reviewer to come to false conclusions, especially if the literature is of poor or variable quality.

Information on the source of publication may be important because some journals are known to have rigorous peer review processes and publish high-quality studies, whereas others have less rigorous processes, and the articles they published may be of lesser quality. Knowing the source of financial support may be a signal to reviewers to watch out for biases in favor of the funder.

ELIGIBILITY AND ACTUALITY

A study that is eligible for review contains relevant information, is accessible, meets preset standards for methodological quality, and does not have any features that justify its exclusion. Inclusion criteria alone often yield many more articles for review than a combination of inclusion and exclusion criteria yields. For instance, suppose you want to review the literature to identify the cause of the decline in rates of heart disease in the United States. You specify that you will include in the review only studies reported in English and that have been published within the past 5 years. Say you identify 250 eligible studies. If you also stipulate that you plan to exclude any reports that do not provide data on males *and* females, the number of articles for review will be reduced. If you further specify that you will review only experimental studies that provide clear descriptions of treatment programs and will exclude all studies focusing on rates of heart disease for people younger than 65, the pool of articles will be reduced even more. Once you have assembled the articles that have passed the practical and methodological screen and are eligible, the reviewer begins the process of determining if each study is well done. The reviewer asks the following: Is this article "worth" reviewing because it is soundly designed and its findings come from valid data?

The following is an excerpt from a review of the literature on alcohol use by older people. As you can see, the reviewers describe their data sources, search terms, and practical and quality (inclusion and exclusion) criteria. In keeping with best practices, they start with a description of how many studies were available (the "universe") and were put through the first—the practical—screen. Often, reviewers use the abstracts (rather than the entire study) to get them through the practical screen.

Data Sources and Eligibility: An Excerpt From a Report of a Literature Review

We searched PubMed and PsycINFO using the following search terms: Alcoholism and aged, alcoholism and elderly, alcohol and elderly, alcohol abuse and elderly, alcohol abuse and aging, problem drinking and elderly, alcohol problems and elderly, substance abuse and elderly, elderly and determinants of alcohol use, elderly and consequences of alcohol use. We identified 401 unique citations using our search terms. After reviewing their abstracts, we omitted 67 that did not address alcohol use or that studied the effects of alcohol in animals. The remaining 334 articles were potentially eligible for review.

After the practical comes the methodological quality screen. Because numerous standards must be met for a study to be characterized as of the highest quality, selecting the quality screen is a fairly complicated job. Must all conceivable methodological criteria be applied to all potentially eligible studies? Suppose, after applying a methodological screen, you find that the resulting studies do not meet the highest quality standards? Should you still review them? Questions such as these are inherent in nearly every literature review (except for the few that have access to large randomized controlled trials). Listen in on a conversation between two reviewers who are beginning their review.

Two Reviewers Discuss Quality Standards

Reviewer 1:   I think we should focus on whether the study's sample is any good and if its research design is internally and externally valid.

Reviewer 2:   OK. What would you look for?

Reviewer 1:   Well, I would read each study and ask, Was the sample randomly selected? Is the design internally valid? Externally valid?

Reviewer 2:   Is that it?

Reviewer 1:   What more do you want?

Reviewer 2:   Well, I can think of a whole bunch of things. For instance, I wouldn't just be concerned with random sampling because sample size counts, too. Also, I don't know how you would decide if a design was internally valid on the whole. Don't you need to ask specific questions like, Is this design subject to maturation, selection, history, instrumentation, statistical regression, or history? In fact, when it comes to sampling and research design, I think you need to evaluate each study in terms of its answers to these questions:

If more than one group is included in the study, are the participants randomly assigned to each?

Are participants measured over time? If so, is the number of observations explained? Justified?

If observations or measures are made over time, is the choice and effect of the time period explained?

Are any of the participants "blinded" to the group— experimental or control—to which they belong?

If historical controls are used, is their selection explained? Justified?

Are the effects on internal validity of choice, equivalence, and participation of the sample subjects explained?

Are the effects on external validity (generalizability) of choice, equivalence, and participation of the subjects explained?

If a sample is used, are the subjects randomly selected?

If the unit sampled (e.g., students) is not the population of main concern (e.g., teachers are), is this addressed in the analysis or discussion?

If a sample is selected with a nonrandom sampling method, is evidence given regarding whether they are similar to the target population (from which they were chosen) or to other groups in the study?

If groups are not equivalent at baseline, is this problem addressed in analysis or interpretation?

Are criteria given for including subjects?

Are criteria given for excluding subjects?

Is the sample size justified (say, with a power calculation)?

Is information given on the size and characteristics of the target population?

If stratified sampling is used, is the choice of strata justified?

Is information given on the number and characteristics of subjects in the target population who are eligible to participate in the study?

Is information given on the number and characteristics of subjects who are eligible and who also agree to participate?

Is information given on the number and characteristics of subjects who are eligible but refuse to participate?

Is information given on the number and characteristics of subjects who dropped out or were lost to follow-up before completing all elements of data collection?

Is information given on the number and characteristics of subjects who completed all elements of data collection?

Is information given on the number and characteristics of subjects for whom some data are missing?

Are reasons given for missing data?

Are reasons given explaining why individuals or groups dropped out?

Reviewer 1:   Well, I can see you know your sampling and research design topics, but I am not sure that all the questions you raise are relevant to this literature review. For example, I doubt we will find any blinded studies. If we use this criterion, then we won't have any studies to review. Also, I am not certain we have the resources to collect this information on each and every study in the review.

Reviewer 2:   Let us examine each criterion to see how important and pertinent it is to our review.

Reviewer 1:   Good idea.

Reviewer 2 is correct in urging restraint in selecting methodological quality criteria. Not all may be relevant or appropriate for each literature review. For example, very few social experiments involve blinding of all participants. Each review has unique requirements. The following are two examples taken from the published literature.

Example 1. Evaluations of Child Abuse Prevention Programs: Review Eligibility Criteria

Randomized controlled trial or true experiment

Clearly defined outcomes

Valid measures

Explicit participant eligibility criteria

Example 2. Evaluations of 36 Criminal Justice Programs: Review Eligibility Criteria and Results

Criterion	Number	Percentage
Data are collected prospectively	35	97
Research questions and objectives are described clearly and precisely	35	97

(Continued)

(Continued)

Criterion	Number	Percentage
Program is clearly described (i.e., includes detail on goals, activities, settings, resources)	32	89
Statistics reported are sufficient to determine clinical/educational/policy cost significance or relevance	29	81
Sample losses (i.e., refusals, unavailable for follow-up, missing and partial data) are described and dealt with to the extent possible	21	58
Potential biases due to sampling method, sample size, or data collection methods are explained	21	58
Data are provided on the validity of the data collection methods	19	53
Sample size is justified	5	4

Some researchers (and philosophers) argue that only perfect or nearly perfect studies count because only they can produce accurate information. Because few studies are perfect or even nearly perfect, reviewers are typically on their own in deciding which criteria to apply and whether the quality of the data in a body of literature is acceptable. Although uniform methods for selecting the "best" studies are not available, reviewers tend to rely on three standard quality assessment methods.

Some literature reviews include all eligible studies, regardless of methodological quality. Reviews of this type typically rate studies according to how much confidence you can have in their findings based on the adequacy of their research design. So even though a relatively poor-quality study is not excluded, its low rating automatically diminishes its credibility. The U.S. Preventive Services Task Force uses this approach in making recommendations regarding preventive health care (such as for vaccinations and screening tests). Each recommendation (e.g., the frequency and timing of flu shots, prenatal care, and screening tests such as mammography and colonoscopy) is accompanied by references from the literature, and each study referenced is "graded" according to the quality of its evidence.

Scoring systems are often used to assess quality. Reviewers first evaluate the extent to which each potentially eligible study achieves preset quality standards. Scores from 1 to 100 points, for example, may be assigned, with a score of 100 points meaning the study has achieved all standards. The reviewers next select a cutoff score, say 74 points, and review only studies with scores of 75 points or more.

Another method of selecting among eligible studies is to insist that one or more preset standards must be met. For instance, in some reviews, only randomized controlled trials are acceptable. In other reviews, studies are considered acceptable if they meet some number of the standards. For example, a study may be considered acceptable if it meets five of eight preset standards. The following illustrates these methods of distinguishing among studies on the basis of their quality.

Classifying Eligible Studies by Methodological Quality

We categorized studies as falling into one of five categories: Randomized controlled trials (Category A); prospective, nonrandomized controlled trials (Category B); retrospective studies with clearly defined sources of information (Category C); probably retrospective studies with unspecified or unclear data sources (Category D); and essays, including editorials, reviews, and book chapters (Category E).

The following is a partial list of our references and the categories into which each study fits.

Reference (by first author and year of publication)	Category
Abel, M. (2010)	B
Arlington, S. (2008)	B
Bethany, Y. (2012)	E
Betonay, A. (1996)	A
. . .	. . .
Caldwell-Jones, R. (2011	C
. . .	. . .
Uris, M. (2000)	D

Scoring Methods

- We assigned each study a score of 1 to 10. Studies with scores of 8 or more are reviewed.
- We selected eight standards of quality. To be included, a study had to have achieved at least five.

REPORTING STANDARDS: CHECKLISTS FOR
RESEARCH WRITING AND REVIEWING

Standardized reporting checklists describe the study characteristics that researchers should include—at a minimum—in their reports. The idea is that to be transparent, a published study must provide the reader with a clear and comprehensive description of the intervention and comparison conditions, settings, participants, and outcomes. Most importantly, transparency requires that researchers report all information related to the study's outcomes, especially the information that readers will need to assess possible biases. Many medical and public health journals will only publish study reports that prove that they meet a given checklist's criteria.

Perhaps the most famous reporting checklist is the **Consolidated Standards of Reporting Trials (CONSORT)**. The CONSORT Statement—its common name—consists of standards for reporting on randomized controlled trials (http://www.consort-statement.org). The statement is available in several languages and has been endorsed by prominent medical, clinical, and psychological journals.

CONSORT consists of a checklist and flow diagram. The checklist includes items that need to be addressed in the report. Example 4.1 contains sample items from the CONSORT statement.

Example 4.1   An Excerpt from the CONSORT Statement

Methods		
Trial design	3a	Description of trial design (such as parallel, factorial) including allocation ratio
	3b	Important changes to methods after trial commencement (such as eligibility criteria), with reasons
Participants	4a	Eligibility criteria for participants
	4b	Settings and locations where the data were collected
Interventions	5	The interventions for each group with sufficient details to allow replication, including how and when they were actually administered

Methods		
Outcomes	6a	Completely defined pre-specified primary and secondary outcome measures, including how and when they were assessed
	6b	Any changes to trial outcomes after the trial commenced, with reasons
Sample size	7a	How sample size was determined
	7b	When applicable, explanation of any interim analyses and stopping guidelines

Source: Kenneth F. Schulz, Douglas G. Altman, and David Moher, for the CONSORT Group. "CONSORT 2010 Statement: Updated Guidelines for Reporting Parallel Group Randomized Trials."

The CONSORT Web site provides an explanation of each of the items on the checklist as shown in Example 4.2. For instance, to better understand how to report on participant' eligibility (4a on the checklist), CONSORT gives an example and offers a justification for the item.

Example 4.2   An Excerpt from CONSORT: A Reporting Checklist for Randomized Controlled Trials (http://consort-statement.org)

Source: Kenneth F. Schulz, Douglas G. Altman, and David Moher, for the CONSORT Group. "CONSORT 2010 Statement: Updated Guidelines for Reporting Parallel Group Randomized Trials."

The CONSORT Statement's required flow diagram is designed to give readers a clear picture of the study participants' progress from the time they are evaluated for eligibility until the end of their involvement (Example 4.3). The intent is to clarify the experimental process for the reader.

The CONSORT Statement is not just about reporting on study methods. It requires researchers to include information on the scientific rationale for the study, the source of funding, the funders' roles, and other factors that may affect the study's transparency and quality.

Of course not all studies are randomized trials, and so checklists have been developed for nonrandomized studies. One commonly used checklist for

Example 4.3   CONSORT Statement Flow Diagram

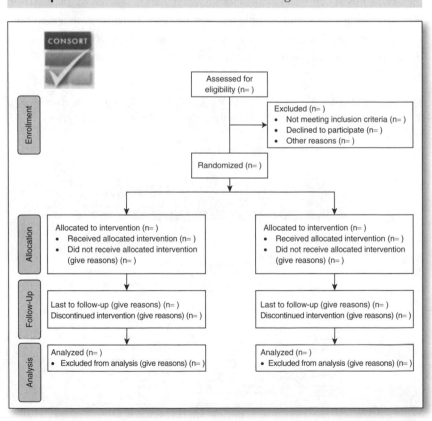

Source: Kenneth F. Schulz, Douglas G. Altman, and David Moher, for the CONSORT Group. "CONSORT 2010 Statement: Updated Guidelines for Reporting Parallel Group Randomized Trials."

these studies is the **TREND** (Transparent Reporting of Evaluations with Non-randomized Designs) Statement of the American Public Health Association and Centers for Disease Control and Prevention (CDC). You can find TREND on the EQUATOR Web site (http://www.equator-network.org/about-equator/equator-publications0/equator-network-publications-2010/) or the CDC's (http://www.cdc.gov/trendstatement/).

Example 4.4 contains an excerpt from TREND. The example shows TREND's emphasis on providing a complete description of the interventions and explaining how the researchers minimized potential biases due to nonrandomization.

Example 4.4 An Excerpt from the TREND Statement: A Checklist for Reporting Non-Randomized Trials

Interventions	4	Details of the interventions intended for each study condition and how and when they were actually administered, specifically including:
		o Content: What was given?
		o Delivery method: How was the content given?
		o Unit of delivery: How were the subjects grouped during delivery?
		o Deliverer: Who delivered the intervention?
		o Setting: Where was the intervention delivered?
		o Exposure quantity and duration: how many sessions or episodes or events were intended to be delivered? How long were they intended to last?
		o Time span: how long was it intended to take to deliver the intervention to each unit?
		o Activities to increase compliance or adherence (e.g., incentives)
Objectives	5	Specific objectives and hypotheses
Outcomes	6	Clearly defined primary and secondary outcome measures Methods used to collect data and any methods used to enhance the quality of measurements

(Continued)

Example 4.4 (Continued)

		Information on validated instruments such as psychometric and biometric properties
Sample Size	7	How sample size was determined and, when applicable, explanation of any interim analyses and stopping rules
Assignment Method	8	Unit of assignment (the unit being assigned to study condition, e.g., individual, group, community)
		Method used to assign units to study conditions, including details of any restriction (e.g., blocking, stratification, minimization)
		Inclusion of aspects employed to help minimize potential bias induced due to nonrandomization (e.g., matching)

Source: Des Jarlais DC, Lyles C, Crepaz N, and the TREND Group. "Improving the reporting quality of nonrandomized evaluations of behavioral and public health interventions: The TREND statement." *American Journal of Public Health*, 2004.

Here is an example of how TREND was used in a systematic literature review of treatments for pathological gambling.

HOW TREND WAS USED IN A LITERATURE REVIEW

In this study, the authors reviewed the transparency of reports of behavioral interventions for pathological gambling and other gambling-related disorders. They used three databases to identify studies: Pubmed, Web of Science, and PsychINFO for experimental evaluations of behavioral interventions published between 2000 and 2011 that aimed to reduce problem gambling behaviors or decrease problems caused by gambling. Experts were contacted for information on other relevant study reports. Twenty-six reports met the inclusion criteria. These were reviewed by two reviewers who used the 59-item Adapted TREND Questionnaire (ATQ). A third reviewer abstracted a 10% sample of all study reports and resolved any differences in interpretation. The reviewers found that that published reports received an average of

38.4 (65%) positive responses to the 59-question ATQ, and the average question received a positive response by 55% of studies. An excerpt of the table describing how the studies did when compared to each of the Adapted TREND Questionnaire items is given below:

Table 4.1 Frequency of Studies (N = 26) That Received a Positive Response to 24 of the 59 ATQ Questions (in descending order)

Adapted Trend Item	N	%
Introduction		
1. Described theories used in designing behavioral interventions	26	100
Methods		
2. Described the eligibility criteria for participants, including criteria at different levels in recruitment/ sampling plan	24	92.3
3. Described the method of recruitment (e.g., referral, self-selection)	24	92.3
4. Reported the recruitment setting (e.g. gay bar, city)	14	53.8
5. Described the sampling method	4	15.4
6. Described the content of interventions intended for each study condition	25	96.2
7. Described the delivery method	26	100
8. Described the unit of delivery or how subjects were grouped during delivery	25	96.2
9. Reported the person who delivered the intervention	21	80.8
10. Described the intervention setting	13	50.0
11. Reported the number of sessions or events that were intended to be delivered	25	96.2
12. Reported the duration of each session	19	73.1
13. Reported activities to increase compliance or adherence (e.g. incentives)	12	46.2

(Continued)

Table 4.1 (Continued)

Methods		
14. Described specific objectives and hypotheses	26	100
15. Clearly defined primary and secondary outcome measures	26	100
16. Provided justification for outcomes measures	20	76.9
17. Described the methods of data collection for each study variable	21	80.8
18. Reported the psychometric properties of each outcome measure	15	57.7
Items 19 to 32 left out of this example		
33. Described protocol deviations from study as planned along with reasons	1	3.8
34. Reported the dates defining the periods of recruitment	8	30.8
35. Reported dates defining the periods of treatment and follow-up	0	0.0
36. Described baseline demographic and clinical characteristics of participants in each study condition	23	88.5
37. Described baseline characteristics for each study condition relevant to the gamblers being studied	25	96.2
38. Described baseline characteristics of those lost to follow-up and those retained, overall	6	23.1
39. Described baseline characteristics of those lost to follow-up and those retained, by study condition	3	11.5

Source: Fink A, Parhami I, Rosenthal RJ, Campos MD, Siani A, Fong TW. How transparent is behavioral intervention research on pathological gambling and other gambling-related disorders? A systematic literature review. *Addiction*. 2012.

For more on this study, see Fink A, Parhami I, Rosenthal RJ, Campos MD, Siani A, Fong TW. How transparent is behavioral intervention research on pathological gambling and other gambling-related disorders? A systematic literature review. *Addiction*. 2012. Epub 2012/04/11.

CONSORT and TREND come from medicine and health, but other fields have begun to develop reporting checklists that reflect their special research n requirements.

The American Psychological Association has produced its checklist, which is called "Journal Article Reporting Standards (JARS): Information Recommended for Inclusion in Manuscripts That Report New Data Collections regardless of Research Design." Attempts are also under way to prepare checklists for reporting mixed-methods and qualitative studies. Qualitative research checklists differ markedly in their emphasis on the researchers' potential motives and perspectives and on the theoretical framework for the study as illustrated in Example 4.5

Example 4.5 A Reporting Checklist for Qualitative Research

Reflexivity

Are the researcher's motives, background, perspectives, and preliminary hypotheses presented, and is the effect of these issues sufficiently dealt with?

Method and design

Are qualitative research methods suitable for exploration of the research question? Has the best method been chosen with respect to the research question?

Data collection and sampling

Is the strategy for data collection clearly stated (usually purposive or theoretical, usually not random or representative)? Are the reasons for this choice stated?

Has the best approach been chosen, in view of the research question?

Are the consequences of the chosen strategy discussed and compared with other options?

Are the characteristics of the sample presented in enough depth to understand the study site and context?

Theoretical framework

Are the perspectives and ideas used for data interpretation presented? Is the framework adequate, in view of the aim of the study?

Does the author account for the role given to the theoretical framework during analysis?

Excerpted from: Malterud K. Qualitative research: Standards, challenges, and guidelines. *Lancet.* 2001;358(9280):483-8. Epub 2001/08/22.

Reporting checklists can simplify the reviewer's task. However, not all research publications require authors to complete checklists, and even if they do, keep in mind that just because something is reported does not guarantee its quality is high. High quality studies are designed to minimize bias so that you can trust the findings.

RELIABLE AND VALID REVIEWS

A reliable review is one that consistently provides the same information about methods and content from time to time from one person ("within") and among several ("across") reviewers. A valid review is an accurate one.

Relatively large literature reviews nearly always have more than one reviewer. Each reviewer examines each study, and the results of the examinations are compared. Perfect agreement between (or among) reviewers means perfect interrater reliability. Sometimes, to promote objectivity, one or more of the reviewers are not told (they are "blinded") the names of the authors of the study, the name of the publication, or when or where the study took place. In relatively smaller reviews (reviews with scant resources and just one reviewer), objectivity can be improved by having the single reviewer review again a randomly selected sample of studies. Perfect agreement from the first to the second review is considered perfect intrarater reliability.

Measuring Reliability: The Kappa Statistic

Suppose two reviewers are asked to independently evaluate the quality of 100 studies on the effectiveness of prenatal care in preventing low-weight births. Each reviewer is asked the following: Do the study's authors include low-risk as well as high-risk women in their analysis? Here are the reviewers' answers to this question.

Reviewer 2

Reviewer 1	No	Yes	
No	20[c]	15	35[b]
Yes	10	55[d]	65
	30[a]	70	

Reviewer 2 says that 30 (superscript a) of the studies fail to collect prospective data, whereas Reviewer 1 says that 35 (b) fail to do so. The two reviewers agree that 20 (c) studies do not collect prospective data.

What is the best way to describe the extent of agreement between the reviewers? Twenty percent (c) is probably too low; the reviewers also agree that 55% (d) of studies include low-risk women. The total agreement: 55% + 20% is an overestimate because with only two categories (yes and no), some agreement may occur by chance.

A commonly used statistic for measuring agreement between two reviewers is called *kappa,* defined as the agreement beyond chance divided by the amount of agreement possible beyond chance. This is shown in the following formula in which O is the observed agreement and C is the chance agreement.

Measuring Agreement Between Two Reviewers:
The Kappa (κ) Statistic

$$\kappa = \frac{O - C \,(\text{Agreement beyond chance})}{1 - C \,\left(\text{Agreement possible beyond chance}\right)}$$

Here is how the formula works with the example of the two reviewers.

1. Calculate how many studies the reviewers may agree by chance *do not* collect prospective data. This is done by multiplying the number of "no" responses and dividing by 100 because there are 100 studies: $30 \times 35/100 = 10.5$.

2. Calculate how many studies they may agree by chance *do* collect prospective data by multiplying the number of studies that each found collected prospective data. This is done by multiplying the number of "yes" responses and dividing by 100: $70 \times 65/100 = 40.5$.

3. Add the two numbers obtained in Steps 1 and 2 and divide by 100 to get a proportion for chance agreement: $(10.5 + 45.5)/100 = 0.56$.

The *observed agreement* is $20\% + 55\% = 75\%$ or 0.75. Therefore, the agreement beyond chance is $0.75 - .56 = 0.19$: The numerator.

The *agreement possible beyond chance* is 100% minus the chance agreement of 56% or $1 - 0.56 = 0.44$: The denominator.

$$\kappa = \frac{0.19}{0.44}$$

$$\kappa = 0.43$$

What is a "high" kappa? Some experts have attached the following qualitative terms to kappas: $0.0-0.2$ = slight, $0.2-0.4$ = fair, $0.4-0.6$ = moderate, $0.6-0.8$ = substantial, and $0.8-0.10$ = almost perfect. In a literature review, you should aim for kappas of 0.6 to 1.0.

How do you achieve substantial or almost perfect agreement—reliability—among reviewers? You do this by making certain that all reviewers collect and record data on the same topics and that they agree in advance on what each important variable means. The "fair" kappa of 0.43 obtained by the reviewers above can be due to differences between the reviewers' definitions of high- and low-risk women or between the reviewers' and researchers' definitions.

UNIFORM DATA COLLECTION: THE LITERATURE REVIEW SURVEY QUESTIONNAIRE

Literature reviews are surveys. In other words, they are systematic observations, and they are also usually recorded. Survey methods, particularly those pertaining to self-administered questionnaires, are often applied to the development of efficient ways to record information extracted from the literature.

Suppose a review has the following as practical and methodological quality screens.

Sample Practical and Methodological Quality Screens

Practical screen (must meet *all* the following four criteria):

1. Study is available in English.
2. Data collection takes place after March 1, 2009.

3. Study includes males and females.

4. Study provides data on persons 65 years of age and older living independently in the community.

Methodological screen (must meet a total of five of the eight following criteria):

1. Key terms are defined.

2. Psychometric evidence is offered to demonstrate that the instrument is pertinent to persons 65 years or older.

3. The study data are collected prospectively.

4. The sample is obtained randomly from a specifically defined population, or the entire eligible population is chosen.

5. The choice of sample size is explained.

6. The adequacy of the response rate is discussed.

7. Information is offered that is specifically pertinent to alcohol-related problems of older persons.

8. The researchers provide psychometric evidence for the validity of the data sources used for the main variables.

To ensure that each reviewer records the same information as the others and that the recording process is uniform, you can translate the criteria into a survey questionnaire form. Look at this portion of a questionnaire to record the process of selecting studies for a review of the literature on alcohol use in the elderly.

A Sample Questionnaire Form for Collecting Information About Study Eligibility

Directions

Part 1: Practical Screen

Answer all questions. If the answer is **no** to ANY question, **stop.** Do not complete Part 2 (Methodological Screen).

Study ID: _____

Date: _____

Name of Reviewer: _____

1. Is the study available in English?

   Yes 1

   No 2

2. Have the study's data been collected after March 1, 2009?

   Yes 1

   No 2

3. Does the study include information on males and females?

   Yes 1

   No 2

4. Are persons over 65 years of age a primary focus of the study?

   Yes 1

   No 2

5. Are persons living independently in the community (as opposed to a nursing home, board and care facility, etc.)?

   Yes 1

   No 2

Part 2: Methodological Quality Screen

Assign 1 point for each yes. Studies must receive a score of 5 or more to be included in the review.

Criterion	Yes (1)	No (2)
1. Main outcome variables are defined.		
2. Psychometric evidence is offered to demonstrate that the instrument used to study alcoholism, heavy drinking, problem drinking, alcohol abuse, alcohol dependence, and alcohol-related problems is pertinent to persons 65 years or older.		

Criterion	Yes (1)	No (2)
3. The study data are collected prospectively.		
4. The sample is obtained randomly from a specifically defined population, or the entire eligible population is chosen.		
5. The choice of sample size is explained.		
6. The adequacy of the response rate is discussed.		
7. Information is offered that is specifically pertinent to alcohol-related problems of older persons.		
8. The researchers provide psychometric evidence for the validity of the data sources used for the main variables (e.g., social isolation, health status).		
Total Score:		

Data from forms such as these tell you relatively quickly which studies are included and excluded from the review and why (practical reasons? methodological reasons?). They also make data entry easier.

Once you have identified literature that is eligible for review, you must design a questionnaire to standardize the information collection process. Look at these portions of a survey questionnaire used to abstract the literature on alcohol use in people 65 years of age and older.

Portion of a Questionnaire for Surveying the Literature on Alcohol Use

1. Are main variables defined? (Circle one)

    No . . . . 1 *(Go to Question 3)*

    Yes 2

1a. If yes, please give definitions in authors' own words.

Term	Definition (if given by authors)
Alcoholism	
Heavy drinking	
Problem drinking	
Alcohol abuse	
Alcohol dependence	
Alcohol-related problems	

2. Do the researchers provide psychometric evidence for the validity of the data sources used for the main variables? (Circle one)

No . . . . 1 *(Go to next question)*

Yes 2

2a. If yes, tell which data source (e.g., achievement test), name the variable it measures (e.g., knowledge), and name the types of validity for which evidence is given.

Use these codes for the type of validity:

Face	1
Content	2
Predictive	3
Construct	4
Convergent	5
Divergent	6
Sensitivity	7
Specificity	8

Data Source	Variable	Validity Code

3. Describe the eligible sample.

	65 to 74 Years of Age (n =)	75 Years of Age and Older (n =)
Men		
White		
African American		
Latino		
Other		
Women		
White		
African American		
Latina		
Other		
Total		

4. Describe the participating sample.

	65 to 74 Years of Age (n =)	75 Years of Age and Older (n =)
Men		
White		
African American		
Latino		
Other		
Women		
White		
African American		
Latina		
Other		
Total		

5. Are reasons given for incomplete or no data on eligible partici-
    pants? (Check all that apply)

    No . . . . 1 *(Go to next question)*

    Yes 2

5a. If yes, what are they?

☐ Incorrect address

☐ Medical problems; specify:

☐ Failure to show for an appointment

☐ Other; specify:

6. Which of the following variables are explored in the study? (Check all that apply)

☐ Use of medicine (Check all that apply)

☐ Antihypertensives

☐ Antipsychotics

☐ Antidepressants

☐ Nonsteroidal anti-inflammatories (NSAIDs)

☐ Aspirin

☐ Barbiturates

☐ Other; specify:

☐ Quantity and frequency of alcohol consumption

☐ Medical conditions or problems

☐ Social functioning

☐ Mental/psychological functioning

☐ Physical functioning

☐ Other; specify:

7. For each variable included in the study, summarize the results and conclusions.

Variables	Results	Conclusions

   8. From which settings are the study's participants drawn? (Check all that apply)

   ☐ Retirement communities

   ☐ General community

   ☐ Community health centers

   ☐ Senior centers

   ☐ Medical clinics

   ☐ Veterans Administration

   ☐ Other; specify:

   9. Who funded this study? (Check all that apply)

   ☐ Federal government

   ☐ State government

   ☐ Local government

   ☐ National foundation

   ☐ State or local foundation

   ☐ University

   ☐ Health care agency. If yes,

   ☐ Public

   ☐ Private

   ☐ Other; specify:

Literature review questionnaires, sometimes called literature review abstraction forms, have several important advantages over less formal approaches to recording the contents of the literature. These include promoting reproducibility and consistent data collection across every reviewed study. If properly designed, they also facilitate data entry, analysis, and reporting. Questionnaires may be completed by hand, on a laptop, or on the Web. Because each review is different, it is likely that computer- or Web-based reviews will require special data entry and analysis programming.

UNIFORM DATA COLLECTION: DEFINITIONS AND MORE

Literature review surveys typically include many terms that are subject to differing interpretations. Phrases and words such as *psychometric evidence* and *content* and *face validity* (see the survey above) may mean different things to different people. For instance, psychometric evidence may mean construct validity to me, whereas you may interpret it to mean any kind of validity or reliability. Some people do not distinguish between face and content validity or do not think the distinction is important.

Some reviewers may not be familiar with terms used in a literature review survey. What are antihypertensives? Antidepressants? Is hydro-chlorothiazide an antihypertensive? What is chlordiazepoxide?

To ensure that the reviewers are familiar with all terms used in the survey and that all interpret the literature in the same way, make certain that definitions and explanations are given of all potentially misleading terms and phrases. These should be written down and discussed. Some people advocate producing a separate manual that includes instructions for the entire literature review process and definitions. Others recommend including instructions and definitions directly on the survey form. Nearly everyone agrees that before beginning the review, a test of the process should be undertaken.

Training Reviewers

Training is essential in large literature reviews, especially if there are two or more reviewers. The following is a sample table of contents for a literature review training manual.

Sample Table of Contents for a Literature Review Training Manual

 I. Introduction
   A. Why the review is being conducted
   B. Who will use the results?

 II. Applying eligibility criteria: The screening survey
   A. Practical screen (e.g., language, years of publication, journals)
     1. Examples of practical criteria

    2. Practice exercises using practical criteria; answers to exercises

B. Methodological screen

    1. Screening for research design: Study must be true or quasi-experiment

      a. Definitions and examples of each type of experiment

      b. Exercises in which you distinguish between true and quasi-experiments and between those types of research design and others

    2. Screening for sampling: Study must justify sample selection with inclusion and exclusion criteria

      a. Definitions and examples of inclusion and exclusion criteria and how they are justified

      b. Exercises in which you select the inclusion and exclusion criteria and explain how the researchers justified them

    3. Screening data collection: Must provide statistical data that measures of outcomes have been validated with appropriate populations

      a. Example of outcomes and measures (e.g., to find out about birth weight, use vital statistics database; to find out about consequences of alcohol use, rely on medical records)

      b. Definitions of terms such as *validate* and *alcohol-related problems* and examples of evidence of validation with different populations, such as people 65 years of age and older and low-risk women who seek prenatal care

      c. Exercises in which you distinguish among types of evidence for validation and for alcohol-related problems

    4. Screening data analysis: Must provide evidence that findings have clinical as well as statistical meaning

      a. Definitions of clinical and statistical meaning; examples of both

      b. Exercises in which you determine if analysis results are meaningful statistically, clinically, or both

III.   Reviewing the Literature
Use the literature abstraction form to review each study in terms of the contents and methods listed below. To do this, you will be given five studies and a form to complete. You may enter data directly on the form or onto the computer. You will be asked to record

A.   Objectives: Purposes and hoped-for outcomes

B.   Research design (such as parallel controls, nonrandom assignment)

C.   Sampling: Eligibility criteria; method of selection; size

D.   Intervention or program: Description of main objectives and activities

E.   Settings

F.   Main outcome variables and measures

G.   Results

H.   Conclusion

I.   First author's name

J.   Funding agency

IV.   Pilot Test of Review Process

Two raters:

A.   Read 10 studies

B.   Apply practical screen

C.   Apply methodological screen

D.   Review 10 eligible studies

E.   Compare results between raters

PILOT TESTING THE REVIEW PROCESS

The aim of the pilot test is to maximize reliability. The first step in the pilot is to test the eligibility criteria: Do all reviewers agree on which articles to include and which to exclude? Does each reviewer accept or reject studies for the same reasons? Do all reviewers complete every item?

If only one reviewer is involved in the review, take a sample of abstracts and review them twice—for example, today and a week from today. Do your selections match from Time 1 to Time 2? Over time, did you include and exclude studies for the same reasons?

The second step of the pilot test is to try out the actual reviewing process. Usually, between 5 and 10 studies are selected for the test. You can select them at random or because they exemplify some particular aspects of the review process; for example, 5 are experimental and 5 are descriptive. Using the actual abstraction form, reviewers review the articles. The results are compared. If differences are found, the reviewers can negotiate until they reach agreement or they can call in a third person to adjudicate. You continue the pilot test until a "satisfactory" level of agreement is reached. Some reviews use very strict standards and accept only perfect agreement; other reviews are less strict.

If you are the sole reviewer, do the review twice about a week apart. If your reviews differ over time, you should either continue practicing your reviewing techniques or revisit the abstraction form. Ask questions such as these: Are the definitions of terms clear to you? Do they conform to those used in your field? Should you add anything to the form? Delete anything?

ESTABLISHING VALIDITY

A valid review results in correct information. How do you determine if information taken from the literature is correct? Ideally, a study author would be around to say, "Yes. You have gotten it right. That's exactly what I meant." Because most of us do not have access to the authors of all the articles we review, an alternative method of verifying correctness must suffice. In many literature reviews, a knowledgeable person is appointed as the "gold standard," meaning that his or her reading of a study is the correct one. Consider this example.

The Project Leader as the Gold Standard: A Case Study

Four people were assigned the task of reviewing the literature to find out which programs were effective in helping overweight children lose weight and keep it off. After screening 520 published and 67 unpublished studies, a total of 120 studies were considered eligible for review. Reviewer A is to review Studies 1 through 60, and Reviewer B is to review Studies 61 through 120. Reviewers C and D will each be assigned their 60 articles at random so that sometimes an article will be reviewed by Reviewers A and C or A and

D; at other times, studies will be reviewed by Reviewers B and C or B and D. Reviewers A and B will never review the same article. At the conclusion of the review, the reviewers' results will be compared. The project leader, who is considered the "gold standard," will adjudicate any differences.

In addition, the project leader will review a 10% sample (12 articles) chosen at random. She will compare her findings to those of the two reviewers originally charged with the responsibility of reviewing the studies. If differences are found between her and any of the two reviewers, she will negotiate a resolution of the differences; her findings, however, take precedence over the other reviewers' findings.

In this example, the project leader is the gold standard: Her word is correct. In that capacity, she does two important things: She adjudicates between reviewers and she monitors the quality of the reviews. Because sole reviewers often have no "gold standard," they may never be able to establish truth. At best, they can demonstrate that the review has high test-retest or intraobserver reliability.

MONITORING QUALITY

Quality monitoring means making sure that over time, reviewers continue to adhere to the standards set for the process. Literature reviews require intense concentration, sometimes for extended periods, and it is not uncommon for reviewers to read a study several times to find the needed information. Monitoring the quality of the review means checking the work of all reviewers and making certain that careless reviews are corrected. In large reviews, provisions can be made to retrain the slack reviewer. If so, a system for retraining needs to be set up. It is important, when planning the review, to select someone who will spend time as the quality monitor and to determine if that person will also do the retraining or if someone else will.

The following is a checklist of activities to accomplish when abstracting information from the literature.

Collecting Data From the Literature: A Checklist

✓   Select practical and quality eligibility criteria.

✓   Define all terms.

✓ Translate eligibility criteria into questionnaire format.

✓ Pilot test the questionnaire with a sample of eligible studies.

✓ Modify the questionnaire using the pilot test results as a guide.

✓ If there are two or more reviewers, decide if they should be "blinded" to authors' and publication names.

✓ Train the reviewers.

✓ Develop a training manual.

✓ Provide practice exercises.

✓ Develop a quality monitoring system.

✓ Decide on a system for negotiation in case of disagreement between reviewers or with one reviewer, from one time to the next.

✓ Collect statistics on extent of agreement between reviewers or over time.

SUMMARY OF KEY POINTS

Collecting data about study methods (research design, sampling, data collection, and data analysis) *and* content (e.g., objectives, participants, settings, interventions, results, findings, and conclusions) enables the reviewer to describe the quality of evidence supporting each study, summarize the quality of evidence across several studies, report individual study conclusions, and summarize conclusions across several studies.

- You may review all eligible studies or select among them. If you review all, categorize each according to its quality.
- A reliable review is one that consistently provides the same information about methods and content from time to time from one person ("within") and among several ("across") reviewers. A valid review is an accurate one.
- A statistic often used in measuring agreement between two reviewers is called *kappa,* or κ, defined as the agreement beyond chance divided by the amount of agreement possible beyond chance.
- Literature reviews are surveys or systematic observations. Survey methods, particularly those pertaining to self-administered questionnaires, are often applied to the development of efficient ways to record information that is extracted from the literature.

- Training is essential in large literature reviews, especially if there are two or more reviewers.
- The literature review's methods should be pilot tested. The aim of the pilot test is to maximize reliability. The first step in the pilot is to test the eligibility criteria: Do all reviewers agree on which articles to include and which to exclude? Does each of the reviewers accept or reject studies for the same reasons? Do all reviewers complete every item? The second step of the pilot test is to try out the actual reviewing process.
- A valid review is correct. In many literature reviews, a knowledgeable person is appointed as the "gold standard," meaning that his or her reading of a study is the correct one.
- Quality monitoring means making sure that, over time, reviewers continue to adhere to the standards set for the process. Make sure (especially in large reviews) that provisions are made to assign someone as the quality monitor. Also, consider the possibility that some reviewers may need to be retrained periodically.
- Standardized reporting checklists are helpful in guiding a research literature review's contents and format. These checklists are based on the principle that transparent reporting is essential if readers and reviewers are to fully understand the biases within a study that can affect its validity. Keep in mind that just because something is reported does not automatically mean that it is high quality.

EXERCISES

1. Two reviewers evaluate 110 studies on the impact of home safety education in preventing accidents. The reviewers are asked to tell if the study investigators adequately describe the education intervention by defining its objectives, activities, participants, and settings. Reviewer 1 says that 30 of the studies do not adequately describe the intervention, but Reviewer 2 says that 45 do. The two reviewers agree that 20 studies do not adequately describe the intervention. Use the kappa statistic to describe the extent of agreement between the reviewers. Is the kappa slight, fair, moderate, or nearly perfect?

2. Prepare a questionnaire that literature reviewers can use in the following situation.

Situation: The Center for the Study of Employee Satisfaction is planning a review of the literature to find out what factors contribute most to employee loyalty. They are especially concerned with identifying ways to promote job satisfaction in highly trained employees. To be eligible for inclusion in the review, the study must be available to the reviewers within 6 months of their projects' starting date (March 1); the cost of obtaining the study must be U.S.$25 or less; the study's methods and results must be reported in English, German, or Italian; and the participants must include male and female employees.

3. Prepare a questionnaire that can be used in the following situation.

Situation: The Center for the Study of Employee Satisfaction sets criteria to ensure that the studies in its review are the best available. Their criteria for high quality include the following:

• All main outcomes (e.g., satisfaction, loyalty) must be defined.
• All measures must be demonstrably consistent with the definitions *plus* three or more of the following:

The study must include data on the same employees for a period of 2 or more years.

The research design must be described in detail.

The sampling methods must be described in detail.

The intervention must be described in detail.

ANSWERS

1. The following describes the way in which the two reviewers' responses look.

Reviewer 2

Reviewer 1	No	Yes	
No	20[c]	15	35[b]
Yes	10	55[d]	65
	30[a]	70	

This is the formula for deriving the kappa statistic:

$$\kappa = \frac{O-C\,(\text{Agreement beyond chance})}{1-C\,\left(\text{Agreement possible beyond chance}\right)}$$

Here is how the formula works with this example.

1. Calculate how many studies the reviewers may agree by chance *do not* adequately describe the intervention. This is done by multiplying the number of "no" responses and dividing by 110 because there are 110 studies: $30 \times 45/110 = 12.3$.

2. Calculate how many studies they may agree by chance do describe the intervention by multiplying the number of studies each found included an adequate description. This is done by multiplying the number of "yes" responses and dividing by 110: $80 \times 65/110 = 47.3$.

3. Add the two numbers obtained in Steps 1 and 2 and divide by 110 to get a proportion for *chance agreement:* $(12.3 + 7.3)/110 = 0.54$.

   The *observed agreement* is 20/110 (18%) + 55/110 (50%) = 68%, or 0.68. Therefore, the agreement beyond chance is $0.68 - 0.54 = 0.14$: The numerator.

   The *agreement possible beyond chance* is 100% minus the chance agreement of 54% or $1 - 0.54 = 0.46$: The denominator.

$$\kappa = \frac{0.14}{0.46}$$

$$\kappa = 0.30$$

A kappa of 0.30 is considered fair.

2. The following is a prototype questionnaire for the Center for the Study of Employee Satisfaction to use in its review.

Eligibility Criteria

Name of Reviewer: _____

Date of Review: _____

Study ID: _____

Instructions: _____

If the answer to any of the questions below is "no," the study is not eligible for this review.

1. Will the study be available by August 30? *(Circle one)*

   Yes 1

   No 2

2. Is the cost associated with obtaining a copy of the study U.S.$25 or less? *(Circle one)*

   Yes 1

   No 2

3. Is the study available in the any of the following languages? *(Circle all that apply)*

   English 1

   German 2

   Italian 3

4. Are both men and women included in the study? *(Circle one)*

   Yes 1

   No 2

---

3. The following is a prototype questionnaire for the Center for the Study of Employee Satisfaction to use to ensure quality.

Quality Criteria

Name of Reviewer: _____

Date of Review: _____

Study ID: _____

1. Are *all* main outcomes defined? *(Circle one)*

   No . . . . 1 *Reject Study*

   Yes 2

2. Are all measures consistent with the definition of the outcome? *(Circle one)*

   No . . . . 1 *Reject Study*

   Yes 2

3. Are data collected on all employees over a period of 2 years or more? *(Circle one)*

   No . . . . 1 *Reject Study*

   Yes 2

4. Is the research design described in detail? A detailed design includes "yes" to all of the following:

   Justification of choice of design

   Description of its implementation (e.g., if random assignment, how randomization was accomplished)

   Explanation of risks from internal validity

   Explanation of risks from external validity

5. Is the sampling method described in detail? Detail includes "yes" to all of the following:

   Explicit eligibility criteria

   Justification of size

   Explanation of how sample is assigned to intervention (or control)

6. Is the intervention described in detail? Detail includes "yes" to all of the following:

   Explicit objectives

   Activities are potentially reproducible

   Results are explained in terms of the objectives

❧ FIVE ❧

WHAT DID YOU FIND?

Synthesizing Results

❧

A Reader's Guide

❧

Purpose of This Chapter

The final outcome of a research review is a synthesis of the literature's contents and an evaluation of its quality. This chapter discusses how the synthesis is used in describing the status of current knowledge about a topic, justifying the need for and significance of new research, explaining research findings, and describing the quality of the available research. The synthesis can be a separate document (such as a stand-alone report), or it may be incorporated into articles, papers, and proposals. The chapter also explains how to do descriptive syntheses and meta-analyses.

Descriptive syntheses rely on the reviewers' knowledge and experience in identifying and interpreting similarities and differences in the literature's purposes, methods, and findings. They are often used when randomized trials and good observational studies are not available. When they are available, meta-analysis may be appropriate.

Meta-analytic reviews draw on formal statistical techniques to combine separate studies into a larger "meta" study. This chapter provides an introduction to meta-analysis that is specifically designed for users of meta-analytic results. Relevant statistical subjects are covered (such as the computation of odds and risks and the concepts behind statistical testing and confidence intervals) because they are essential components of meta-analytic studies. The research literature reviewer needs to understand the purposes and outcomes of these statistical techniques.

Checklists and flow diagrams are available to guide reviewers in conducting and reporting their reviews. Two of the most useful and comprehensive are the Preferred Reporting Items for Systematic Reviews and Meta-Analyses or PRISMA Statement and the Institute of Medicine's Standards for Systematic Reviews.

Figure 5.1 shows the steps in conducting a research literature review. This chapter deals with the shaded areas: Combine the results to produce a descriptive review, or perform a meta-analysis.

NOW THAT YOU HAVE DONE IT, WHAT DO YOU DO WITH IT?

The final step in conducting a research literature review is to synthesize the results. The synthesis provides answers to research questions and describes the quality of the evidence on which the answers are based.

Figure 5.1   Steps Involved in Conducting a Research Literature Review

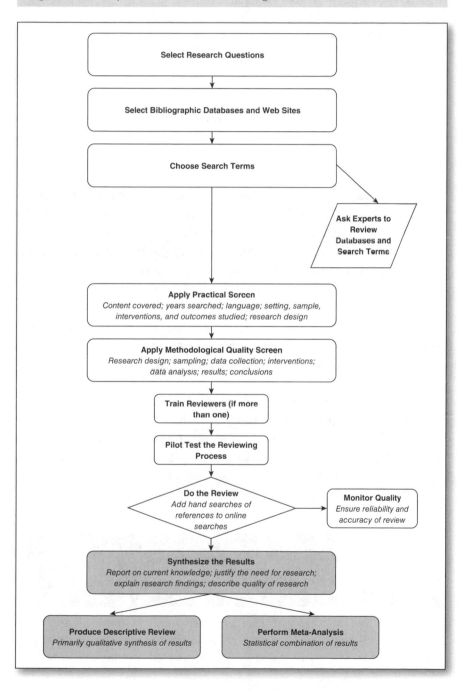

The research literature review process concludes by synthesizing the results. The synthesis has four main purposes:

1. Describe current knowledge about a topic or body of research

2. Support the need for and significance of new research

3. Explain research findings

4. Describe the quality of a body of research

Reviews Describe Current Knowledge

One primary use of the literature is to describe how much is currently known about a topic or body of research. Reviews of the current status of knowledge are integral components of proposals and research papers.

Suppose you are writing a proposal to evaluate an intervention to reduce symptoms of depression in children who have been exposed to violence. The proposal will contain the answers to at least four research questions: How widespread is the problem of children and exposure to violence? What are the physical, psychological, and behavioral effects on children of exposure to violence? Is depression one of the symptoms associated with exposure to violence? If so, how frequently is it seen among children who have been exposed to violence?

A first step in answering these questions is to review the literature in order to synthesize current knowledge on topics such as these: children and violence, consequences of children being exposed to violence, depressive symptoms in children who have been exposed to violence, and interventions to reduce symptoms of depression in children who have been exposed to violence. The hypothetical results of the review are illustrated next.

What Is Known About the Need to Intervene With Children Who Have Been Exposed to Violence and Have Depressive Symptoms?

Large numbers of American children personally witness or are the victims of violence, and an even greater number may experience symptoms after personally witnessing violence directed at others (references needed here). Exposure to violence is associated with depression (references needed here) and behavioral problems (references needed here). In addition, youth exposed to violence are more likely to have poorer school performance (references needed here), decreased IQ and reading ability (references needed here), lower grade point average (references needed here), and more days of school absence (references needed here). Exposure to violence may also interfere with the important developmental milestones of childhood and adolescence (references needed here).

These wide-ranging negative consequences of violence have resulted in calls for interventions to address the needs of children who are experiencing a range of symptoms after being exposed to violence (references needed here). Yet no randomized controlled trials of interventions for these symptomatic children exposed to violence have been conducted. (Note: although you do not need to include references for this statement, you should be prepared to defend it. Your best defense is a comprehensive review.) Based on our previous work (references needed here), we conducted a randomized controlled trial to test the effectiveness of the intervention in reducing depressive symptoms.

All statements in a proposal or research paper that can be challenged with the request, "Prove this," should be accompanied by references to the literature. Restrict your references to high-quality studies for scientific and ethical reasons. Also, if you plan to publish your work, some journals limit the number of references you can include.

Literature reviews that describe current knowledge are often published as stand-alone reports. If you review any high-quality medical or nursing journal, you will find numerous examples of stand-alone literature reviews that systematically examine the state of the art and science on a particular topic. These reviews are extremely important in health and medicine, where new technologies and studies appear continuously and need to be described and evaluated. But health professionals are not the only ones who depend on stand-alone reviews. Consumer groups such as the Consumer's Union use them to help consumers make decisions about products.

Reviews Support the Need for and Significance of New Research

Literature review syntheses provide evidence that a proposed study is needed and significant. Suppose, for example, that you have developed an educational program to encourage students to become interested in public service as a career choice. Suppose also that you would like to get a grant to evaluate the program's effectiveness. To get the grant, you will need to do a literature review to answer questions such as these: Why is this program needed? What benefits will society gain if more students become interested in public service as a career choice? Are other programs available, and if so, why are they not as effective as the one you are proposing? The idea is to convince the grant makers that the literature supports your claims that a new program is needed to achieve the objective of getting students to choose public service for their careers. Here is an example of the use of literature review results in justifying the need for and significance of new research.

Do South Asian Women Who Live in the United States Receive Appropriate Preventive Health Care?

South Asians are a rapidly growing population in the United States. Immigrants from South Asia originate from India, Pakistan, Bangladesh, and Sri Lanka. Asian Indians far outnumber other South Asians, with 11.8% of the entire Asian American population in the United States or 786,000 persons. Pakistanis follow with 82,000 individuals living in the United States. From 1980 to 1990, both groups increased in proportion by 110%. Furthermore, the Asian and Pacific Islander group (API) is expected to increase to four times its current size by the year 2050 [Census of Population and Housing, 1993, #143]. Given this expected increase, the United States must be prepared to integrate these immigrants into its health care system.

Unfortunately, there are multiple challenges to providing health care for immigrants. Barriers such as language difficulties, resettlement concerns, problems acculturating, cultural health beliefs, and low self-efficacy [Jenkins, 1996, #125; Phillips, 2000, #127; Stephenson, 1999, #128] may influence the receipt of preventive care services more than acute care services. Failure to obtain preventive care can increase health care costs and cause significant morbidity and mortality [Fries, 1993, #26; Kattlove, 1995, #27].

Although many immigrants to the United States do not obtain necessary preventive services, scant data are available on South Asians. In their homelands, South Asians usually obtain medical treatment only when they are acutely ill; only rarely do they receive comprehensive primary care [Berman, 2000, #140]. It is unknown if this type of patient behavior carries over when these immigrants arrive in the United States.

A comprehensive study of this subject is needed to adequately ascertain which preventive services this unstudied group obtains. Gaps in the provision of preventive care services need to be identified so that policy makers can create culturally appropriate outreach programs that encourage the use of preventive services. Factors associated with the use of these services need to be identified so that physicians caring for South Asian patients can maximize the appropriate use of preventive services.

The names and numbers in the brackets in the example above (such as [Berman, 2000, #140]) are the references that justify the statements that together make up the authors' argument. The format is typical of a reference manager program. In this case, Berman, 2000, is the 140th reference listed in the reviewer's library.

Reviews Explain Research Findings

Literature review results explain research findings by demonstrating how a particular study's outcomes compare to all others, as illustrated below.

South Asian Women Do Not Obtain a Very Important Preventive Health Care Test

Papanicolaou (Pap) smears have been shown to detect early cervical cellular abnormalities, thereby reducing morbidity and mortality from cervical cancer.[1] Lower proportion of lifetime spent in the United States is a negative predictor of Pap smear receipt for Vietnamese women.[12] Similarly, other measures of acculturation based on acculturation "scores" have found that acculturation predicts Pap smear receipt for Native Americans and Hispanics[37,38] and that language barriers and fewer years in the United States negatively affect access to the health care system for Chinese Americans.[39] Thus, our study supports prior research noting the positive correlation between acculturation, health services use in general, and Pap smear receipt in particular.

Unlike previous studies, we did not find age to be an important predictor of Pap smear receipt.[40] This may have been due to the small number of elderly women in our cohort, which limited the power of our study to assess effectively the impact of age on Pap smear receipt in this sample.

The references in the example above are used to defend the following finding: "Thus, our study supports prior research noting the positive
correlation between acculturation, health services use in general, and
Pap smear receipt in particular." The references have been formatted by
the reference manager program to appear as superscripts such as [1] or [40].
Reference manager programs have hundreds of formats to correspond to
the needs of different journals. You may switch from one format to another
quite easily.

Reviews Describe the Quality of Current Research

The quality of current research refers to its methodological quality.
The best reviews have detailed descriptions of the quality of the literature. This description is essential because the accuracy of the review
depends on the quality of the literature available to it. Also, the higher the
quality of the literature, the more likely you are to feel confident in and
accept its conclusions.

Among the questions reviewers should ask about each article or studies
are these: How internally valid is the research design? Are the outcome measures valid? Was the sample selection process explained and justified? Are the
data current? Are there any obvious biases in each study, say, due to failure to
"blind" participants or because of financial conflict of interest?

Suppose you were interested in finding out if prenatal care helps prevent
premature births (duration of pregnancy less than 37 weeks from last men-
strual period) and low birth weight (less than 2,500 grams). You do a literature
review and prepare the next two tables.

In the first table (Table 5.1), you list the methodological features of 22
evaluations of prenatal care programs. That is, the table is used to summarize
the number and characteristics of articles on prenatal care that met your first
set of screening criteria. In the second table (Table 5.2), you present the findings of seven studies that met five of the second set of screening or quality
criteria. In this case, there are eight quality criteria.

Table 5.1. Screening Criteria: Part I

Question: What are the methodological characteristics of 22 studies that
evaluated prenatal care?

Table 5.1 Methodological Features of 22 Studies of Prenatal Care Programs

Features	N (%)	References
Health status of mothers	19 (86.4)	21 23–29 31–38 40–42
Clear description of experimental program	17 (77.3)	21 23–28 30 33 36 37 39 42
Statistical presentation	14 (63.6)	21 24 26–30 32 34 35 37 39 41
Valid data collection	13 (59.1)	21 25 29 32 34 35 39 41
Prospective data collection	8 (36.4)	24 27 28 32 36 37 41 42
Follow-up data on women and infants	6 (27.3)	23 24 28 32 36 41
Randomization into study	6 (27.3)	21 22 30 35 40 42
Random assignment to groups	4 (18.2)	27 32 37 41

The table tells you that 86.4% of the studies looked at mother's health status, and more than three fourths (77.3%) have a clear description of the experimental program, but only 27.3% have follow-up data or randomly selected participants for the study or randomly assigned participants to groups once they were selected. Now look at Table 5.2.

Table 5.2. Screening Criteria: Part II—Quality

Question: What programs and outcomes are examined in the seven studies that contain five or more of the eight methodological characteristics?

Looking at Table 5.2, you can conclude that at the time of the review, prenatal care programs varied considerably in their focus (e.g., sometimes on who should deliver care and at other times on providing information on nutrition or smoking cessation). You are not surprised to find that the outcomes also differed considerably from study to study and include infant mortality, quality of diet, infections, and smoking reduction and smoking cessation.

The review's findings suggest that only one prenatal care program (parent education and family support) had a beneficial effect on the baby's birth weight and gestational age (Olds et al.), although a nutritional program (Huggins et al.) had a positive effect on the baby's gestational age.

You prepare Table 5.3 to describe more about each study and present it in this format.

Question: In what geographical area was the study conducted, with how many women, and of what age, ethnicity, marital status, and education?

As you can see from Tables 5.2 and 5.3, the specific study that had significant, positive effects on birth weight and gestational age (Olds) had a sample of 189 women. These women were from a relatively suburban part of California. Nearly two thirds were unmarried, and almost half (47%) were 19 years of age and younger.

The choice of data to present depends on the problem and your audience. For instance, you might just have a table describing the objectives of each included study for a group of people who are interested in deciding on how to focus a program. In Table 5.4, only study objectives are given.

Table 5.2   Seven Prenatal Care Programs Meeting the Review Criteria

Author	Program Description	Birth Weight	Effects on Gestational Age	Other Outcomes
Able et al.	Case management service	*	NA	*Infant mortality *Costs *Immunizations *Knowledge of child development
Eddie et al.	Medical, psychosocial, and nutritional assessments and services	o	o	*Immunizations
Frank and Kine	Nurse midwives	o	o	NA

Author	Program Description	Birth Weight	Effects on Gestational Age	Other Outcomes
Huggins et al.	Nutritional assessment	o	*	* Perinatal mortality *Fetal growth retardation
Olds et al.	Parent education and family support	*	*	*Kidney infections *Childbirth education *Knowledge of services o Weight gain o Alcohol consumption
Spender	Family workers	o	ʋ	NA
Winston	Smoking cessation	NA	NA	*Smoking cessation *Smoking reduction

*Statistically significant beneficial effect; o = no statistically significant effect.

Note: NA = not assessed.

Other descriptive tables can contain information on the number of studies that met their research objectives, were published during certain periods of time (such as between 1950 and 1960 or 1990 and 2005, etc.), collected data from their participants for 12 months or more, included children in their programs, excluded children in their programs, and so on.

Why do you need all this additional information if the purpose of the review is to synthesize the findings from high-quality studies? Why not just give summary information (as in Table 5.1)? The reason is that you must make the literature review synthesis as accurate as possible, and one way to ensure accuracy is to place all studies in their context. The context includes the methodological quality and other study characteristics. With information on context, you are able to report on how high quality the best available studies are and to identify the populations and programs that have contributed to current knowledge or have not been studied well or completely.

Table 5.3   Demographic Characteristics of Experimental Program Participants

Author	Sample Size	Geographic Area	Age	Marital Status	Education
Able et al.	15,526	North Carolina	15% < 18	66% unmarried	48% < 12 years
Eddie et al.	125	Salt Lake City, Utah	100% < 20	11% married	97% < high school graduate
Frank and Kine	667	Charleston, South Carolina	32% < 20	45% unmarried	63% < high school graduate
Huggins et al.	552	St. Louis, Missouri	Average: 22	82% married	Not stated
Olds et al.	189	San Fernando Valley, California	47% < 19	41% married	Average: 11 years
Spender	626	London, England	45% < 19	25% married	45% high school graduates
Winston	102	Birmingham, Alabama	23	Not stated	Average: 11 years

Table 5.4   Objectives of the Studies in a Review of the Literature on Screening Measures Used in Older Persons

First Author	Objectives
Willenbring	Study the validity of the Michigan Alcoholism Screening Tests scored with weighted (MAST) and unit scoring (UMAST) and two short versions: the BMAST and the SMAST
Tucker	Determine the adequacy of verbal reports of drinking using three questionnaires: the SMAST, Drinking Practices Questionnaire, and the Questionnaire Measure of Habitual Alcohol Use
Werch	Compare three measures for estimating alcohol consumption: a 7-day and a 21-day diary and a quantity/frequency index
Colsher	Examine two measures of alcohol consumption: quantity/frequency and history of heavy drinking
Moran	Determine the sensitivity and specificity of a two-question alcoholism screening test not previously tested in the elderly and compare the results to MAST scores

First Author	Objectives
Buchsbaum Fulop Jones	Assess the performance of the CAGE questionnaire in identifying elderly medicine outpatients with drinking problems Examine the utility of the CAGE and MAST as brief screening instruments for alcoholism and depression Assess the validity of CAGE and the MAST in distinguishing between elderly patients with and without alcohol disorders
Chaikelson	Determine the validity of a retrospective self-report measure, the Concordia Lifetime Drinking Questionnaire
Clay Bradley Fink	Compare the AUDIT and CAGE questionnaires in screening for alcohol use disorders in elderly primary care outpatients Examine the AUDIT alcohol consumption questions: reliability, validity, and responsiveness to change in older male primary care patients Evaluate the validity of the Alcohol-Related Problems Survey, a measure designed to detect nonhazardous, hazardous, and harmful drinking in older adults

Descriptive Syntheses or Reviews

Descriptive literature reviewers use their own knowledge and experience to synthesize the literature by evaluating similarities and differences in the purposes, methods, and findings of high-quality research. The validity of a descriptive synthesis or review's findings depends on the subject matter expertise and critical imagination of the reviewer and on the quality of the available literature.

Descriptive reviews are particularly relevant when randomized controlled trials or rigorous observational studies are scarce or even unavailable. If randomized trials and good observational studies are available, then statistical analyses—meta-analyses—are appropriate. This type of review uses formal statistical techniques to sum up the outcomes of separate studies.

Examples of Descriptive Literature Reviews

The following are examples of descriptive literature review reports.

Example 1. Placebo Effects in Pain Treatment and Research[1]

Purpose of the Review. The reviewers aimed to estimate the importance and implications of placebo effects in pain treatment and research. A placebo is an intervention designed to simulate medical therapy but not believed to be a specific therapy for the target condition. It is used either for its psychological effect or to eliminate observer bias in an experimental setting. A placebo effect is a change in a patient's illness that can be attributed to the symbolic import of a treatment rather than a specific pharmacologic or physiological property. A placebo response refers to any change in patient behavior or condition following the administration of a placebo.

Methods. English-language articles and books identified through MEDLINE (1980 through 1993) and PsycLIT (1967 through 1993) database searching, bibliography review, and expert consultation.

Results. Three books and 75 articles were included in the review. The reviewers found that placebo response rates vary greatly and are often much higher than previously believed. (Current belief is that about one third of patients will have a placebo effect.) As with medication, surgery can produce substantial placebo effects. Individuals are not consistent in their placebo responses.

Conclusions. Placebo effects influence patient outcomes after any treatment, including surgery, that a clinician and patient believe is effective. Placebo effects plus the natural history of diseases and regression to the mean can result in high rates of good outcomes that may be incorrectly attributed to specific treatment effects. The true causes of improvement in pain after treatment remain unknown in the absence of independently evaluated randomized controlled trials.

Limitations. The criteria for selecting the 75 articles and three books are not described, nor are the quality of the studies the reviewers discuss prominently in their analysis. In the absence of such information, we may lose confidence in the conclusions.

Example 2. The Cost-Savings Argument for Prenatal Care[2]

Purpose of the Review. Public spending for prenatal care in the United States has been justified by the cost-savings argument. Prenatal care, it is said, can prevent the costs and medical complications associated with low birth weight. What is the evidence for this claim?

Methods. Refereed journals and government publications were reviewed. Of 100 studies on effectiveness and economics made available over an 18-year period, 12 addressed issues of cost and cost savings. Four studies used data from experiments of prenatal care that included objectives other than evaluation of costs, four were surveys of groups of patients, and four used hypothetical calculations of cost savings.

Conclusions. In each study, methodological problems were identified that could have resulted in the overestimation of cost savings. These included non-comparable control groups, unsupported assumptions, underestimation of the cost of prenatal care, underestimation of the cost of overcoming nonfinancial barriers to access prenatal care, and oversimplification of the relation between changes in the frequency of low birth weight and actual cost savings.

Limitations. This review does not demonstrate that prenatal care is not cost-effective. In fact, the authors point out that with better data, the cost savings due to prenatal care might even be convincingly demonstrated. In addition, costs savings may not be the appropriate criterion for evaluating prenatal care programs.

Example 3. Adequacy of Reporting Race/Ethnicity in Clinical Trials in Areas of Health Disparities[3]

Purpose of the Review. Research in the United States has shown disparities in health by race and ethnicity. Because of this, U.S. government-supported initiatives have mandated broader inclusion of minorities in clinical research on diseases that have such disparities. The reviewers in this study examined the reporting of race/ethnicity in clinical trials in areas of known disparities in health (i.e., diabetes, cardiovascular disease, HIV/AIDS, and cancer) to determine the success of the mandates.

Methods. The reviewers performed a MEDLINE search covering the period from January 1989 to October 2000 to identify clinical trials of diabetes, cardiovascular disease, HIV/AIDS, and cancer published in the *Annals of Internal Medicine, Journal of the American Medical Association,* and *New England Journal of Medicine.*

Conclusions. The reviewers found that of 253 eligible trials, analysis of results by race/ethnicity was reported in only 2 trials. In diseases with known racial and ethnic disparities, almost none report analyses by race/ethnicity. Thus, although federal initiatives mandate inclusion of minority groups in research, the reviewers conclude that the inclusion has not translated to reporting of results that might guide therapeutic decisions.

Limitations. One important limitation to the review's findings is that it focused only on reports of clinical trials in selected and excellent general medicine journals. Because the sampling frame included only these journals, it is possible that reporting may have been different in other journals with a different readership.

Example 4. Exercise for Women with Anorexia Nervosa[4]

Purpose of the Review. This review aimed to identify exercise interventions to help inform decision-making in the treatment of underweight individuals with anorexia nervosa (AN) and also to uncover recommended differences in how to plan to care for those who excessively exercise and those who do not.

Methods. The reviewers relied on PubMed and PsycINFO to identify relevant studies. They also searched the study's' references for additional articles. The search terms were: anorexia nervosa, eating disorders, excessive exercise, compulsive exercise, obligatory exercise, physical activity (PA) and intervention. Peer-reviewed research articles that focused on weight restoration using any form of exercise or structured PA program with women diagnosed with AN were included. The reviewer evaluated six studies.

Conclusions. The review revealed that few studies have systematically explored exercise as a part of treatment among patients with AN. The authors suggest a need for developing further research, but currently the field may benefit from standardized guidelines for treating excessive exercisers with AN.

Limitations. All studies were included in the review without regard to their quality.

The list below contains sample descriptive literature reviews.

Blank, L., Peters, J., Pickvance, S., Wilford, J., & MacDonald, E. (2008). A systematic review of the factors which predict return to work for people suffering episodes of poor mental health. *Journal of Occupational Rehabilitation, 18,* 27–34.
Coffey, M. (2006). Researching service user views in forensic mental health: A literature review. *Journal of Forensic Psychiatry & Psychology, 17,* 73–107.

Connolly, C. M., Rose, J., & Austen, S. (2006). Identifying and assessing depression in prelingually deaf people: A literature review. *American Annals of the Deaf, 151*, 49–60.

Connolly, T. M., Boyle, E. A., MacArthur, E., Hainey, T., & Boyle, J. M. (2012). A systematic literature review of empirical evidence on computer games and serious games. *Computers & Education, 59*(2), 661–686.

Griffiths, K. L., Mackey, M. G., & Adamson, B. J. (2007). The impact of a computerized work environment on professional occupational groups and behavioural and physiological risk factors for musculoskeletal symptoms: A literature review. *Journal of Occupational Rehabilitation, 17*, 743–765.

Magill-Evans, J., Harrison, M. J., Rempel, G., & Slater, L. (2006). Interventions with fathers of young children: Systematic literature review. *Journal of Advanced Nursing, 55*, 248–264.

McMaster, K., & Espin, C. (2007). Technical features of curriculum-based measurement in writing: A literature review. *Journal of Special Education, 41*(2), 68–84.

Mechling, L. C. (2007). Assistive technology as a self-management tool for prompting students with intellectual disabilities to initiate and complete daily tasks: A literature review. *Education and Training in Developmental Disabilities, 42*, 252–269.

Shaw, W., Hong, Q. N., Pransky, G., & Loisel, P. (2008). A literature review describing the role of return-to-work coordinators in trial programs and interventions designed to prevent workplace disability. *Journal of Occupational Rehabilitation, 18*, 2–15.

Stallwitz, A., & Stover, H. (2007). The impact of substitution treatment in prisons: A literature review. *International Journal of Drug Policy, 18*, 464–474.

Yudko, E., Lozhkina, O., & Fouts, A. (2007). A comprehensive review of the psychometric properties of the Drug Abuse Screening Test. *Journal of Substance Abuse Treatment, 32*, 189–198.

Zunker, C., Mitchell, J. E., & Wonderlich, S. A.(2011). Exercise interventions for women with anorexia nervosa: A review of the literature. *International Journal of Eating Disorders, 44*(7), 579–584.

META-ANALYSIS

Take this true-false test.		
True or false?		
Coaching raises SAT scores.	T	F
Using sunscreen with an SPF of 15+ is more protective of wrinkling than skin creams.	T	F
Reducing serum cholesterol concentration with diets or drugs or both reduces the incidence of major coronary events in men.	T	F

The answers are false, true, and true. How do we know? The answers come from the findings of a combination of several high-quality studies. The studies were combined using a method called meta-analysis.

A meta-analysis uses formal statistical techniques to sum up the results of similar but separate studies. Put another way, a meta-analysis integrates or combines data from more than one study on a given topic to arrive at conclusions about a body of research. The idea is that the larger numbers obtained by combining study findings provide greater statistical power than any of the individual studies. In the true-false test above, for example, the results of 36 studies on the effects of coaching on SAT scores were combined. A meta-analysis has qualitative features, too, because it takes into account more subjective issues, such as strength of study design and extent of content coverage.

The discussion that follows is specifically designed for users of meta-analytic results. Some statistical issues are covered (such as the computation of odds and risks and the concepts behind statistical testing and confidence intervals) because they are essential components of most meta-analyses. Even if you do not plan to do your own meta-analysis, you should continue reading because you will definitely encounter meta-analytic studies (and those that call themselves meta-analyses) as part of the literature-reviewing process.

What to Look for in a Meta-Analysis: The Seven Steps

Meta-analysis is a statistical synthesis of relevant studies to reach conclusions about a body of research. The concept of *effect size* is central to meta-analysis. An effect is the extent to which an outcome is present in the population. It is an index of how much difference there is between two groups, usually a treatment (experimental) group and a control group. If the outcome of a study is continuous (e.g., a score from 1 to 100 or blood pressure measurements), then the effect size is defined as the difference in means or average scores between the intervention and control groups divided by the standard deviation of the control or both groups. Effect sizes can be based on proportions, if the outcome is nominal, or on correlations, if the outcome is an association. Effect sizes can also be expressed as differences between odds ratios or relative risks (see the section under "Statistical Interlude" later in this chapter).

The effect sizes are combined statistically in meta-analysis. Suppose you do a literature review to find out the effect of a low-fat diet on your blood pressure. Typically, an effect size that expresses the magnitude and direction of the results would be calculated for each study in the review. For example, a positive effect of fish oil might be expressed as the difference in mean blood pressure levels between a group given a low-fat diet and a group not on a low-fat diet (possibly divided by a within-group standard deviation). A positive sign can be given if the low-fat diet group has lower postintervention blood pressure and a negative sign given when the opposite is true. As a second example, think of a group of studies examining whether attitude toward reading is associated with age. The effect size can be the correlation between age and satisfaction (as a component of the concept of "attitude"), with positive correlations indicating that older students are more satisfied than younger students. In this example, the effect size is an expression of the degree of relationship between two variables.

There are many ways to define the average or typical effect size. Among the most commonly reported is the weighted mean, where weighting is by the size of the study. The idea is that effect sizes based on larger studies have more stability and should be weighted more heavily than the more variable effect sizes based on smaller studies. But this may be misleading. Suppose, for example, that interventions in larger studies were intrinsically weaker and had less impact than the more intensive interventions that might be possible in smaller studies; the average effect size weighted by study size would be systematically biased toward the weaker interventions and could lead to a pessimistic conclusion. Because of this, many meta-analytic practitioners urge the reporting of both weighted and unweighted average effect sizes.

The following are seven steps that should be taken to complete a comprehensive, valid meta-analysis. When using a meta-analysis, check to determine how adequately each step is performed.

Seven Steps to a Meta-Analysis

1. Clarify the objectives of the analysis.

2. Set explicit criteria for including and excluding studies.

3. Describe in detail the methods used to search the literature.

4. Search the literature using a standardized protocol for including and excluding studies.

5. Use a standardized protocol to collect ("abstract") data from each study regarding study purposes, methods, and effects (outcomes).

6. Describe in detail the statistical method for pooling results.

7. Report results, conclusions, and limitations.

As a reviewer of a meta-analysis, check how well each of the seven steps is implemented.

Step 1. Are the Objectives of the Meta-Analysis Clear? The objectives are the purposes of doing the analysis. Meta-analyses have been done about subjects as diverse as school-based smoking prevention programs, adolescent gambling disorders, consumer choice and subliminal advertising, cesarean childbirth and psychosocial outcomes, the effectiveness of intravenous streptokinase during acute myocardial infarction, and the use of electroshock in the treatment of depression.

Meta-analysis is a research method, and so the objectives (research questions, hypotheses) must come before any other activity. As a user, you need to know the objectives of the meta-analysis so that you can subsequently evaluate the appropriateness of the included (and excluded) literature, determine the adequacy of the methods used to combine studies, and evaluate the soundness of the researchers' conclusions.

Step 2. Are the Inclusion and Exclusion Criteria Explicit?[5] Conservative meta-analysis practitioners assert that only true experiments or randomized trials are eligible to be included in meta-analysis. More liberal practitioners will accept all high-quality studies. They often group them by study design characteristics, such as random or nonrandom assignment, in order to estimate if differences exist between the findings of higher and lower quality studies. The technique used to conduct separate analyses of different quality studies is called *sensitivity* analysis. As a reviewer or user, you should check that the meta-analyst specifies and justifies quality criteria and that high-quality studies are not (without good reason) analyzed together with lower quality studies.

Step 3. Are the Search Strategies Described in Great Detail?[6] Reviewers should describe all databases and search terms they used to obtain literature. It is also crucial to make sure that all potentially relevant studies are included. This means tracking down studies that have negative results and even those that are still in progress. The idea is to avoid becoming a victim of "publication bias."

Publication bias is a term used to mean that a review unfairly favors the results of published studies. Published studies may differ from unpublished ones in that they tend to have positive findings. The general rule in estimating the extent of the bias is to consider that if the available data uncovered by the review are from high-quality studies and reasonably consistent in direction, then the number of opposite findings will have to be extremely large to overturn the results.

A number of statistical techniques are available to help deal with publication bias. Formulas are available that you can use to estimate the number of published studies showing no differences between programs that are needed to convert a statistically significant pooled difference into an insignificant difference. If the number of unpublished studies is small relative to the number of published studies pooled in the meta-analysis, then you should be concerned about potential publication bias.

Other methods include estimating the size of the population from which each study group is drawn. Using this information and the study's sample size, potential publication bias can be calculated for individual study. Software is available for investigating publication bias by graphically displaying sample size plotted against effect size. Some researchers suggest that this graphic display (which is called a *funnel plot*) should always be examined as part of a meta-analysis, if a sufficient number of studies are available.

Step 4. Is a Standardized Protocol Used to Screen the Literature?[7] The fourth step of the meta-analysis is to screen each identified study. Usually two or more reviewers determine the quality of the universe of studies. To ensure a consistent review, a screening protocol should be prepared. This means that each study is reviewed in a uniform manner. The following are typical of the types of questions included in a standardized protocol.

Portions of a Quality Screen for Studies of Alcohol Use in Older People

Are these terms defined?	1. Yes	2. No
Alcoholism	1	2
Heavy drinking	1	2

(Continued)

(Continued)

Are these terms defined?	1. Yes	2. No
Problem drinking	1	2
Alcohol dependence	1	2
Alcohol abuse	1	2
Alcohol-related problems	1	2
Hazardous drinking	1	2
Harmful drinking	1	2

Is evidence offered that the instrument used to measure each of the following is valid in persons 65 years of age or older?

Alcoholism	1	2	NA
Heavy drinking	1	2	NA
Problem drinking	1	2	NA

Are study data collected prospectively?

Yes	1
No	2

Does the analysis include all participants regardless of whether they completed all aspects of the program?

Yes	1
No	2

To minimize bias, reviewers are sometimes not told the authors' names, the objectives of the study, or where the study was conducted. After each reviewer completes the questionnaires for all studies, the results are compared between reviewers. Usually, differences in results are negotiated either by discussion between the reviewers themselves or by a third person who is the arbitrator or "gold standard." This method is used across all types of literature review.

In selecting studies for inclusion into a meta-analysis, a commonly used method relies on scoring. For example, each study is assigned a numerical score between 1 and 100, and a cutoff score is selected. If the cutoff is 75, and higher scores are better, that means that only studies having scores of 75 or more are included in the meta-analysis. In other cases, certain minimum standards are set, and the analysis includes only studies meeting those standards. If eight quality criteria are chosen, for example, the meta-analysis can be designed to include only those studies that meet at least six. Alternatively, if eight quality criteria are set, the analysis can be designed so that all studies with randomly selected participants (or valid data collection or follow-up for more than 1 year or data collection that endures for at least 10 months, etc.) are included if they also meet a certain number of the eight criteria.

The choice of screening criteria and the method of determining if they have been met are subjective. Check to see that the meta-analysis authors have adequately justified their choice of screening and selection criteria.

Step 5. Is Standardized Protocol or Abstraction Form Used to Collect Data?[8] Once studies are selected, they are reviewed and information is abstracted. As with the screening process, valid data collection often requires at least two reviewers using a standard protocol. These forms should be described and made accessible to the reader either in the review, on a Web site, or directly from the reviewers.

Check the report of the analysis to see if nonexpert reviewers are used to abstract literature. These nonexperts may not be knowledgeable about the topic or even about literature reviews. If nonexperts are used in data collection, determine if the authors discuss the type of training the reviewers received and if a "quality control" method was employed. A typical quality control method involves having experts keep watch. Often one or more meta-analysis authors act as a quality controller. These people—the gold standards—abstract some or all studies. The results are compared among all reviewers and differences are negotiated. The level of agreement among reviewers should be discussed. A statistical measure called the kappa (κ) is available to evaluate the extent of agreement by adjusting for agreements that might have arisen by chance.[9]

Step 6. Do the Authors Fully Explain Their Method of Combining or "Pooling"
Results? An underlying assumption of one of the most commonly used meta-
analytic approaches is that you can pool (merge) individual study results to produce a summary measure because all study results are homogeneous in that they
reflect the same "true" effect. Differences, if you find any, are due to chance alone
(sampling error). If the assumption is correct, then when the results are combined,
any random errors will be canceled out, and one meta-study will be produced. A
meta-study—a merging of many studies—is presumed to be better than just one.

In large meta-analyses, you can expect disagreement in results among studies. Sometimes the differences may be due just to chance. But not always. Other
factors, such as variations in study settings or the age or socioeconomic status of
the participants, may be the culprits. Rather than being *homogeneous* (with any
observed variations due to chance), studies may be *heterogeneous* (with
observed variations due to initial differences in design, setting, or sample).

In reviewing the results of a meta-analysis that assumes that study results
are homogeneous, check to see if the authors systematically examine their
assumption of homogeneity or compatibility of the study results. Investigations of homogeneity (also called tests of heterogeneity) may be done graphically or statistically or both ways. Among the statistical methods used to test
for homogeneity are the chi-square for proportions and regression. It is generally
considered good practice for a meta-analysis to examine sources of variation
based on theoretical or other empirical considerations regardless of the outcomes
of the homogeneity tests. These tests alert the investigator to the likelihood
that differences in effect size may be due to influences on the intervention that
vary from study to study. Thus, a significant test result for homogeneity obli-
gates the meta-analyst to search for variations in study settings or participants'
characteristics; a nonsignificant test does not preclude the search.

Pooling Results: A Case Study

Suppose you are interested in finding out how television watching affects
children's behavior. Suppose also that you really believe that television has a
profound effect on children's behavior (particularly in encouraging violent acts)
and you want to obtain evidence to support your belief. In a meta-analysis, you
(or the authors of a meta-analysis) first gather the pertinent studies: those that
compare children who watch television with those who do not. You next
compare the findings of each study to the hypothesis that television has no

effect on behavior. The hypothesis that there is no effect is called the *null*. So in a meta-analysis, you compare each finding to the null. If the null (no effect) is true, the series of study-by-study comparisons should differ only randomly from a zero effect. Adding them together should give a result near zero because the other chance results will cancel each other out. But if the studies consistently observe an effect, such as an increase in violent acts among children, the comparisons should add up and provide a sharp contrast to the null hypothesis.

A popular statistical technique—the Mantel-Haenszel-Peto method—assumes that studies addressing similar questions should—except for chance occurrences—result in answers pointing in the same qualitative direction. The only direct comparisons made are between experimental and control participants within the same experiment. The basic idea is that one statistic and its variance are calculated from each study. The separate statistics are then added together and divided by the sum of their variances to produce a statistic that summarizes the totality of the evidence. This method is illustrated for three hypothetical studies.

Calculating the Grand Total of Differences in Three Studies

Study 1: Difference 1 (experimental vs. control)

Study 2: Difference 2 (experimental vs. control)

Study 3: Difference 3 (experimental vs. control)

Grand total: Difference 1 + Difference 2 + Difference 3

The variance of the grand total can be calculated by adding the separate variances of the separate differences from each study.

The first step in applying the meta-analysis method involves taking each study at a time and computing the number of outcomes (e.g., children performing violent acts) that would be expected in the experimental group if, in reality, the experimental intervention or program (say, selective television viewing) had no effect. This number of *expected* outcomes (E) is then subtracted from the number of outcomes that were actually *observed* (O) in the experimental group. If the program actually has no effect on the outcome, the two numbers will be the same, except by chance. If, however, the experimental program is more effective than the control in reducing the incidence of the outcomes, fewer outcomes (i.e., fewer violent acts) than expected will be seen in the experimental group (and subtracting E from O will result in a negative value). If the experimental program increases the occurrence of the outcome, more outcomes than expected will be observed in the experimental group (and subtracting E from O will result in a positive value).

Adding these separate differences $(O - E)$ and their variances allows the calculation of a statistic (and its variance) that is "typical" of the difference observed between experimental and control groups in the collection of studies assembled for the analysis. The typical statistic then can be used in a test of the null hypothesis and also to estimate how large and worthwhile any differential effects are likely to be. (The null hypothesis says that the experimental and control programs have equivalent effects, or said another way, no difference exists between experimental and control.) An estimate of the differential effects can be described by the odds ratio (or relative risks) and associated confidence interval. A confidence interval provides a plausible range for the "true" value of the difference. For more information on risks and odds, see the section "Statistical Interlude" on page 224.

Step 7. Does the Report Contain Results, Conclusions, and Limitations? The results of a meta-analysis refer to numbers, percentages, odds ratios, risk ratios, confidence intervals, and other statistical findings. The conclusions are inferences from the statistical data. The limitations are the threats to internal and external validity[10] caused by sampling, research design, data collection, and unexplored or unanswered research questions.

The following are typical results, conclusions, and limitations from meta-analyses.

Sample Results of Several Meta-Analyses

Reporting the Facts

1. Keeping Medical Appointments
   - A total of 164 articles were identified from all sources; more than 95% were identified from electronic searches. Simple agreement for assessing the potential relevance of citations was 83% ($\kappa = 0.66$)[11] for citations retrieved from PubMed and 98% for citations from PsycLIT ($\kappa = 0.95$). Eighty-eight articles were selected as potentially

relevant. Thirty-three of the 88 articles were randomized controlled trials. Ten of these 33 studies did not report attendance as the primary outcome measurement or did not provide sufficient data to develop contingency tables, leaving 23 articles of high relevance and scientific merit for detailed review (82% agreement; $\kappa = 0.62$).

- The average rate of compliance with appointments was 58%. Mailed reminders and telephone prompts were consistently useful in reducing broken appointments (odds ratio of 2.2, 95% confidence interval [CI] = 1.7 to 2.9; odds ratio of 2.9, CI = 1.9 to 4.3).

2. Reducing Blood Pressure

- The mean reduction (95% CI) in daily urinary sodium excretion, a proxy measure of dietary sodium intake, was 95 mmol/d (171–119 mmol/d) in 28 trials with 1,131 hypertensive subjects and 125 mmol/d (95–156 mmol/d) in 28 trials with 2,374 normotensive subjects. Decreases in blood pressure were larger in trials of older hypertensive individuals and small and nonsignificant in trials of normotensive individuals whose meals were prepared and who lived outside the institutional setting.

3. Using Estrogen

- For women who experienced any type of menopause, risk did not appear to increase until at least 5 years of estrogen use.

Sample Conclusions of a Meta-Analysis

Inferences From the Data

1. Keeping Appointments

- In clinic settings where kept appointments can be an accurate measure of patient compliance with health care interventions, broken appointments can be reduced by mail or telephone reminders.

2. Reducing Blood Pressure

- Dietary sodium restriction for older hypertensive individuals might be considered, but the evidence in the normotensive population does not support current recommendations for universal dietary sodium restriction.

3. Using Estrogen

- Although the overall benefit of estrogen replacement after meno-pause may outweigh the risks for many women, our analysis supports a small but statistically significant increase in breast cancer risk due to long-term estrogen use.

Sample Limitations

Threats to Internal and External Validity

- Our interest was in those settings where keeping appointments ensured achievement of the intended health care objective, such as flu shots. The results cannot be safely extrapolated to settings where patients attend appointments for ongoing care that they administer themselves between visits.
- There was evidence of confounding, resulting in reductions in blood pressure with no change in sodium intake, but the source could not be identified from the reports.

A meta-analysis should be subject to the same methodological rigor as the studies it reviews. You should examine the threats to internal and exter-nal validity and decide if the reviewers have justified the merits of their analysis despite the threats. In the meta-analysis of estrogen replacement therapy, for example, the reviewers note that further studies are needed to determine whether different estrogen preparations affect breast cancer risk differently and whether progestin use affects breast cancer risk.

Meta-Analysis Illustrated

One method of describing the results of a meta-analysis is by plotting the results on a graph, as in Figure 5.2. The graph compares the number of violent acts in experimental and control studies and contains information on violent acts for five studies. Each study is assigned an identification number (e.g., 1013 or 1016). The identification numbers are arbitrary and are given in the first column.

The second column lists the number of participants in each study. So, 36 participants were in the control group in Study 1013, while 211 were in the control group in Study 1016. The third column describes the number and percentage of violent acts committed by persons in the control. There were five violent acts committed by control participants in Study 1013, for example, and that is 13.9% of the entire number of control participants.

The fourth column consists of the number of persons in the experimental group, and the fifth contains the number of violent acts. (We are assuming for this example that no person commits more than one violent act.)

The graph to the right of each study consists of the 95% confidence interval for the odds ratios resulting from the comparisons between experiment and control groups. The study's confidence intervals overlap (the lines emanating from the blackened circles) and, as you can easily see, tend to favor the experimental group.

Fixed Versus Random Effects

In reviewing meta-analyses, critics often focus on the reviewers' choice of one or two models called **fixed effects** versus **random effects.** The fixed effects model assumes that all experiments are similar in that they share the same underlying treatment effect. Thus, the observed differences in their results are considered to be due to chance alone (sampling error within each study).

The random effects model incorporates the potential heterogeneity of the treatment effect among different studies by assuming that each study estimates a unique treatment effect that, even given a large amount of data, might still differ from the effect in another study. Compared with the fixed effects model, the random effects model weights smaller studies more heavily in its pooled estimate of treatment effect. The fixed effects and random effects models are equivalent when there is no heterogeneity of the treatment effect among different studies.

Which approach—fixed or random effects—is better? Although each may have its supporters, the choice probably depends on the situation. It is not uncommon for researchers first to use a fixed effects model and to statistically test for homogeneity of treatment effect. If the effect is not constant across studies, the researchers then apply a random effects model to derive an estimate (using statistical methods) of the between-study component of variance.

Some researchers frame the debate between fixed and random effects as a conflict in the analysis between numbers of persons participating in all studies versus the number of studies, as in this discussion.

Figure 5.2 Hypothetical Results of Individual Experiments and Meta-Analysis by Participant

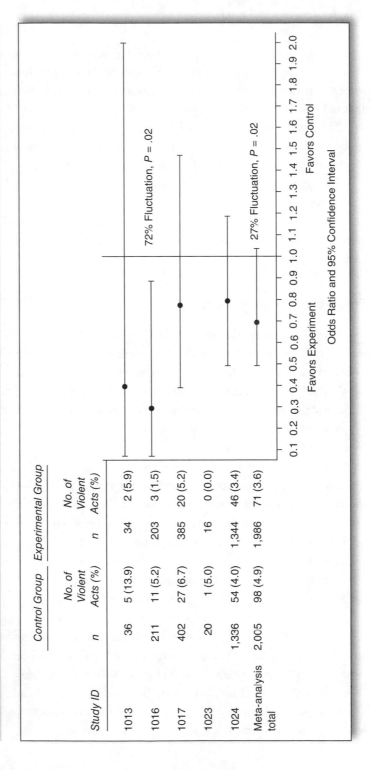

	Control Group		Experimental Group	
Study ID	n	No. of Violent Acts (%)	n	No. of Violent Acts (%)
1013	36	5 (13.9)	34	2 (5.9)
1016	211	11 (5.2)	203	3 (1.5)
1017	402	27 (6.7)	385	20 (5.2)
1023	20	1 (5.0)	16	0 (0.0)
1024	1,336	54 (4.0)	1,344	46 (3.4)
Meta-analysis total	2,005	98 (4.9)	1,986	71 (3.6)

72% Fluctuation, P = .02

27% Fluctuation, P = .02

0.1 0.2 0.3 0.4 0.5 0.6 0.7 0.8 0.9 1.0 1.1 1.2 1.3 1.4 1.5 1.6 1.7 1.8 1.9 2.0

Favors Experiment   Favors Control

Odds Ratio and 95% Confidence Interval

One View of Fixed Effects and Random Effects: Number of Participants Versus Number of Studies

Meta-Analysis A. We have reviewed 10 studies of methods to improve the welfare system. More than 25,000 people participated in the 10 studies. Our conclusions are based on these 25,000 people. With such a large sample, our confidence intervals are relatively small.

Meta-Analysis B. Yes, the confidence intervals are small, but you can generalize your findings only to new persons eligible for the original studies. We are interested in generalizing our findings to other studies. So we are going to focus instead on the 10 studies. This is a random effects model. With it, we have smaller samples and wider confidence intervals but greater generalizability.

Cumulative Meta-Analysis

A cumulative meta-analysis is a technique that permits the identification of the year when the combined results of many studies (almost always randomized, controlled trials or true experiments) first achieve a given level of statistical significance. The technique also reveals whether the temporal trend seems to be toward superiority of one intervention or another or whether little difference in treatment effect can be expected and allows investigators to assess the impact of each new study on the pooled estimate of the treatment effect.

Large Studies Versus Meta-Analysis of Smaller Trials: Comparing Results

The literature is sparse with respect to comparing the results of meta-analyses with each other and with large studies. Some evidence is available to suggest that the results of smaller studies are usually compatible with the results of large studies, but discrepancies do occur. These differences may be due to the quality of the primary studies in the meta-analysis, differences in protocols, and publication bias.

The results of many diverse smaller studies may actually reflect the natural heterogeneity of treatment effectiveness found in the real world, and this may be an advantage of doing a meta-analysis. Large studies, however, may produce a more precise answer to a particular question, especially when the treatment effect is not large but is important in practical terms. Both large studies and the combined results of smaller studies are useful sources of information.

Supporters and Critics

Many influential supporters of meta-analysis insist that only properly randomized trials can be put into a meta-analysis. They also maintain that studies must use an *intention-to-treat analysis* to be valid. An intention-to-treat analysis includes all participants (e.g., patients, students, employees) who are randomized into the analysis, regardless of whether they comply with all experimental rules or complete the program or intervention. So, for example, a study that excludes dropouts from its data analysis is not eligible for inclusion in an intention-to-treat analysis.

Critics of meta-analysis point out that the technique is essentially observational and is subject to all the pitfalls of observational studies. An observational study (unlike an experiment) must cope with whatever data are available.

Critics of meta-analysis also say that the technique's uncertainty may actually produce misleading results. Many statistical issues are still being debated, including which methods and models to use, when and if odds ratios overestimate the relative change in risk (especially if the event rate is high), and the effect of publication and other sources of bias.

Supporters point out that despite its flaws, meta-analysis is a systematic method for dealing with important issues when results from several studies disagree, when sample sizes of individual studies are relatively small, or when a larger study is unlikely to be performed in time to answer a pressing question. Even detractors agree that a meta-analysis can be viewed as a way to present the results of disparate research studies on a common scale.

You can purchase software that will actually do some of the work of a meta-analysis for you. These programs can create or import study databases, analyze the effects for all samples included in the analysis or for subgroups, and provide graphs to show the results. To get to these programs, go to your favorite search engine and use the key word *meta-analysis*.

Displaying Meta-Analysis Results

Meta-analytic results are shown in tables and in graphs. Table 5.5 is an example of a table that describes the results of a meta-analysis studying the effect of a hypothetical intervention when compared with a control group.

What does the table reveal? Looking at the last row, which is labeled "Subtotal," you can see that the pooled absolute risk reduction was 10.5% (95% CI: 7.1% to 13.9%). The pooled *number needed to treat* (NNT), which is defined as 1 divided by the absolute risk reduction, was 10 (7 to 14). The NNT is a concept that is central to understanding the results of a meta-analysis. It is defined as the number of persons who need to be "treated" (given an intervention) to prevent one bad outcome. It is the inverse of the risk difference. In this example, the NNTs of single studies ranged from 6 to 61, and all results favored intervention to some degree. Two studies had notably higher NNTs (References 24 and 40).

Table 5.5   Outcomes in Studies Included in Hypothetical Meta-Analysis

Reference #	Intervention Group*	Control Group*	Absolute Risk Reduction or ARR (%) (Intervention–Control)	Number Needed to Treat(1 ÷ ARR)
36	83/103	71/102	11.0 (–0.9 to 22.5)	9 (4 to –113)
24	9/33	10/39	1.6 (–18.1 to 21.9)	61 (5 to –6)
42	66/87	44/71	13.9 (–0.5 to 27.9)	7 (4 to –195)
37	102/274	66/256	11.4 (3.5 to 19.1)	9 (5 to 28)
41	277/392	247/382	6.0 (–0.6 to 12.5)	17 (8 to –171)
40	16/96	13/93	2.7 (–7.8 to 13.1)	37 (8 to –13)
38	116/48	48/459	15.4 (10.5 to 20.4)	6 (5 to 10)
39	14/80	4/74	12.1 (1.8 to 22.4)	8 (4 to 54)
Subtotal (pooled estimate)	600/1,410	432/1,374	10.5 (7.1 to 13.9)	10 (7 to 14)

*Proportions of people who showed benefit at follow-up.

Note: Values in parentheses are 95% confidence intervals.

META-ANALYSES IN PRACTICE: EXAMPLES

The following are examples of published meta-analyses. They have been chosen because of the importance of their topics and methods. No attempt is made to include all methods, results, and conclusions. No attempt has been made to choose only studies that contain very common methods. A reviewer may find terms and methods that are unfamiliar unless he or she is familiar with the methods used in all social, behavioral, and health sciences. The examples below have been selected because they illustrate important points about the conduct and review of meta-analyses.

Example 1. A Meta-Analysis of the Effect of Estrogen Replacement Therapy on the Risk of Breast Cancer[12]

Purpose of the Review. The reviewers investigated the impact of duration of estrogen replacement therapy on the risk of breast cancer.

Methods. The authors conducted an electronic search supplemented by studies referenced in bibliographies and recommendations of experts. Two reviewers applied explicit inclusion and exclusion criteria and negotiated differences in conference. Three epidemiologists reviewed the methods in studies that met the eligibility standards. A score was assigned to each study based on its methodological properties. The results were pooled separately for high-, medium-, and low-quality studies. To quantify the effect of estrogen replacement therapy on breast cancer risk, the reviewers combined "dose-response" slopes of the relative risk of breast cancer against the duration of estrogen use. (A dose-response curve refers to a representation of the extent to which risk increases with an increased "dose" or, in this case, duration of "exposure" to estrogen replacement therapy. A dose-response slope refers to the average change in the log relative risk for breast cancer associated with the use of estrogen for 1 month.) Using the summary dose-response slope, the reviewers calculated the proportional increase in risk of breast cancer for each year of estrogen use.

Results. The meta-analysis found that for women who experienced any type of menopause, risk did not appear to increase until after at least

5 years of estrogen use. After 15 years of estrogen use, the reviewers found a 30% increase in the risk of breast cancer.

Conclusions. Although the overall benefit of estrogen replacement after menopause may outweigh the risks for some women, the analysis supports a small but statistically significant increase in breast cancer risk due to long-term estrogen use. Further studies are needed to determine whether the risk of breast cancer due to estrogen use differs in perimenopausal and postmenopausal women, whether different estrogen preparations affect breast cancer risk differently, and whether progestin use affects breast cancer risk. Family history may also be an important consideration.

Example 2. The Relationship Between Dietary Sodium Restriction and Blood Pressure[13]

Purpose of the Review. The review was performed to find out whether restricting dietary sodium (salt) lowers blood pressure in people with high blood pressure and also with normal blood pressure.

Methods. An English-language computerized literature search, restricted to human studies with medical subject heading terms (*hypertension, blood pressure, vascular resistance, sodium and dietary, diet and sodium restricted, sodium chloride, clinical trial, randomized controlled trial,* and *prospective studies*) was conducted. Bibliographies of review articles and personal files were also searched. Reviewers selected only trials that had randomized allocation to control and dietary sodium intervention groups, monitored by timed sodium excretion, with outcome measures of both systolic and diastolic blood pressure selected by blinded review of the methods section. Two reviewers abstracted the data.

The reviewers conducted an electronic search of the English-language literature and supplemented it with bibliographies of review articles and in personal files. Eligibility criteria included the following study characteristics: randomized controlled trial, random allocation to treatment groups, a dietary sodium intervention, and reporting of diastolic and systolic blood pressure and urinary sodium excretion.

Methodological quality criteria included the adequacy of the method of randomization, the degree of blinding, the percentage of participants who completed the trial, and the percentage of target sodium achieved. The kappa statistic was to measure agreement between reviewers, a test of homogeneity was performed, and a regression method was used to explore the sources of variation in blood pressure effect among studies.

Results. Fifty-six studies were included. Decreases in blood pressure were larger in experiments with older hypertensive individuals and small and nonsignificant in trials of normotensive individuals whose meals were prepared and who lived outside the institution setting.

Conclusions. Dietary sodium restriction for older persons with high blood pressure might be considered, but the evidence in the population with normal blood pressure does not support current recommendations for universal dietary sodium restriction. The reviewers also found evidence of publication bias in favor of small studies reporting a reduction in blood pressure and significant heterogeneity in the blood pressure response among studies.

Example 3: The Effects of Isoflavones (Soy Phytoestrogens) [Found in Soybeans, Clover, and Legumes] on Cholesterol[14]

Purpose of the Review. To determine the effects of isoflavones (soy phytoestrogens) on serum total cholesterol (TC), low-density lipoprotein cholesterol (LDL), high-density lipoprotein cholesterol (HDL), and triglyceride (TG).

Methods. The reviewers searched the databases from the ACP Journal Club, 1991 to October 2002; Cochrane Controlled Trials Register, 3rd Quarter 2002; Cochrane Database of Systematic Reviews, 4th Quarter 2002; Database of Abstracts of Reviews of Effectiveness, 4th Quarter 2002; British Nursing Index (BNI), 1994 to October 2002; CANCERLIT, 1975 to October 2002; CINAHL, 1982 to October Week 4 2002; CSA–Life Sciences Collection, 1982 to October 2002; EMBASE, 1980 to 2002 Week 45; International Pharmaceutical Abstracts, 1970 to October 2002; PREMEDLINE, October 27, 2002; and MEDLINE, 1996 to October Week 4 2002. We searched the following keywords with Ovid software version re16.2.0: *soy, soy protein, soybean, tofu, phytoestrogen, isoflavone, genistein, daidzein, formononectin,* and *biochanin A.* The reviewers did not restrict any languages during the searching. Hand searching was made by retrieving relevant articles from the obtained studies, and unpublished data were obtained through contacting experts. The reviewers identified ongoing trials by searching Clinical Trials.gov, the UK National Research Register, and Meta-register of controlled trials on the Internet. Review Manager 4.2 was used to calculate the pooled risk differences with a fixed effects model.

Results. Seventeen studies (21 comparisons) with 853 subjects were included in the meta-analysis. Isoflavone tablets had insignificant effects on serum TC, 0.01 mmol/L (95% CI: −0.17 to 0.18, heterogeneity $p = 1.0$); LDL, 0.00 mmol/L (95% CI: −0.14 to 0.15, heterogeneity $p = 0.9$); HDL, 0.01 mmol/L (95% CI: −0.05 to 0.06, heterogeneity $p = 1.0$); and TG, 0.03 mmol/L (95% CI: −0.06 to 0.12, heterogeneity $p = 0.9$). Isoflavone interventions in the forms of isolated soy protein (ISP), soy diets, or soy protein capsule were too heterogeneous to combine.

Conclusions. Isoflavone tablets, isolated or mixtures with up to 150 mg per day, seemed to have no overall statistical and clinical benefits on serum lipids. Isoflavone interventions in the forms of soy proteins may need further investigations to resolve whether synergistic effects are necessary with other soy components.

Example 4. Lifestyle Determinants of the Drive to Eat: A Meta-Analysis[15]

Purpose of the Review. Obesity is emerging as the most significant health concern of the 21st century. The purpose of this article was to provide a meta-analysis of the relation between lifestyle choices and increases in acute food intake.

Method. The reviewers did an initial search of PubMed to collect articles relating television, sleep deprivation, and alcohol consumption to food intake. They only included articles published before February 2013. Studies were analyzed by using three meta-analyses with random-effects models. In addition, a 1-factor ANOVA was run to discover any main effect of lifestyle.

Results. The three most prominent lifestyle factors—television watching, alcohol intake, and sleep deprivation—had significant short-term effects on food intake, with alcohol being more significant (Cohen's d = 1.03) than sleep deprivation (Cohen's d = 0.49) and television watching (Cohen's d = 0.2).

Conclusions. The reviewers concluded that watching television, alcohol intake, and sleep deprivation are not merely correlated with obesity but likely contribute to it by encouraging excessive eating.

Statistical Interlude

Risks and Odds

Typically, meta-analyses rely on risks and odds to describe the likelihood that a particular effect will or will not take place. They are alternative methods for describing effects. For example, suppose that for every 100 persons who have headaches, 20 people have headaches that can be described as severe. The *risk* of a severe headache is 20/100 or 0.20. The *odds* of having severe headaches is calculated by comparing the number of persons with severe headaches (20) against the number without (100 − 20 or 80) or 20/80 = 0.25. The difference between risks and odds is shown below.

Odds and Risks: Compare and Contrast

Number of Persons With Outcome	Risk	Odds
20 of 100	20/100 = 0.20	20:80 = 0.25
40 of 100	40/100 = 0.40	40:60 = 0.66
50 of 100	50/100 = 0.50	50:50 = 1.00
90 of 100	90/100 = 0.90	90:10 = 9.00

Because risks and odds are really just different ways of talking about the same relationship, one can be derived from the other. Risk converts to odds by dividing it by 1 minus the risk, and odds can be converted to risk by dividing odds by odds plus 1.

$$\text{Odds} = (\text{Risk})/(1 - \text{Risk}).$$

$$\text{Risk} = (\text{Odds})/(1 + \text{Odds}).$$

When an outcome is infrequent, little difference exists in numerical values between odds and risks. When the outcome is frequent, however, differences emerge. If, for instance, 20 of 100 persons have headaches, the risks and odds are similar: 0.20 and 0.25, respectively. If 90 of 100 persons have headaches, then the risks are 0.90 and the odds are 9.00.

Relative Risks (Risk Ratios) and Odds Ratios

Both risks and odds are used to describe the likelihood that a particular outcome will occur within a group (e.g., the group with or the group without headaches). But risks and odds can also be used in comparing groups (e.g., the experimental and control groups). When they are, you are comparing the *relative* likelihood that an outcome will take place. The *relative risk* expresses the risk of a particular outcome in the experimental group relative to the risk of the outcome in the control group. The *odds ratio* is a description of the comparison of the odds of the outcome in the experimental group with the odds in the control group.

Relative risks and odds ratios are compared in the following table.

The Relationship Between Relative Risk and Odds Ratio

	Experimental: Selective Television Viewing	*Control: Usual Viewing*	*Total*
Violence	a	b	a + b
No violence	c	d	c + d
Total	a + c	b + d	a + b + c + d
Experimental		a/a + c	a/c
Control		b/b + d	b/d

Relative risk =

$$\frac{\text{Experimental risk}}{\text{Control}} = \frac{a/a + c}{b/b + d}$$

Odds ratio =

$$\frac{\text{Experimental odds}}{\text{Control odds}} = \frac{a/c}{b/d} = \frac{a \times d}{b \times c}$$

The relative risk and the odds ratio will be less than 1 when an outcome occurs less frequently in the experimental group than in the control group. Similarly, both will be greater than 1 if the outcome occurs more frequently in the experimental group than in the control group. The direction of the relative risk and odds ratio (less than or greater than 1) is always the same. The extent to which the odds ratio and relative risk deviate from unity can be quite different.

Combining Studies

To consider combining studies in which one of two outcomes or effects are possible, you construct a 2×2 table (2 rows and 2 columns) for each study included in the analysis. In the television-viewing study, the table would consist of the numbers of children who do and do not watch television and who do and do not commit violent acts.

The 2×2 table looks like this:

	Television Viewing	No Television Viewing
Effect		
Violent acts	a	b
No violent acts	c	d

The figure is divided into the observed number of children (O) in the experimental group with the effect (violent acts) and the expected number (E), which is the number of children who would have performed violent acts if the experiment had not worked—that is, had no effect.

Statistically, it works this way: O is equal to a, but the expected number is $(a + b)(a + c)/N$, where N is the total population in the experimental and control groups. The difference $(O - E)$ is then figured for each trial. This procedure is repeated for all i trials.

If the treatment has no effect, the difference $(O - E)$ should differ only randomly from zero. Thus, the grand total (GT),

$$GT = (\Sigma\, O_i - E_i),$$

should differ only randomly from zero, and as N approaches infinity, GT should approach zero asymptotically. A nonzero GT is a strong indication that the experiment has had some effect. The odds ratio (exp [T/V], where V is the sum of the individual variances) is an estimate of the validity of the nonnull hypothesis, with 95% confidence limits being given by exponent ($T/V \pm 1.96/S$), where S is the number of standard deviations by which GT differs from zero.

Some experts in the field use logistic regression to derive a "maximum likelihood estimator of the pooled odds ratios" (an estimate of the relative risk). The advantages of logistic regression are the ability to control simultaneously for the influence of study design characteristics such as the participants' age or health status—variables that might be hypothesized to influence a study's outcomes. Logistic regression enables you to include variables such as age and health status in the regression equation to estimate adjusted treatment effects. These variables are independent variables (also sometimes called covariates). When the assumption of homogeneity is rejected statistically, logistic regression can be used to search for systematic differences among studies. If the homogeneity assumption is rejected, and the logistic models produce no convincing results to explain the basis of the heterogeneity, some analysts recommend using a components-of-variance analysis.

The estimated values of the treatment effect can be supplemented with weighting techniques based on the precision of the estimate, the relative importance or quality of the studies in the analysis, or a reference population used for standardization of results.

DESCRIPTIVE REVIEW VERSUS META-ANALYSIS

The best descriptive reviews and meta-analyses are identical in being systematic and reproducible. They both rely on explicit search strategies; unambiguous criteria for selecting pertinent, high-quality studies; and a standardized review process. They differ, however, in how they deal with the findings and conclusions of each study included in the review. Descriptive reviews rely on experience and evidence in their interpretations, whereas meta-analyses use statistical techniques to combine study results. It is appropriate to combine results only if the studies meet maximum, preset quality requirements. You need to know the difference between descriptive and statistical reviews so that you can decide which is better for your purposes.

The following examples of meta-analyses are typical of those found in the literature.

Aderka, I. M., Nickerson, A., Boe, H. J., & Hofmann, S. G. (2012). Sudden gains during psychological treatments of anxiety and depression: A meta-analysis. *Journal of consulting and clinical psychology, 202*(80), 93–101.

Al, C. M. W., Stams, G. J. J. M., Bek, M. S., Damen, E. M., Asscher, J. J., & van der Laan, P. H. (2012). A meta-analysis of intensive family preservation programs: Placement prevention and improvement of family functioning. *Children and Youth Services Review, 34*(8), 1472–1479.

Chapman, C. D., Benedict, C., Brooks, S. J., & Schiöth, H. B. (2012). Lifestyle determinants of the drive to eat: A meta-analysis. *The American Journal of Clinical Nutrition, 96*(3), 492–497.

Feder, G. S., Hutson, M., Ramsay, J., & Taket, A. R. (2006). Women exposed to intimate partner violence. *Archives of Internal Medicine, 166,* 22–37.

Goldberg, W. A., Prause, J., Lucas-Thompson, R., & Himsel, A. (2008). Maternal employment and children's achievement in context: A meta-analysis of four decades of research. *Psychological Bulletin, 134,* 77–108.

Grabe, S., Ward, L. M., & Hyde, J. S. (2008). Role of the media in body image concerns among women: A meta-analysis of experimental and correlational studies. *Psychological Bulletin, 134,* 460–476.

Juffer, F., & van Uzendoorn, M. H. (2007). Adoptees do not lack self-esteem: A meta-analysis of studies on self-esteem of transracial, international, and domestic adoptees. *Psychological Bulletin, 133,* 1067–1083.

Lemstra, M., Bennett, N. R., Neudorf, C., Kunst, A., Nannapaneni, U., Warren, L. M., et al. (2008). A meta-analysis of marijuana and alcohol use by socio-economic status in adolescents aged 10–15 years. *Canadian Journal of Public Health, 99,* 172–177.

Makarios, M. D., & Pratt, T. C. (2012). The effectiveness of policies and programs that attempt to reduce firearm violence. *Crime & Delinquency, 58*(2), 222–244. doi: 10.1177/0011128708321321

Rhodes, R. E., & Smith, N. E. I. (2006). Personality correlates of physical activity: A review and meta-analysis. *British Journal of Sports Medicine, 40,* 958–965.

Ried, K., Frank, O. R., Stocks, N. P., Fakler, P., & Sullivan, T. (2008). Effect of garlic on blood pressure: A systematic review and meta-analysis. *BMC Cardiovascular Disorders, 8,* 13.

Wood, S., & Mayo-Wilson, E. (2012). School-based mentoring for adolescents. *Research on Social Work Practice, 22*(3), 257–269.

REVIEWING THE REVIEW

Until this point, the reviewer has been in charge of evaluating the transparency and quality of other people's work. Once the review is complete, it, too, may be subject to an evaluation. Reporting standards for reviews are available to help reviewers receive outstanding evaluations. The most commonly used set of guidelines for reporting literature reviews and meta-analyses is the PRISMA Statement.

PRISMA (http://www.prisma-statement.org/index.htm) stands for Preferred Reporting Items for Systematic Reviews and Meta-Analyses. It describes the minimum set of items that reviewers should include in their systematic reviews and meta-analyses. Although PRISMA focuses on reviews of randomized trials, it can also be used as a basis for reporting systematic reviews of other types of interventional research such as program evaluation and effectiveness research.

The PRISMA Statement consists of a 27-item checklist, an explanation of its items with examples, and a flow diagram. The example below illustrates two items in the Statement. The first asks the reviewer to describe where the information for the review comes from. The second item calls for a description of how the data for the review were collected.

Example Sample of Explanation of Two Items in the PRISMA Statement*

Item 7: Information sources

Describe all information sources in the search (such as databases with dates of coverage, contact with study authors to identify additional studies) and date last searched.

Example. "Studies were identified by searching electronic databases, scanning reference lists of articles, and consultation with experts in the field and drug companies . . . No limits were applied for language and foreign papers were translated. This search was applied to Medline (1966 – Present), CancerLit (1975 – Present), and adapted for Embase (1980 – Present), Science Citation Index Expanded (1981 – Present), and Pre-Medline electronic databases. Cochrane and DARE (Database of Abstracts of Reviews of Effectiveness) databases were reviewed . . . The last search was run on 19 June 2001. In addition, we hand searched contents pages of Journal of Clinical Oncology 2001, European Journal of Cancer 2001, and Bone 2001, together with abstracts printed in these journals 1999 – 2001. A limited update literature search was performed from 19 June 2001 to 31 December 2003."

Explanation. The National Library of Medicine's Medline database is one of the most comprehensive sources of healthcare information in the world. Like any database, however, its coverage is not complete and varies according to the field. Retrieval from any single database, even by an experienced searcher, may be imperfect, which is why detailed reporting is important within the systematic review.

At a minimum, for each database searched, authors should report the database, platform, or provider (such as Ovid, Dialog, PubMed) and the start and end dates for the search of each database. This information lets readers assess the currency of the review, which is important because the publication time-lag outdates the results of some reviews. This information should also make updating more efficient. Authors should also report who developed and conducted the search.

In addition to searching databases, authors should report the use of supplementary approaches to identify studies, such as hand searching of journals, checking reference lists, searching trials registries or regulatory agency Web sites, contacting manufacturers, or contacting authors. Authors should also report if they attempted to acquire any missing information (such as on study methods or results) from investigators or sponsors; it is useful to describe briefly who was contacted and what unpublished information was obtained.

*References are left out of the text for convenience.

Item 10: Data Collection Process

Describe the method of data extraction from reports (e.g., piloted forms, independently by two reviewers) and any processes for obtaining and confirming data from investigators.

Example. "We developed a data extraction sheet (based on the Cochrane Consumers and Communication Review Group's data extraction template), pilot-tested it on 10 randomly selected included studies, and refined it accordingly. One review author extracted the following data from included studies and the second author checked the extracted data . . . Disagreements were resolved by discussion between the two review authors; if no agreement could be reached, it was planned a third author would decide. We contacted five authors for further information. All responded and one provided numerical data that had only been presented graphically in the published paper."

Explanation. Reviewers extract information from each included study so that they can critique, present, and summarize evidence in a systematic review. They might also contact authors of included studies for information that has not been, or is unclearly, reported. In meta-analysis of individual patient data, this phase involves collection and scrutiny of detailed raw databases. The authors should describe these methods, including any steps taken to reduce bias and mistakes during data collection and data extraction

Source: Alessandro Liberati , Douglas G. Altman, Jennifer Tetzlaff, David Moher, Cynthia Mulrow, Peter C. Gøtzsche, John P. A. Ioannidis, Mike Clarke, P. J. Devereaux, and Jos Kleijnen. "The PRISMA Statement for Reporting Systematic Reviews and Meta-Analyses of Studies That Evaluate Health Care Interventions: Explanation and Elaboration." Retrieved from http://www.plosmedicine.org/article/info%3Adoi%2F10.1371%2Fjournal.pmed.1000100

Additional guides for undertaking and evaluating systematic reviews and meta-analyses include the Meta-analysis of Observational Studies in Epidemiology (MOOS) statement (http://www.cochrane.org/about-us/evidence-based-health-care/webliography/books/reporting) and the Center for Review and Dissemination's guidelines for doing reviews (http://www.york.ac.uk/inst/crd/SysRev/!SSL!/WebHelp/SysRev3.htm).

For those in the health field, the most comprehensive standards for systematic reviews of comparative effectiveness research of therapeutic medical or surgical interventions have been issued by the Institute of Medicine or IOM (Institute of Medicine). (2011). *Standards for systematic reviews.* Retrieved from http://www.iom.edu/Reports/2011/Finding-What-Works-in-Health-Care-Standards-for-Systematic-Reviews/Standards.asp). Even though these guidelines are especially relevant to health, many, if not all, of the standards can be used to guide literature review reports in all fields. The example below contains an excerpt from the IOM's standards.

Example: Excerpt From the Institute of Medicine's Standards for Systematic Reviews

Standard 3.1: Conduct a comprehensive systematic search for evidence

3.1.1 Work with a librarian or other information specialist trained in performing systematic reviews to plan the search strategy

3.1.2 Design the search strategy to address each key research question

3.1.3 Use an independent librarian or other information specialist to peer review the search strategy

3.1.4 Search bibliographic databases

3.1.5 Search citation indexes

3.1.6 Search literature cited by eligible studies

3.1.7 Update the search at intervals appropriate to the pace of generation of new information for the research question being addressed

3.1.8 Search subject-specific databases if other databases are unlikely to provide all relevant evidence

3.1.9 Search regional bibliographic databases if other databases are unlikely to provide all relevant evidence

Standard 3.2: Take action to address potentially biased reporting of research results

3.2.1 Search grey literature databases, clinical trial registries, and other sources of unpublished information about studies

3.2.2 Invite researchers to clarify information about study eligibility, study characteristics, and risk of bias

3.2.3 Invite all study sponsors and researchers to submit unpublished data, including unreported outcomes, for possible inclusion in the systematic review

3.2.4 Hand search selected journals and conference abstracts

3.2.5 Conduct a Web search

3.2.6 Search for studies reported in languages other than English if appropriate

Source: Jill Eden, Laura Levit, Alfred Berg, and Sally Morton, Editors; Committee on Standards for Systematic Reviews of Comparative Effectiveness Research; Institute of Medicine. *Standards for Systematic Reviews*. The National Academies Press. 2011.

The PRISMA Statement requires that reviewers provide a flow diagram that shows selection process for the qualitative (descriptive) or quantitative (meta-analysis) review. The flow diagram begins with a statement of the number of studies that were identified through electronic databases and other sources (such as expert recommendations), describes the numbers of studies that were screened and found eligible, and concludes with the number that was finally included in the review as shown in the Figure 5.3.

SUMMARY OF KEY POINTS

- Literature reviews are used to describe current knowledge, justify the need for and significance of new research, explain research findings, and describe the quality of the available research.
- Descriptive reviews rely on knowledge and experience in identifying and interpreting similarities and differences in the literature's purposes, methods, and findings. These reviews are done when randomized controlled trials or rigorous observational studies are scarce or unavailable.
- If randomized trials and good observational studies are available, then a meta-analysis may be appropriate. This type of review uses formal statistical techniques to combine the outcomes of separate studies.
- The following are seven questions to ask when using a meta-analysis.
  1. *Are the objectives of the meta-analysis clearly defined?* The objectives are the purposes of doing the analysis. Meta-analyses have been done about subjects as diverse as school-based smoking prevention programs, adolescent gambling disorders, consumer choice and subliminal advertising, cesarean childbirth and psychosocial outcomes, the effectiveness of intravenous streptokinase during acute myocardial infarction, and the use of electroshock in the treatment of depression.

     Meta-analysis is a research method, and like any such endeavors, the objectives (research questions, hypotheses) must come before any other activity. As a user, you need to know the objectives of the meta-analysis to evaluate the appropriateness of the criteria for including and excluding articles and to determine the adequacy of the methods used to combine studies and the soundness of conclusions.

Figure 5.3   PRISMA Statement Flow Diagram

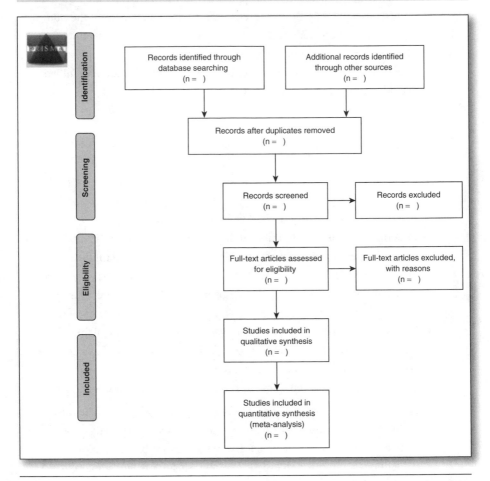

Source: Alessandro Liberati, Douglas G. Altman, Jennifer Tetzlaff, David Moher, Cynthia Mulrow, Peter C. Gøtzsche, John P. A. Ioannidis, Mike Clarke, P. J. Devereaux, and Jos Kleijnen. "The PRISMA Statement for Reporting Systematic Reviews and Meta-Analyses of Studies That Evaluate Health Care Interventions: Explanation and Elaboration."

2. *Are the inclusion and exclusion criteria explicit?* A literature review— regardless of whether it is a descriptive review or meta-analysis—is usually filtered through two eligibility screens. The first screen is primarily practical. It is used to identify studies that are potentially usable in that they cover the topic of concern, are in a respectable publication, and so forth. The second screen is for quality, and it is used to identify

the best available studies in terms of their adherence to methods that scientists and scholars rely on to gather sound evidence.

3. *Are the search strategies satisfactory?* Electronic and manual literature searches supplemented by consultation with experts in the field are the order of the day for all literature reviews. In meta-analyses, it can be especially important to make certain that data are included from ongoing studies that have not yet been published in peer-reviewed journals. If they are not, the analysis may fall victim to *publication bias,* a term used to mean that a review unfairly favors the results of published studies. Published studies may differ from unpublished ones in that they tend to have positive findings; negative findings or findings of no difference between groups do not get published as frequently.

4. *Is a standardized protocol used to screen the literature?* Usually two or more reviewers determine the quality of the universe of studies. To ensure a consistent review, you should prepare a screening protocol. This means that each study is reviewed in a uniform manner. To minimize bias, reviewers are sometimes not told the authors' names, the objectives of the study, where the study was conducted, or the nature of the interventions or programs. After each reviewer completes the questionnaires for all studies, the results are compared between reviewers. Usually, differences in results are negotiated either by discussion between the reviewers themselves or by a third person who is the arbitrator or "gold standard."

5. *Is a standardized protocol used to collect data?* Once studies are selected, they are reviewed and information is abstracted. As with the screening process, valid data collection often requires at least two reviewers using a standard protocol.

6. *Do the authors justify their method of combining or "pooling" results?* One common underlying assumption of meta-analytic procedures is that you can pool individual study results to produce a summary measure because all study results are homogeneous and reflect the same "true" effect. If this assumption is correct, then when the results are combined, any random errors will be canceled out, and one meta-study will be produced. Another assumption is that each study estimates a unique treatment effect and provides greater weight to smaller studies. The two approaches are equivalent when there is no heterogeneity of treatment effect among studies.

7. *Does the report contain results, conclusions, and limitations?* The results refer to the actual numbers, percentages, odds ratios, risk ratios, confidence intervals, and other statistical findings. The conclusions are inferences from the data. The limitations are the threats to internal and external validity caused by sampling, research design, data collection, and unexplored or unanswered research questions.

- Check the transparency and quality of the review by using standardized guidelines like PRISMA or those developed by the Institute of Medicine (even if you are in a different field).

EXERCISES

1. Are the following statements comparing descriptive literature reviews and meta-analysis true or false? Explain your choice.

1a. Descriptive reviews generally rely on observational—rather than experimental—studies.

1b. Meta-analyses produce better information than descriptive reviews.

1c. You need to have formal training in statistics to do a meta-analysis.

1d. Meta-analyses are appropriate only in fields—such as medicine and health—that support randomized trials or true experiments.

2. A meta-analysis was done of studies evaluating programs to improve attendance at school. Read the abbreviated (e.g., research design, search strategy, and quality criteria omitted for brevity) abstract of the meta-analysis and its results. Using the information provided in the abstract, write the results.

Objective: To improve attendance at school.

Participants: The participants fell into one of four age categories: 8–10 years of age, 11–13 years, 14–16 years, and 17 years and older.

Programs: Five types of programs are discussed in the literature. They are (a) letters to parents from the principal; (b) telephone calls from the principal; (c) educational materials for the whole family regarding the importance of school attendance; (d) contracts with students in which students agree to certain school-related behaviors, including regular attendance; and (e) meetings with family and the principal or teachers.

Analysis: The odds of attending school were calculated as the proportion of students in a given age category who attended school divided by the proportion who did not attend. Odds ratios (ORs) were calculated as the odds of attendance in the group that received the program divided by the odds of attendance in the control group. ORs greater than 1.0 indicated a positive effect of the program on attendance. The estimates from individual studies of the same type of program were tested for homogeneity—that is, the compatibility of the results from different studies. A statistical method was used to pool homogeneous ORs from individual studies of the same type of intervention. Test-based 95% confidence intervals (CIs) were calculated for the individual ORs and the summary OR.

Results:

Type of Program and Age Category of Participant	No. of Participants	Odds Ratio (95% Confidence Interval)
Letter[a]		
11–13	662	1.91 (1.30 to 2.70)
14–16	192	5.60 (2.40 to 13.60)
17 plus	883	1.69 (0.86 to 3.35)
Pooled total	**1,737**	**2.17 (1.69 to 2.92)**
Telephone		
8–10	50	7.70 (1.30 to 59.30)
11–13	50	2.70 (0.74 to 10.17)
14–16	184	4.90 (1.90 to 13.30)
17 plus	424	2.10 (1.16 to 3.73)
Pooled total	**708**	**2.88 (1.93 to 4.31)**

(Continued)

(Continued)

Type of Program and Age Category of Participant	No. of Participants	Odds Ratio (95% Confidence Interval)
Educational materials		
8–10	247	0.84 (0.48 to 1.46)
11–13	60	3.82 (1.00 to 15.87)
14–16	60	2.10 (0.63 to 7.19)
17 plus	50	3.27 (0.87 to 12.72)
Pooled total	**417**	**2.91 (1.51 to 5.61)**
Contracts[b]		
14–16	123	1.36 (0.60 to 2.98)
17 plus	50	4.57 (1.19 to 18.31)
Pooled total	**173**	**1.89 (1.04 to 3.45)**
Meetings[c]		
14–16	195	1.46 (0.79 to 2.71)
17 plus	2,055	1.66 (1.35 to 2.04)
Pooled total	**2,250**	**1.64 (1.36 to 1.98)**

a. Outcome data on 8- to 10-year-olds were heterogeneous.

b. Outcome data on 8- to 10-year-olds and 11- to 13-year-olds were heterogeneous.

c. Outcome data on 8- to 10-year-olds and 11- to 13-year-olds were heterogeneous.

Write the results, using the table as your guide.

ANSWERS

1a. *False.* Descriptive reviews rely on both observational and experimental studies.

1b. *False.* Meta-analysis and descriptive reviews depend on the quality of data available and on the expertise with which the data are handled. It is possible to have an excellent descriptive review and a terrible meta-analysis. In theory, meta-analysis may have the edge over descriptive reviews because of the logical proposition that the power of several excellent but relatively small studies is likely to be greater than the power of all but the most elegant and sweeping true experiment.

1c. *True.* You must have formal training in statistics to do a meta-analysis. You do not need to be a formally trained statistician to understand a meta-analysis. Having knowledge of the logic of statistics and also understanding how to interpret statistical data are essential, however.

1d. *False.* Meta-analysis is appropriate in all fields. It often cannot be done because in many fields, the available research is not experimental, does not focus on outcomes, or does not adequately describe a study's methods and findings. Research methodology has received a great deal of attention in health and medicine. So has meta-analysis as a research method.

2. *Results:* Letters to parents proved effective in improving school attendance among children aged 11 and older (pooled OR = 2.2, 95% CI: 1.7 to 2.9). Telephone calls were effective for all groups. The OR was 2.9 (95% CI: 1.9 to 4.3). Educational materials were also successful in improving attendance for children of all ages (OR = 2.9, 95% CI: 1.5 to 5.6). Contracts and meetings were effective for children ages 14 to 17 plus (OR = 1.9, 95% CI: 1.04 to 3.5 and OR = 1.64, 95% CI: 1.4 to 1.9, respectively). Because the results on younger children were heterogeneous in three of the interventions, they were not included in the pooled total.

SUGGESTED READINGS

Bailar, J. C. (1997). The promise and problems of meta-analysis. *Journal of the American Medical Association, 337,* 559–561.

Cappelleri, J. C., Ioannidis, J. P. A., Schmid, C. H., de Ferranti, S. D., Aubert, M., Chalmers, T. C., et al. (1996). Large trials vs. meta-analysis of smaller trials: How do their results compare? *Journal of the American Medical Association, 276,* 1332–1338.

Chalmers, T. C., & Buyse, M. E. (1988). Meta-analysis: For Mantel-Haenszel-Peto method. In T. C. Chalmers (Ed.), *Data analysis for clinical medicine in gastroenterology: The quantitative approach to patient care* (pp. 75–84). Rome: International Press.

DerSimonian, R., & Laird, N. (1986). Combining evidence in clinical trials. *Controlled Clinical Trials, 71,* 171–188.

Egger, M., Juni, P., Bartlett, C., Holenstein, F., & Sterne, J. (2003). How important are comprehensive literature searches and the assessment of trial quality in systematic reviews? [Monograph]. *Health Technology Assessment, 7*(1), 1–76.

Egger, M., Smith, G. D., & Phillips, A. N. (1997). Meta-analysis: Principles and procedures. *British Medical Journal, 315,* 1533–1537.

Greenland, S. (1994). Invited commentary: A critical look at some popular meta-analytic methods. *American Journal of Epidemiology, 140,* 290–296.

Hall, J. A., & Rosenthal, R. (1995). Interpreting and evaluating meta-analysis. *Evaluation & the Health Professions, 18,* 393–407.

Institute of Medicine. (2011). *Finding What Works in Health Care: Standards for Systematic Reviews.* Retrieved from http://www.iom.edu/Reports/2011/Finding-What-Works-in-Health-Care-Standards-for-Systematic-Reviews/Standards.asp

Ioannidis, J. P. A., Cappelleri, J. C., Lau, J., Skolnik, P. R., Melville, B., Chalmers, T. C., et al. (1995). Early or deferred zidovudine therapy in HIV-infected patients without an AISA-defining illness: A meta-analysis. *Annals of Internal Medicine, 122,* 856–866. (Provides the statistical method for the random effects [DerSimonian and Laird] model)

L'Abbe, K. R., Detsky, A. S., & O'Rourke, K. O. (1987). Meta-analysis in clinical research. *Annals of Internal Medicine, 107,* 224–233.

Petticrew, M. A. (2003). Why certain systematic reviews reach uncertain conclusions. *British Medical Journal, 326,* 756–758.

PRISMA Statement. Retrieved from http://www.prisma-statement.org/

Riegelman, R. K., & Hirsch, R. P. (1996). *Studying a study and testing a test: How to read the health science literature.* Boston: Little, Brown.

Rosenthal, R. (1979). The file drawer problem and tolerance for null results. *Psychological Bulletin, 86,* 638–641.

Sensky, T. (2003). The utility of systematic reviews: The case of psychological debriefing after trauma. *Psychotherapy & Psychosomatics, 72,* 171–175.

Stroup, D. F., Berlin, J. A., Morton, S. C., Olkin, I., Williamson, G. D., Rennie, D., et al. (2000). Meta-analysis of observational studies in epidemiology: A proposal for reporting. Meta-analysis Of Observational Studies in Epidemiology (MOOSE) group. *Journal of the American Medical Association, 283*(15), 2008–2012.

Meta-Analysis

If you are interested in meta-analysis, the place to learn about them is the Cochrane Collaboration. The Web site (http://www.cochrane.org) provides a handbook consisting of definitions of all major terms (such as number needed to treat [NNT], homogeneity, etc.). The site also contains hundreds of meta-analyses. Other readings to consider include:

Ellis, P. D. (2010). *The Essential Guide to Effect Sizes: An Introduction to Statistical Power, Meta-Analysis and the Interpretation of Research Results*. United Kingdom: Cambridge University Press.

O'Rourke, K. (2007). *Just the history from the combining of information: investigating and synthesizing what is possibly common in clinical observations or studies via likelihood*. Oxford: University of Oxford, Department of Statistics.

Owen, A. B. (2009). Karl Pearson's meta-analysis revisited. *Annals of Statistics, 37*(6B), 3867–3892. Supplementary report.

Thompson, S. G., & Pocock, S. J. (1991, November 2). Can meta-analysis be trusted? *The Lancet, 338*(8775), 1127–1130. doi:10.1016/0140-6736(91)91975-Z

Wilson, D. B., & Lipsey, M. W. (2001). *Practical meta-analysis*. Thousand Oaks: Sage publications.

Check out these links:

Cochrane Handbook for Systematic Reviews of Interventions (http://www.cochrane.org/training/cochrane-handbook)

Effect Size and Meta-Analysis (ERIC Digest) (http://www.ericdigests.org/2003-4/meta-analysis.html)

Meta-Analysis in Educational Research (ERIC Digest) (http://www.ericdigests.org/1992-5/meta.htm)

EffectSizeFAQ.com (http://effectsizefaq.com/)

Meta-Analysis in Economics (Reading list) (http://ideas.repec.org/k/metaana.html)

NOTES

1. Turner, J. A., Deyo, R. A., Loeser J. D., Von Korff, M., & Fordyce, W. E. (1994). The importance of placebo effects in pain treatment and research. *Journal of the American Medical Association, 271,* 1609–1614.

2. Huntington, J., & Connell, F. (1994). For every dollar spent: The cost-savings argument for prenatal care. *New England Journal of Medicine, 331,* 1303–1307.

3. Corbie-Smith, G., St George, D. M., Moody-Ayers, S., & Ransohoff, D. F. (2003). Adequacy of reporting race/ethnicity in clinical trials in areas of health disparities. *Journal of Clinical Epidemiology, 56,* 416–420.

4.   Zunker, C., Mitchell, J. E., & Wonderlich, S. A. (2011). Exercise interventions for women with anorexia nervosa: A review of the literature. *International Journal for Eating Disorders, 44*(7), 579-584.

5.   See Chapters 2 and 3 for a full discussion of inclusion and exclusion criteria.

6.   See Chapter 1 for a full discussion of how to search the literature.

7.   See Chapter 3 for a full discussion of standardized protocols.

8.   See Chapter 4 for a discussion of the data collection process.

9.   See Chapter 4 to find out how to calculate the kappa statistic.

10.   See Chapter 2 for a discussion of internal and external validity.

11.   See Chapter 4 for a discussion of kappa.

12.   Steinberg, K. K., Thacker, S. B., Smith, S. J., Stroup, D. F., Zack, M. M., Flanders, D., et al. (1991). A meta-analysis of the effect of estrogen replacement therapy on the risk of breast cancer. *Journal of the American Medical Association, 265,* 1985–1990.

13.   Midgley, J. P., Matthew, A. G., Greenwood, C. M., & Logan, A. G. (1996). Effect of reduced dietary sodium on blood pressure. *Journal of the American Medical Association, 275,* 1590–1597.

14.   Yeung, J., & Yu, T.-F. (2003). Effects of isoflavones (soy phyto-estrogens) on serum lipids: A meta-analysis of randomized controlled trials. *Nutrition Journal, 2,* 15. The electronic version of this article is the complete one and can be found online at http://www.nutritionj.com/content/2/1/15 © 2003 Yeung and Yu; licensee BioMed Central Ltd. This is an Open Access article: verbatim copying and redistribution of this article are permitted in all media for any purpose, provided this notice is preserved along with the article's original URL.

15.   Chapman, C. D., Benedict, C., Brooks, S. J., & Schiöth, H. B. (2012). Lifestyle determinants of the drive to eat: A meta-analysis. *The American Journal of Clinical Nutrition, 96*(3), 492–497.

AUTHOR INDEX

SUBJECT INDEX

⑤SAGE research**methods**

The essential online tool for researchers from the
world's leading methods publisher

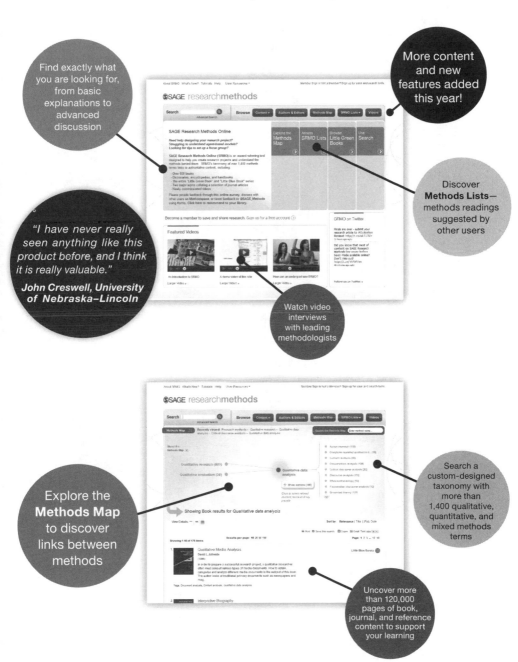

Find exactly what
you are looking for,
from basic
explanations to
advanced
discussion

More content
and new
features added
this year!

Discover
Methods Lists—
methods readings
suggested by
other users

*"I have never really
seen anything like this
product before, and I think
it is really valuable."*

**John Creswell, University
of Nebraska–Lincoln**

Watch video
interviews
with leading
methodologists

Explore the
Methods Map
to discover
links between
methods

Search a
custom-designed
taxonomy with
more than
1,400 qualitative,
quantitative, and
mixed methods
terms

Uncover more
than 120,000
pages of book,
journal, and reference
content to support
your learning

Find out more at
www.sageresearchmethods.com